Fourth Generation Business Systems:

Vendor Support Environments and Systems Generation

Fourth Generation Business Systems:
Vendor Support Environments and Systems Generation

Alex Varsegi

WILEY

JOHN WILEY & SONS
New York   •   Chichester   •   Brisbane   •   Toronto   •   Singapore

Library of Congress Cataloging in Publication Data:

Varsegi, Alex

    Fourth generation business systems / Alex Varsegi
      p. cm.
    Bibliography: p.
    Includes index.
    ISBN 0-471-61548-X
    1. Business—Data processing.   2. Fourth generation computers.
3. Expert systems (Computer science)   4. System design.   I. Title.
HF5548.2.V354 1989
650'.028"5—dc19   88-29157
                                         CIP

Printed in the United States of America

10 9 8 7 6 5 4 3 2 1

To my wife, Marie,
to my children, Mary and George
and to the memory of Brownly Walter

Contents

Preface

"How much experience do you have working with a vendor package?" said the interviewer to the young man "I need to know the sort of projects you're familiar with and, specifically, the vendor associated with some of those applications." The young man had an undergraduate degree in Computer Science from a prestigious university and nearly four years of solid experience as a programmer analyst.

"I did some systems work on an in-house Payroll project" replied the young man, his confidence taking a nose dive, "Unfortunately I never had a chance to acquire hands-on experience with a vendor package..."

More frequently, a job applicant is asked questions of this kind. It is no longer viable for the analyst to be purely a data processing technician. For example, when working on an Accounts Receivable project you need to understand credit management and cash application as much as your colleague in accounting does. Specialists in the industry earn from $95 to $120 an hour and more for their skills. Surprisingly, this area remains either unchallenged, or simply unrecognized by technical writers and universities alike.

"Fourth Generation Systems" is dedicated to two major aspects of business systems. The first concerns the idea of a vendor developed systems design that requires an entirely different set of skills than do those designs for "home grown" applications. This difference must be recognized and its requirements taught as a specialized discipline.

A second, equally important, aspect addresses a thoroughly new technology, which like some of the application packages is also vendor developed. It is commonly referred to as a fourth generation system, or more graphically, a support environment.

Fourth generation systems are catalysts; they produce systems rather than be the end product themsclves. Clearly, they expedite the technical prerequisites for complex or medium-size systems development.

Fourth generation systems enable you to efficiently develop your own design while lending both quality and flexibility to your project. They can also upgrade antiquated systems (some of them still batch) with real time capabilities and a high degree of internal automation. Last, but not least, they can provide a common base for a mixed environment i.e., a variety of different vendor packages working in unison with in-house applications. In the field of fourth generation technology, there is a common misconception regarding fourth generation languages. In reality, the language is merely a building block, one of dozens, that make up the architecture of the business system. Such sophisticated vendor products as McCormack & Dodge's Systems Development Tool (SDT) or MSA's Extended Information Expert environment employ a significant number of innovations in addition to a fourth generation language. Their other features include "smart screens" and tutorial tools, screen painters, dictionaries, report generators, PC-microcomputer interfaces, on demand queries, and relational databases. They provide the user with borderless "navigational" ability among a great number of applications—all accomplished without a single interface and all utilizing a highly-secure environment.

This book is written for a a broad community of readers. Technicians, programmers, and project leaders will find useful information in these pages. Managers on the acquisition of productivity tools will also benefit. Users who perform data processing functions previously within the domain of the Information Systems Department will find much to satisfy their technological needs. And finally, the student who majors in Computer Science will have the opportunity to learn, state of the art technology.

I'd like to express my appreciation for the unusually high level of cooperation I received by Mr. Frank Dodge, President, and Mr. George Cohen of the McCormack & Dodge Corporation, as well as Miss Emma Morris and Mr. Richard Buckley of the MSA Corporation.

Chapter 1

The New Technology
in Systems Design

1.1 Overview

"Fourth Generation Business Systems" is a product of new ideas and concepts in systems design and in programming efficiencies. The term "fourth generation" refers to the technology that enables one a timely delivery of a high-quality product which would be too expensive in a conventional setting. A fourth generation design technology is developed independently from a particular application, then, integrated into that application as a separate step. So, the same support software that drives an automated payroll system, may also be responsible for the upkeep of an accounts receivable system, a general ledger system or for the processing of daily inventory activities.

Given these circumstances, it is possible to make the various applications compatible, regardless of the number of vendors "participating" in the total environment. (Note that the term vendor is also used in reference to some of the internally developed software.)

The first and most dramatic aspect of a fourth generation environment lies in the system's ability to perform borderless inquiries. Before defining the term "borderless," here is an example.

Assume, the accounts payable department is about to produce a check to the Universal Insurance Company in the amount of $7,500. Unknown to accounts payable is the little-known fact that Universal also owes a total of some $10,000, already 120 days delinquent, which is probably uncollectible. Do you still want to pay Universal your recent obligation of $7,500 which would bring your net loss to a total of $17,500, to add insult to injury?

Interestingly enough, in most business environments, the accounts payable department, for one, is completely independent from other operations, and, with some relatively minor exceptions, one has no way of accessing or interrogating the other's database to avoid a costly and embarrassing incidence like the above.

In a true "borderless" situation, of course, there are no boundaries among the various applications. It is, though, as if the entire organization were handled via a giant database with hundreds, if not thousands, of logical views.

The purpose of this book is to give some very specific ideas, not so much about speculating the direction in which mainframe technology is headed (this would merely be fortune telling), but what has already been achieved and utilized. In the pursuit of this, a substantial portion of this book is dedicated to two of the most progressive application developers in the industry: Management Science of America, Inc. (MSA) and the McCormack & Dodge Corporation (M&D).

My primary objective is to present some of the innovative ideas (and strategies) these companies developed and applied in their systems and not simply to discuss their line of products in a light of intense competition and marketing strategies.

1.2   The Reader Community

Background for this book comes from my personal experience in implementing both MSA and M&D application packages. In addition, I was able to utilize proprietary material made available to me by both companies, material that is generally not available for the reader community.

This book is geared to the following technical and administrative personnel:

1. The systems analyst, who will be taught more creativity in designing a particular business application. He or she needs to have some definite ideas in determining what techniques are viable to expedite work and to achieve high quality results. For example, vendors do not create software for highly specialized applications. There is simply no money in this kind of venture.

2. This book is geared to the programmer analyst, who needs to have some basic understanding with regards to the new approach: a good grasp on techniques, so that he or she can understand and utilize some of the fourth generation features discussed and frequently evaluated here. Among these techniques, specifically, are on-demand type of report generations, screen painting, designing queries, and dictionary specifications, etc.

3. The project leader wants to know how the new environment translates into a quick installation scheme of his package. This kind of methodology, as mentioned earlier, is simply not taught anywhere. Chapters 10 through 12, for example, will highlight a comprehensive process, starting with some systems generation type activities, including the use of a vendor-developed demo module and a case study to highlight the entire process.

4. This book is highly recommended for the executive, who has some limited understanding of the above topics. He or she does not need to read this book in its entirety, rather certain topics would suffice: those

Chapter	Systems analyst	Programmer analyst	Project leader	Executive	User	Student
2	yes	yes	yes	yes	yes	yes
3	yes	yes	yes	no	yes	yes
4	yes	yes	yes	no	yes	yes
5	yes	yes	yes	no	no	yes
6	no	yes	no	no	no	yes
7	yes	yes	yes	no	yes	yes
8	yes	yes	yes	no	yes	yes
9	yes	yes	yes	no	no	yes
10	yes	yes	yes	no	no	yes
11	yes	no	yes	no	no	yes
12	yes	no	yes	no	no	yes

Figure 1.1 This matrix suggests who should read what chapters of this book.

in Chapters 2 through 4 and Chapters 7 through 8. In fact, Chapter 2 can be singled out for an executive overview.

5. This book is also geared to the user. After all, once a fourth generation system is implemented and turned over to him or her, it will be this user and not the data processing personnel who will need to rely on Millennium, who will be coding customized procedures in the Expert Language: either by using the step-by-step approach, or else the standard Information Expert (I.E.) programming environment.

6. This book is also geared toward junior- and senior-level computer science graduates. There are not very many colleges or universities today that teach fourth generation languages, let alone fourth generation business system technologies.

Figure 1.1 shows the recommended reading assignment by each of the above group. For example, both the project leader and a systems analyst should read every aspect of the book with the exception of perhaps Chapter 6, which deals with some of the programming conventions in Procedural Development Language (PDL). This section tends to be quite technical. As mentioned during the introduction, students are educated in our system, in an academic environment that is a great deal more restrictive than it ought to be.

Most universities today still emphasize conventional languages, some using purely batch technology, a concept no longer viable without at least some limited real time technology. Structurally speaking, most computer science departments report to the mathematics departments (as if there would be any correlation between the two disciplines).

1.3   Fourth Generation Business Systems Defined

The term "Fourth Generation Business Systems" reflects a number of evolutionary methods to evaluate and process a set of user requirements. Thus, the prevailing concept behind a "fourth generation system" does not necessarily correspond to that of a fourth generation language technology. It is likely to use a fourth generation language such as FOCUS or Natural in conventional design in place of COBOL or PL/I, since the language is merely a single aspect of a total environment.

To understand exactly what a fourth generation system stands for, here is an historical overview of the various capabilities involved.

First and second generation systems were pretty much limited by the architecture of the hardware which was critically weak in providing sufficient internal storage for a program, thus memory. To overcome this kind of handicap, systems had to be designed where not all the initial user requirements could be automated. Also, some of the programs that were developed were done so, using extensive overlays. Overlays are necessary to cram more logic and more procedures into an application program that requires so much (core) memory by the hardware.

Third generation systems design (which is referred to as "conventional systems" throughout this book) came into play with extended machine capabilities, virtual memories, and the reliance on interactive, real time technology.

Conventional design has not been stagnant for the duration: it utilized extensive batch technology in the early seventies, some, heavily dependent on the use of formal databases. A third generation systems technology today consists of features such as prototyping capabilities to establish and process a set of user requirements. This is further highlighted through the use of a data dictionary and by a variety of externally developed productivity tools previously unavailable. A fourth generation system, actually, is an environment that is made up of two separate systems. The first one is a specific application such as a payroll or a general ledger package, while the latter is the actual fourth generation support module. You need to acquire (or develop) the latter only once, and as soon as that technology is disseminated among the various applications, it will drive those applications single handedly. Figure 1.2 shows how such a composite environment can drive any number of applications through a centralized dictionary.

A fourth generation system approaches problem solving by standardizing what is common to the various applications and then providing each one of those applications with internally (rather than externally) developed productivity tools acquired piecemeal, such as the ability to do prototyping, screen painting, on-demand reporting, querying, the ability to use database technology and a fourth generation language, migration technology, the borderless access of information, help functions, and a thoroughly enhanced communication between the host mainframe system and its corresponding PC network.

Here is an example of a fourth generation system, as opposed to a conventional one that only uses fourth generation language technology. In a fourth generation system, each application is tied to a particular Help module. In order to find the problem with a job classification, all you need to do is to position the cursor over to the first character of the field and then, press a predesignated function key. This will enable temporary escape from the current procedures and the ability to look up the needed explanation to

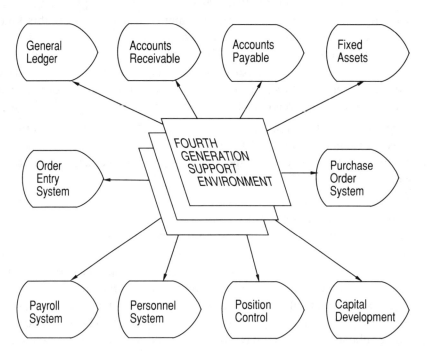

Figure 1.2 Each fourth generation business system is made up of an application module and a full-blown support environment.

the problem which is automatically generated on secondary and tertiary level Help screens. Once the problem is found and resolved, if it is indeed resolvable in that module, you can page back to your original panel and continue processing where you left off.

Now, think for a moment about all the extra steps that would be required if you were to develop a "Help" module on your own in lack of a powerful support environment. The effort would be substantial even if you were to achieve it through a fourth generation language such as IDEAL or FOCUS. To be responsive to the new requirements, you would need to define every element in the system practically from scratch. You would also need to draw up new criteria for field attributes such as intensification and field protection, since you are dealing with hundreds, if not thousands of data elements populating a typical application. The task to develop source code for the above procedures would be overwhelming.

In utilizing a fourth generation support environment, however, all that is already provided for you as long as you remain within the framework of a vendor application. Only the new elements, the new criteria, would have to be formulated. Even those, however, would require minimal effort.

1.4   Scope of Vendor Technology: an Overview

As mentioned in Section 1.1, the purpose of this book is to be explicit about a state-of-the-art technology used in systems design and analysis as well as programming today, and not to elaborate on the degree of innovativeness by the particular software company in discussion. Thus, this book is geared to an individualized, rather than to a comparative review of a number of topics.

With regards to MSA, I heavily concentrated on reporting through the Expert Language, on security, and on the versatility of the vendor's powerful data dictionary which pretty much drives the I.E. environment. Likewise, in my coverage on the M&D based technology, I reviewed yet some different aspects of the software, such as the system's ability to query, screen paint, its powerful Help module, as well as its extended utilities contained in the Systems Development Tool Software.

The idea of providing partial coverage on each vendor is simply that you can theoretically consolidate the above products and arrive at a single entity fourth generation model of your own. Note that there are currently other vendor companies on the market utilizing similar fourth generation techniques at various stages of development. Some of these are computer Associates' "Masterpiece" model as well as Global's "Globalview" product.

Not too long ago, I attended two separate seminars: one by MSA which was their "Interact" convention in Chicago, and another one by M&D in Huntsville, Alabama. Through these sessions, I was fortunate enough to have a glimpse into some of the planning sessions of the preceding vendors. Interestingly enough, both vendors at that time were very serious about developing a new language that would combine both batch and on-line coding techniques in a single application program. If you are familiar with COBOL and CICS Command level coding, I'm sure you realize the vast differences that exist among these products.

1.4.1   The McCormack & Dodge Technology

M&D's fourth generation technology is commonly referred to as the "Millennium" system. Figure 1.3 gives a somewhat high-level overview of how

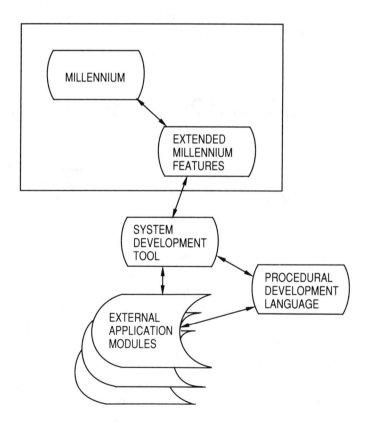

Figure 1.3   This flowchart provides a structural overview of the Millennium environment.

the pieces fit together. Millennium actually contains two distinct technologies: one that is only functional with M&D based applications alone, and another one that is an extended version of the above system made compatible with non-M&D files and procedures.

"Extended" or "enhanced" Millennium is heavily supported by two auxiliary modules, these being the Systems Development Tool (SDT) and the vendor's fourth generation language called Procedural Development Language (PDL). Actually, PDL, as will be seen, is a subset of SDT designed to access external programs (mostly COBOL), and other subroutines. Millennium is described in detail in Chapters 3 through 6 in a progressive manner. Chapters 3 and 4 discuss the basic product, which provides borderless communications only among M&D's own line of applications. SDT, which is part of the extended Millennium environment reviewed in Chapter 5, provides a high level of integration with regards to external, non-M&D systems. Chapter 5 contains an entire section describing the mechanics of the query process, using McCormack & Dodge's SDT (Systems Development Tool) technology.

1.4.2   The MSA Technology

MSA's fourth generation support environment is referred to as Information Expert. Like M&D's extended product, Information Expert (I.E.) is made up of two major components: the first is geared to MSA's own line of application products, and another one, which is an extended version of the above accommodates foreign file structures, meaning non-MSA applications. An overview of this is presented in Figure 1.4. Four chapters are dedicated to describing the MSA model.

Chapter 2, which is also an executive overview of a fourth generation I.E. environment, tells about the components of the system, such as report generation through the Expert Language, queries, screen painting, data dictionary, a Help module, extended product security, a particular vendor developed data frame technology, up and down loading into a PC network through Expertlink, and so on.

Chapters 7 and 8 deal with two types of language technology available in the I.E. model. The first one is what MSA refers to as a step-by-step approach in generating code. Simply define a program through a set of continuous questionnaires, which will automatically create some executable statements.

Chapter 8 focuses on standard programming conventions. This chapter provides for a fairly comprehensive coverage of the specific capabilities of the language inherent in the Expert product.

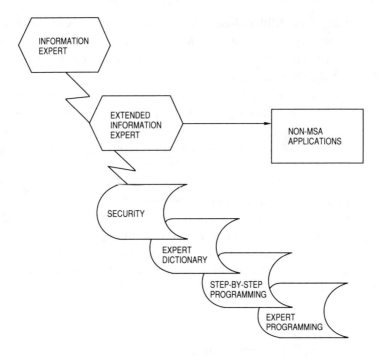

Figure 1.4   This flowchart presents a standard overview of the Information Expert environment.

Chapter 9 is segregated into two major, but related, topics such as:

1. How to build a data frame, and
2. How to provide an extensive data dictionary security.

The second topic is also illustrated through several practical examples.

1.5   Systems Generation Process and a Case Study

The third major area of technology covered in this book deals with the installation of a vendor package, which pretty much reinforces the above topics. This specific technology is arranged in two units: the first one deals with the systems generation process (Chapter 10), and a second (Chapters 11 and 12) describes an actual case study.

An overview of some of the activities associated with the above is presented in Figure 1.5.

define   create GDG's
define application   create VSAM clusters
define interface requirements set up runstreams
describe procedures   load demo tape
describe systems idiosyncrasies test batch/on-line modules
describe hierarchies   reinitialize demo environment
describe sequences of events   customize and enhance
analyze problems   reload own test environment
recommend solutions   using the demo module
implement fourth generation   bench mark process
  technology   create a production environment
enhance via exit points
install application
run parallel systems

Figure 1.5   This list gives an overview of systems installation activities.

The systems generation process involves answering some very specific questions, those that pertain to the physical environment, to virtual and auxiliary storage facilities, to a telecommunications monitor, to the various library systems, loading files, setting up runstreams, compiling and linking the vendor's source code, and so on.

Note that the case study at the end of this book is segregated into two major aspects. The first one (Chapter 11) provides a very elaborate overview of a case study describing every file and procedures required to conceptualize the problem.

Chapter 12, on the other hand, highlights a number of possible approaches and solutions associated with the above case study. Briefly, the case study deals with the implementation process of two parallel systems; a vendor-developed accounts receivable system set into a fourth generation environment and billing system designed in-house. The latter is in its early programming activities.

Summary

"Fourth Generation Business Systems" is a product of new ideas and concepts in systems design and in programming efficiencies. The term "fourth generation" refers to the technology that enables one a timely delivery of a high-quality product which would be too expensive in a conventional setting.

Fourth generation systems technologies are developed independently from a particular application, then, integrated into that application as a separate step. So, the same fourth generation software that drives an automated payroll system, may also be responsible for the upkeep of an accounts receivable system, a general ledger system or for the processing of the daily inventory cycle.

The first and most dramatic aspect of a fourth generation environment lies in the system's ability to perform borderless inquiries.

This book is geared to the following types of readers:

1. Systems analysts
2. Programmer analysts
3. Project leaders
4. Executives
5. Users, and
6. Senior level computer science graduates.

The term "Fourth Generation Business Systems" reflects a number of evolutionary methods to evaluate and process a set of user requirements. Thus, the prevailing concept behind a "fourth generation system" does not necessarily correspond to that of a fourth generation language technology. It is likely to use a fourth generation language such as FOCUS or Natural in the conventional design in place of COBOL or PL/I, since the language is merely a single aspect of a total environment.

A fourth generation system approaches problem solving by standardizing what is common to the various applications. It then provides each one of those applications with internally (rather than externally) developed productivity tools acquired piecemeal, such as the ability to do prototyping, screen painting, on-demand reporting, querying, the ability to use database technology and a fourth generation language, migration technology, the borderless access of information and a thoroughly enhanced communication between the host mainframe system and its corresponding PC network.

Chapter 2

The Building Blocks of a Fourth Generation System

2.1   Overview

Until recently, systems analysis was approached in a conventional way starting with the requirements study, followed by subsequent activities, part of a dynamic project cycle, then, implementation as the final event.

Not until recently has this process been challenged and some of the steps thoroughly automated, as the result. The problem is that, unlike developing a fourth generation compiler, which is a purely technical aspect, systems analysis, and, therefore design, requires a great deal more than pure technical know-how. It requires a strong sense of direction and creativity. It also requires a thorough understanding of the problem and the options involved in resolving it.

When one talks about a fourth generation language within this frame of reference, one is only talking about a mere building block that is part of a thoroughly new architecture. The big picture, however, points to a whole new environment that contains dozens of such technical innovations. So in reality, this gamut of innovations is what will be referred to as a fourth generation system, or more correctly a fourth generation support environment.

Apart from the physical make up previously mentioned, what is the overall merit of such a support environment?

A fourth generation support environment is a productivity tool that enables the development of other systems in the application area with unprecedented efficiency and quality. It is a tool necessary for developing new generations of systems design with great effectiveness.

Historically speaking, fourth generation support systems were developed by applications software companies with a vision. The underlying marketing strategy was that this methodology would seriously influence the corporate buyer to do business with the particular vendor company in possession of such a powerful product. The buyer can now access and freely navigate through an unlimited number of applications without as much as a single interface module to worry about—and what more can you ask?

This is great, but the problem is that very few users could actually be persuaded into putting all their eggs into one basket, that is, to buy all their application packages from the same vendor. After all, what happens when the vendor company of their choice declares bankruptcy or is forced into a merger by a much larger corporation for a mere tax write-off. Besides, a support environment of this kind is usually not persuasive enough for the potential user to acquire a weaker, or a less complete software product.

In most data centers, there is a healthy mix between a number of different vendor packages and in-house systems. In order to utilize these systems in a cohesive manner, some extended support mechanism beyond the current capabilities is needed to consolidate the various vendor products into a functional environment.

Let's face it, in a real life situation you're seldom dedicated to a particular vendor package, rather you wear several hats. One has to do with the implementation of different vendor-systems, another, with your very own in-house applications and so on.

This prompted some of the software giants, Management Science America, Inc. (MSA), the McCormack & Dodge Corporation (M&D), and Global, C. A. to develop products far more comprehensive than were intended originally, a product that could expedite the development of an in-house system without the user having to acquire as much as a single application from the vendor of such a system. One of these packages is M&D's Systems Development Tool (SDT) which is simply a derivative of the Millennium software. Another one is MSA's Information Expert environment.

These systems are tools either to develop new systems from scratch or to enhance and upgrade existing applications. So, a fourth generation environment is merely a catalyst to expedite systems development—it does not have to be redeveloped with every application, rather you may clone it into those systems that need such a tool. In Figure 2.1, the true building blocks

DATA DICTIONARY	requirements study, detail design
DATABASE MANAGEMENT	general design
SCREEN PROCESSING TECHNOLOGY	detail design
SCREEN PAINTING	detail design
SCREEN EDITING	detail design
PROTOTYPING	requirements study
REAL TIME "BORDERLESS" QUERYING	detail design
REPORT GENERATING	detail design
HELP SUBSYSTEM	detail design
ERROR MESSAGE MANAGEMENT	detail design
FOURTH GENERATION LANGUAGE	programming
AUTOMATIC DOCUMENTATION	detail design, implementation
PROJECT CONTROL FACILITIES	project management
TESTING AND DEBUGGING	unit, integration, volume testing
BATCH JOB SUBMISSION	production
SECURITY	detail design, systems software
PC LINK TO UPLOAD AND DOWNLOAD	detail design

Figure 2.1   This list presents potential building blocks, components of a full-blown fourth generation system.

of a fourth generation architecture are summarized. Note how these building blocks permeate through the life cycle of an entire project. For example, you can utilize the system's prototyping capabilities during the requirements study. Database technology is almost mandatory in this sort of
environment even though you need not get too involved in building such a
complex apparatus yourself. (Note, that a formal database environment
such as DB2 or IDMS is not referred to.) The kind of database I'm suggesting is vendor developed and remains transparent to the user.

There are at least nine functional areas referenced during the detail
design. These range from comprehensive screen processing techniques to
real time, borderless querying facilities giving you full access to any number of databases in the system.

Finally, think of a fourth generation support system as acquiring a telecommunications monitor. Once you have it, it will certainly drive all your
interactive requirements, and you need not re-implement it every time a
new application is developed. The comprehensive model of a fourth generation support system is now presented based in most parts on MSA's
extended I.E. The word "extended" also refers to the various building blocks
that make up such a system, and the fact that it can be used globally, which
in this case would mean functionality even in a purely non-MSA environment.

2.2   The Fourth Generation
Data Dictionary Concept

The data dictionary is the very foundation of this fourth generation environment. Unlike some of the conventional packages, dictionaries in the so-
called extended model can accommodate three types of situations. These
are as follows:

1. The vendor's various proprietary software,

2. Applications developed in-house, and

3. Applications developed through other third-party vendors.

So, in the extended I.E. environment, for example, you may integrate
an MSA payroll system, Global's Personnel module and your own position
control system into a single cohesive unit. Data dictionaries in the conventional sense are used to create a central repository of data to eliminate
redundancies and whatever inconsistencies they encompass. This is to say,
the Gross Earnings field will be defined only once, it will be updated in one

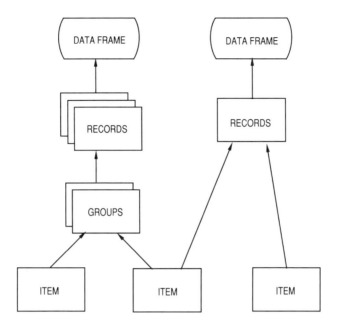

Figure 2.2   This flowchart shows the architecture of the Expert Dictionary.

place, and made available to a particular application, as required. All information about the data maintained in an application is assigned identifiers and default characteristics.

This leads to a fairly important issue, which is that in a fourth generation environment, the various databases are promptly integrated into an active data dictionary, which is the driving force. Since the use of the dictionary is mandatory in this kind of a system, just about any number of physical or logical databases can be referenced through such a powerful vehicle. Figure 2.2 depicts the MSA architecture used in defining its "Expert" dictionary. Although the I.E. data dictionary will be discussed in more detail in Chapter 9, let me briefly acquaint you with this concept.

As can be seen, data items represent the smallest unit in MSA's "Expert" architecture. They essentially specify data in a required detail, such as an item or a field name, type, decimal alignment, date and print formats along with the corresponding column headings. After defining each individual field, these items are now clustered into groups, a process similar to defining a record, or part of it, referred to as a *segment*.

The most comprehensive unit in this architecture is the Data frame, which can be equated to a physical file, or simply to a logical database.

There is tremendous flexibility in such a dictionary. As previously mentioned, you can define the above items, groups, records, and files to a dictionary regardless of the physical data structure or database being used. An additional role of such an interactive dictionary is to allow the migration of one type of computer environment to another. You may also migrate from one database management system to another. So, if you were to change a specific environment, it would not be necessary to redefine each application in the system to the dictionary.

In the I.E. model, I assumed that all major functions would be performed through the dictionary in order to best handle additions and changes, which is physically from a central location. By relying on the dictionary, users and libraries can also be added and deleted to and from the dictionary's security file. You can also back up, and restore, as the rule, any particular file or data set, as needed. Should more space be required, for example, simply expand the dictionary which will also allow the modification or reformatting of some of the databases in the system. Being responsible for a data dictionary, of course is no small task, and it is normally assigned to someone thoroughly knowledgeable such as a systems administrator. This person should come from data processing, rather than from the user side of the business. The following will demonstrate how one can integrate a function, a record, or part of a record into a dictionary and how a specific report can be generated as the result. Figure 2.3 shows a detailed layout of one of the Employee Profile segments called EMPLOYEE-PROFILE-SEGMENT1.

To approach this simplistically, assume you have a segment of a record, which is part of an old batch system, and you want to go ahead and integrate it into the dictionary for the obvious benefits. In addition, suppose you want to generate some kind of a report—an audit trail perhaps—on this transaction for future references.

In order to generate a report to reflect any additions such as the one above, is like printing and formatting an audit trail for which most dictionaries have standard procedures. If you need any nonstandard features apart from what is built into the dictionary, you will have to define to the system the specific request, or else you will be stuck with a set of default values that may not be satisfactory. As an illustration, assume that the field name"200-XCT-E-RES" denotes the employee's identification number in the data dictionary. When you are ready to print the report, you want to define a meaningful title for the respective column indicating that it is indeed the employee's identifier. If you omit a title description (corresponding to each field) in your dictionary, the system will grab the field name 200-XCT-E-RES for the title. It will print 200 XCT E RES instead of something a lot more meaningful, like EMPLOYEE-ID. (Underlining a title is an automatic function.) Notice the comma between EMPLOYEE, I.D. ,

```
WORKING-STORAGE SECTION.
01   EMPLOYEE-PROFILE-SEGMENT1.
     02   EMP-ID                 PIC   X(09).
     02   EMP-NAME               PIC   X(25).
     02   EMP-DEPARTMENT         PIC   X(05).
     02   EMP-STATUS             PIC   X(01).
     02   EMP-POSITION           PIC   X(03).
```

A Segment from an in-house Personnel file to be integrated into the Information Expert environment.

```
ADD ITEM EMP-ID                 (9A 'EMPLOYEE,ID')
ADD ITEM EMP-NAME               (25A 'EMPLOYEE NAME')
ADD ITEM EMP-DEPARTMENT         (5A 'EMP,DEPART)
ADD ITEM EMP-STATUS             (1A 'EMP,STATUS)
ADD ITEM EMP-POSITION           (3A 'EMP,POS')


ADD RECORD EMPLOYEE-PROFILE-SEGMENT1;
    CONTAINS EMP-ID;
    EMP-NAME;
    EMP-DEPARTMENT;
    EMP-STATUS;
    EMP-POSITION


ADD DATAFRAME PAYPROF;
    TYPE (VSAM);
    LRECL (90);
    RECFM (FB);
    BLKSIZE (9000);
    KEYLEN (9);
    KEYLOC (1);
    ORGANIZED BY EMP-ID;
    CONTAINS EMPLOYEE-PROFILE-SEGMENT1 RECORD
```

Figure 2.3 Systems maintenance listing: data from another system (PAYPROF) can also be defined to the dictionary and utilized in a combined fashion.

for example, meaning that the header will be printed in two lines: EMPLOYEE in the first and I.D. in the second for proper spacing and clarity. In the particular example given below, the term EMPLOYEE, ID is used in place of the actual field name or EMP-ID (Figure 2.4) , for a more meaningful description.

Once all data elements are described, they may be retrieved from the dictionary for the purpose of reporting. As can be seen in Figure 2.4, only part of the personnel profile report comes from the previously described personnel segment: these are EMP-ID, EMP-NAME, and EMP-POSITION. Additional information, such as the employee's gross salary, as well as his voluntary or involuntary deductions are also part of the report. In reality, a

```
REPORT:      PERSPROFL         PERSONNEL PROFILE              PAGE:        1

                                                         DATE:   10/12/88
     EMPLOYEE        EMPLOYEE NAME       EMP    EMP       VOL        INVOL
     ID                                  POS    SALARY    DEDUCT     DEDUCT
     ───────────────────────────────────────────────────────────────────────

     213449871       ARIOLA, JESSE       003    42,752    250        6,798
     245667876       BAILEY, CAROL       402    29,877    308        3,211
     278903254       POREBSKY, DENNIS    203    37,876    200        5,198
     309816453       ALEX VARSEGI        766    29,789     50        4,787
     412847562       WOOD, ADOLF D       908    62,678    300        8,765
     4679835227      FRAZIER, JEFF       908    52,987    219        6,901
     549887612       WALLIN, TOM, Y      100    47,677    100        6,198
     590973426       MATTHEWS, JOHN      234    28,762    192        2,908
     610964536       NAVARRO, MARIE B    134    33,789    402        5,210
     654328761       BURKS, KARON T      112    23,877     50        1,098
     690752435       FLEMING PAUL J      134    40,987    320        4,908
     709263549       SCOEFIELD, KAREN A  334    31,876     29        2,765
     719087655       SCHROEDER, ART G    112    27,766     35        2,376
     ───────────────────────────────────────────────────────────────────────
```

Figure 2.4 This is an example data dictionary reporting using prior definitions.

report, such as the one shown in Figure 2.4 can be easily generated using a number of databases, through simple DB commands.

2.3   Borderless Queries

First of all, what is a query? What does it buy the user? A query provides you with the ability to retrieve information quickly and in real time. You can choose what you want to see and process for an up-to-the-minute response at your terminal. The term "borderless" means that you can retrieve any number of participating systems that are defined in the dictionary, and that you can freely "navigate" through a number of applications that have no formal boundaries.

```
                    PAYROLL QUERY SELECTION SCREEN              PAY.QRYS
     ===>                         11/17/88        10:09:27
     PLACE AN S BY THE DATAFRAME NEEDED TO SELECT ELEMENTS
     -----------------------------------------------------------------------
          _ FRINGE BENEFITS               _ U.S. SAVINGS BONDS
          _ UNION & PROFESSIONAL DUES     S SALARY HISTORY
          _ HEALTH & LIFE INSURANCE       _ EMPLOYEE DEMOGRAPHIC SEGMENT 1
          _ EMPLOYEE DEMOGRAPHIC SEGMENT 2  _ EMPLOYEE DEMOGRAPHIC SEGMENT 3
          _ RETROACTIVE PAY SEGMENT       _ REVERSAL AND INTERIM PAY
          _ CHECK RECONCILIATION          _ TAX SHELTERED ANNUITIES
          _ GARNISHMENT                   _ FEDERAL, STATE & LOCAL TAXES
          _ CHARITIES, CONTRIBUTIONS      _ SYSTEMS PROFILE
```

Figure 2.5   Selection of one or a number of data frames.

Most queries, such as the one developed by MSA, for example, provide you with a list of data frames from which to select. These data frames, through a successive menu screen process, can be further sub-defined into individual items which are the building blocks of a screen. In this fashion, you can define any number of ad hoc displays and keep them, if you need to, for subsequent use. Queries, generally speaking, are menu driven, which is an industry trend.

In Figure 2.5, using the query selection screen, the SALARY-HIS-TORY data frame is selected for a closer review. You will build and display an inquiry screen from it. When you press enter, a query element selection submenu panel comes up, which happens to be the magnification of that data frame on a field-by-field, item-by-item basis. If those items you need to reference are already on the data dictionary, all you have to do is select each item on the payroll query element selection screen, which is to be displayed on the "answer" panel.

In Figure 2.6, seven items have been selected for such a display, meaning that those data fields will "populate" the inquiry screen, for example, the employee's name and identification number, current and previous salaries, as well as corresponding position codes. In addition to simply displaying these items on the output panel, suppose you want to compute the employee's last increase by subtracting the previous from the current salary.

Figure 2.6 This screen shows the selection of individual fields from the salary history data frame.

```
                    PAYROLL PROCESSING                      PAY.QRYS
    ===>                                    11/17/88        10:10:30
    ENTER DESIRED KEY VALUES FOR QUERY AND PRESS ENTER
    ------------------------------------------------------------------
    COMPANY-ID            FROM: 0129
                            TO: 0129
    DEPARTMENT            FROM: 00001_____
                            TO: 99999_____
```

Figure 2.7 This is an example of establishing a set of criteria prior to processing a query.

The next step in the query process is depicted in Figure 2.7, which simply allows you to define certain viable selection criteria to the system. In this particular instance, you want to select company 0129 and all departments within that company, which are shown as a limit, ranging from 1 to 99999. (Note that you can define a great deal more selection values to fit the requirements.)

Once all of the selections have been made for a particular display you can now describe to the system the kinds of computations required prior to such a display. In Figure 2.8, you need to calculate a specific increase for every employee, within company 0129.

After gaining more confidence dealing with the system, you can define more complex arithmetical operations. Figure 2.9 shows the resulting display panel, which is formatted by the system in a purely real time environment.

```
              PAYROLL QUERY CALCULATION DEFINITION SCREEN
    ===>                             11/17/88    10:10:59
    BUILD THE CALCULATION USING THE LETTER ASSIGNED TO THE ITEMS BELOW
    ------------------------------------------------------------------
    OP1    (+.-/*,-)   OP2  =  RESULT   OPTIONAL RESULT NAME
    A_         +       B__  =  R1       INCREASE-AMOUNT_____
    __         __      __   =  R2       _____
    __         __      __   =  R3       _____
    __         __      __   =  R4       _____
    __         __      __   =  R5       _____
    __         __      __   =  R6       _____
    A: CURR-SALARY                      B: PREV-SALARY
    C: _____          D: _____
    E: _____          F: _____
    G: _____          H: _____
    I: _____          J: _____
    K: _____          L: _____
```

Figure 2.8 This screen is a panel used by Information Expert to define a query.

```
                      PAYROLL QUERY
     ===>                                    11/17/88  10:11:02
     ----------------------------------------------------------------
     EMP-ID    EMPLOYEE NAME    CURRENT   POS.  PREVIOUS   POS.  INCREASE
                                SALARY          SALARY
     ------    ---------------  ------    ---   ------     ---   -------
     223455    ARDMORE, ALEX C  29,712    124   28,113     124   1,599
     322344    RUTHER, LEX M    42,700    222   43,700     222   1,000
     345667    ALEXANDER, TOM   34,312    223   36,765     223   2,453
     356555    JONES, SHIRLEY   37,800    221   40,000     221   2,200
     437456    WOODWARD, FRED   29,870    566   32,460     566   2,590
     456322    MUNOZ, JOHN M    33,000    354   35,200     357   2,200
     563424    VARSEGI, ALEX    28,790    112   28,790     112
     578954    LENETZKY, JEFF   42,354    009   45,987     009   3,633
     657484    PRATT, ROBERT    42,900    010   44,300     010   1,400
     765877    LEWANDOWSKI, ART 34,200    887   37,250     900   3,050
     778771    SCOEFIELD, PAUL  52,980    700   56,973     700   3,993
     876553    MCNEAL ANDREW    29,700    887   31,000     887   1,300
     987665    ANDERSON, JOHN   34,590    223   34,590     223
```

Figure 2.9 This screen represents an on-Line display of the above query criteria

2.4   The Fourth Generation Expert Language

A fourth generation language merely represents a single building block in the overall architecture of our support environment model, even though it is an important one. Fourth generation languages are procedural and many aspects of them would be difficult to visualize, let alone flow chart. The language does so many things and many things are triggered automatically as a response. The programmer who is used to having a better understanding and more control over how certain commands are interpreted must settle for less. The programmer no longer has to be concerned about OPENING, CLOSING, and READING files, generating report headings, checking return codes, issuing call statements, and so on.

Fourth generation languages are simple to code and some of the commands used in the process represent a set of complex internal instructions when compared to conventional languages. To give some more specific examples, the reader is referred to MSA's fourth generation Information Expert product. When you say LIST, TOTAL, or BY; these commands perform formatting and totaling. LIST arranges the report in the "optimum" format. TOTAL provides automatic columnar totaling, and BY defines grouping for additional totals. The ORDER command automatically determines the sort sequence of the records for reporting.

Define PAGEHEADINGS/PAGEFOOTINGS describes all the report heading and footing information so that it is not necessary to worry about paging, spacing, and other formatting problems. Information Expert also enables you to view your finished product through the on-line support facility. Report images that are written to the report viewing library may be easily retrieved for browsing on the screen. Once you are satisfied with the way the report looks, it can be routed to the printer and purged from the system once the information is in printed format.

In the I.E. reporting module, there is a report specification referred to as "series" (or report "series") that contains all the commands, items, constants, literals, and whatever else is needed to produce processing requirements for a given report. (Note that most of this information comes from the data dictionary.) Information Expert enables you to describe a particular report series via an on-line dialogue that produces a "source" version of that report in the Information Expert dedicated library.

Every report in the system has a basic structure (more on this under Reporting Systems, Section 2.6). The advantage of such a formal structure is that it makes it easy to define any number of different reports. As I.E. processes the individual series, these series can produce any number of different reports from the same input data. The three I.E. functional sections are as follows:

1. Input section,
2. Common section, and
3. Report request section.

These sections are briefly discussed as follows:

1. The input section, as the term reveals, refers to the data frame handled by the INPUT command, which has been already defined to the data dictionary earlier. The input section is an optional feature. If you are not using a data frame, but instead using I.E.'s data processing facilities to produce such a report, you can skip the input section altogether.

2. The common section pertains to calculations, selections, and exclusion criteria, value assignments, and so on. This section, like the input section is an optional feature.

3. The third section deals with the physical definition of the output report, and it is made up of statements that describe such a format to I.E. Syntax-wise the report request section starts with the key word "REPORT," and ends when the next REPORT statement is found. You need to have at least one such REPORT definition in your Report Request Section for it to be valid.

Reporting functions and fourth generation languages are fairly intertwined. Here, you will need to define your reports to the "Expert

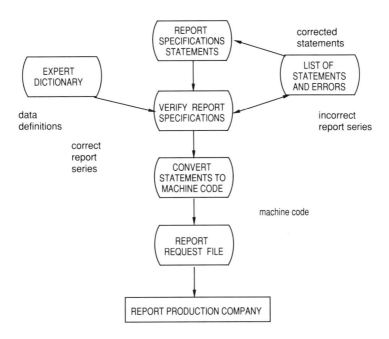

Figure 2.10   This flowchart shows the mechanics of preparing a report in MSA's I.E. environment.

Language" through a report series which contains the specific requirements for each report. You may define not just one, but a number of such reports. Each one of your report specifications is called a request. The statements in a report series define a source of the data for the reports and any processing common to all report requests in a report series. The statements also specify instructions used to produce each report. Once you have completed a set of specifications, and assuming that all syntax checks have been corrected, the system will transform all that into executable modules. The result will then be stored in the Information Expert report library. Figure 2.10 shows how the report preparation works. Once the statements are written, Information Expert verifies that the syntax is also correct and that the names of the data frames and the items within each of those data frames are correct.

Batch reports or report series can be reviewed on-line. Visual verification is a good idea simply because it enables you to verify that, indeed, you have the right report (before printing, say, 1100 pages of it), and that it works properly including spacing and formatting. Assuming that most reports require up to 132 print positions, the system's facilities enable you to scroll from left to right or split the screen to view the left and the right sides

```
PREPARE EXPENSE-ACCNT-BAL-PROJECTIONS
INPUT GLCURRYR(Dataframe containing GL policy and actual budget
                     information for the current year)
 SELECT GL-COMPANY-ID 'CMAG' AND GL-CENTER-ID 'PURCHASING'
 AND GL-CLASS-CODES
 (CMAG is the name of the company and 5 identifies expense account)
 PERIODS-LEFT-IN-YR = GL-NUMBER-OF-PERIODS-OPEN - GL-CURRENT-PERIOD
 PROJ-ACTIV-TO-YR-END = GL-CURRENT-PERIOD-ACTIVITY * PERIODS-LEFT-IN-YR
 PRO-YR-END-BAL = GL-CURRENT-PERIOD-BALANCE + PROJ-ACTIV-TO-YR-END
 PROJ-VARIANCE = GL-CURRENT-YEAR-BUDGET-BALANCE - PROJ-YR-END-BAL
 PERCENT-VARIANCE = (PROJ-VARIANCE/GL-CURRENT-YEAR-BUDGET-BALANCE) * 100


REPORT EXPNPROJ
ORDERED BY #REPORTID
GL-GROUP-CODE
PROJ-YR-END-BAL DESCENDING


DEFINE PAGE HEADING
   'DATE: #SYSDATE';
   'CERMAG MAGNETIC PRODUCTS PURCHASING DEPT';
   'PAGE #PAGE';
NEXT LINE;
   'EXPENSE ACCNT YEAR-END BAL PROJECTIONS'
LIST       GL-GROUP-CODE GL-ACCOUNT-ID GL-CURRENT-PERIOD-BALANCE;
           PROJ-YR-END-BAL GL-CURRENT-YEAR-BUDGET-BALANCE;
           PROJ-VARIANCE PERCENT-VARIANCE;
      TOTAL GL-ACCOUNT-ID GL-CURRENT-PERIOD-BALANCE PROJ-YR-END-BAL;
           PROJ-VARIANCE;
      BY     #REPORTID GL-GROUP-CODE
```

Figure 2.11 This presents the body of the fourth generation Expert Language

of your report simultaneously, or focus in on a single page. In order to design a report under the I.E. concept, you may do the following:

1. Name the report series and the specific report request(s).
2. Identify the data frame to access to create the report series.
3. Define the selection criteria to determine which data from the data frame will actually appear on the report.
4. Specify the sequence or order in which information will appear.
5. Define any calculations or other operations, and specify what information will actually appear on the report.

Here is an example showing how a purchasing manager can use this fourth generation language to create a report from MSA's general ledger system. The purchasing manager needs a rough projection of year-end

```
DATE: 11/17/88    CERMAG MAGNETIC PRODUCTS PURCHASING DEPT           PAGE    1
                  EXPENSE ACCNT YEAR END BAL PROJECTIONS

                    CURRENT PERIOD                      YEAR END
GRP   ACCOUNT    BALANCE       PROJ YR END BAL   BUDGET BAL    PROJ VARIANCE   VAR%
---   -------    -------       ---------------   ----------    -------------   ----

0     99950      134,380,077   258,517,068       208,052,579   50,464,489      24
      =====      ===========   ===========       ===========   ==========      ==

          1      134,380,077   258,517,068                     50,464,489

1     99951      138,380,077   258,517,068       208,052,579   50,464,489      24
      51030       56,313,289    99,454,759        54,969,858   44,484,901      80
      51010       18,396,313    40,528,597         3,664,656   36,863,941   1,005
      51020       18,168,778    39,764,515       100,569,857   60,805,341-     60-
      51050       11,071,470    23,708,442         7,329,313   16,379,129     223
      51060        9,003,487    18,006,207        15,741,366    2,264,841      14
      51040       11,896,354    17,841,076         8,745,204    9,095,872     104
      51070        3,999,996     7,999,992         7,329,314      670,678       9
      51100        2,530,496     5,213,492         4,372,601      840,891      19
      51080        1,999,998     3,999,996         3,498,082      501,914      14
      51090          999,996     1,999,992         1,832,328      167,664       9
      =====      ===========   ===========       ===========   ===========
         11      268,769,154   517,034,136                    100,928,978


                              TOTALS BY EABP-001

         12      403,140,231   775,551,204                    151,393,467

                         * END OF REPORT EABP-001
```

Figure 2.12 This shows a report generated by the fourth generation Expert Language (Fig. 2.11). Note that the decimals were eliminated for a more concise presentation.

Copyright © 1988 Management Science America, Inc. Used by permission.

balances for the appropriate cost center's expense account. Such a projection requires that the system:

1. Calculate the number of periods remaining in the accounting year, multiply them by the current period's net activity to forecast for the remainder of the year, and finally add the result to the current account balance for an annual projection.

2. The manager also wants to compare the current projection with the budget expense totals for the current year, including a variance. Totals should be reported by group code for current and projected year end balances.

Seems like an ambitious, time consuming task? The I.E. fourth generation command structure is presented in Figure 2.11 and the sample report is shown in Figure 2.12. The report can be easily run through the menu-driven on-line support facility. In writing code for the above criteria, you'll be interested to know that the entire source program would take up less than 30 statements—which is a dramatic improvement when compared to a conventional language such as COBOL or PL/I.

2.5 Information Expert Screen Painting Techniques

Screen painting facilities within a fourth generation support environment are usually geared to both the users of an application, as well as to the data processing professional. The most significant aspect of using such a tool is time saving, although some of its strengths also relate to other features as well. Here is a summary of the advantages of this productivity tool:

1. Screen painters need to be simplistic enough so that people other than those with extensive data processing background can use it.

2. The package must be capable of facilitating both the enhancement and the integration among the different products, such as an in-house system versus another vendor package and so on.

3. It must be able to utilize expensive computer resources to the fullest.

4. It must be independent of the operating environment. Such a package should be functional, for example, under DOS or OS/MVS, including a formal data base environment such as an IMS/DLI, or DB2, IDMS/R or DATACOM/DB.

5. Such a model needs to be fully secure in terms of who has access to what panel and in what specific mode, that is, adding or creating a new screen, changing its contents or simply browsing through it.

6. Last, but not least, there must be an ability by the screen painter to perform extensive edit functions, which is the essence of prototyping.

With recent screen painting packages, the data processing professional, as well as the user, now have the ability to build the basic system layout before actually focusing in on the particular systems design or the programming phase of the overall project. So, you can produce an entire system flow including menus, and other detailed screen layouts, Help screens, and paths in a relatively short period of time. And once such a flow is agreed upon, you may go ahead and design your system based on those specifications.

As a rule, screen painters need to be interfaced with other similar "building blocks" in this fourth generation support environment. To perform editing or even to recognize certain edit rules, formats, etc. screen painters need to coordinate all their requirements with an active data dictionary for a number of reasons:

First and foremost, all predefined edits are built into such a dictionary. These include the standard edits associated with a data field for a particular application. Users need to define their own specific edit criteria to the dictionary, as well. These include additional, yet specialized edits for customized screen layouts. In this fashion, you can add new screen edits, and change existing ones while deleting others that are no longer required.

Most screen painters normally perform a number of functions. Among these is the one that enables you to create or "activate" new panels or simply change existing ones. With other utility type functions, you can also copy a panel, then customize it to fit the new requirements.

You can display a sample of your newly created screen, as it would appear during normal processing, which is great for prototyping. Finally, you can also list an entire library of existing screens you created and delete all those no longer functional. With this background, what follows is a bit more specific discussion of the overall process as it relates to the Information Expert environment.

How do you create a new screen using the extended I.E. package? Figure 2.13 shows a menu screen which is the first step in this process.

As can be seen, all such "functional" modes have been selected, that is, inquiry, add, update, and delete including a sequential "browse" mechanism which is a form of inquiry.

The following explains the difference between a pure inquiry mode versus a browse mode. When performing in an inquiry mode, you need to know the search key to find the specific information, the specific record to make a "hit."

For example, if you are looking for an employee whose key identification happens to be 123456, you need to know that exact number, or else you will be locked out of the system failing to meet the required criterion. This is rather harsh, when considered. It is preferable to be in a browse mode because it allows you to scroll up and down the panel, even if you are not quite familiar with the specific search requirements. Browsing through a file gives you generic search capabilities. Using this technology, for example, assume you need to find employee 123456. However, also assume that you only have part of the search key. (The more you know about the key, the more specific is your inquiry, that is, your chances of making a

Figure 2.13 This is the I.E. Systems menu to select one of the "building blocks" from the I.E. architecture.

direct hit.) If you were to enter the partial key of 123, then your search would commence with the employee whose first three digits of the key identifier comply with the partial key of 123, that is, 123000, 123007, 123098, etc. You may browse your file from that specific point on, certainly you will not get locked out of the system for lack of any specific information. As can be seen, an initial menu screen (Figure 2.13) is used to describe the entire MSA fourth generation support system. Function 1 (expert screen painting) was selected, after which enter was pressed to invoke a more specific panel (Figure 2.14) for a further selection. In Figure 2.14, Function 1 was selected (having entered the character 'S' or select, next to the build a screen task), which will then trigger the general screen information panel for me. This panel is shown in Figure 2.15. Figure 2.16 is the data frame selection menu, which is similar to the one displayed during the overview of the I.E. query facilities. Here, again, the personnel demographic data frame was selected, simply by placing an 'S' next to that function. This will bring into focus the entire contents of that data frame showing all the building blocks on an item-by-item basis. This is the purpose of the Item Selection Screen, which is shown in Figure 2.17.

On the item selection menu screen, 10 out of the 13 data items listed were selected. A paint the items blank screen (Figure 2.18) will be triggered by the system, which will look like the one presented in Figure 2.19

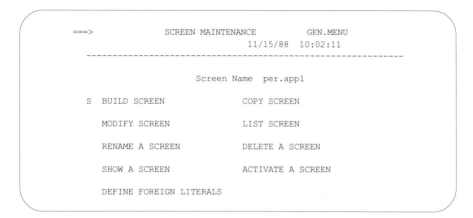

```
    ===>            SCREEN MAINTENANCE        GEN.MENU
                          11/15/88  10:02:11
        ------------------------------------------------------------

                      Screen Name  per.appl

     S  BUILD SCREEN              COPY SCREEN

        MODIFY SCREEN             LIST SCREEN

        RENAME A SCREEN           DELETE A SCREEN

        SHOW A SCREEN             ACTIVATE A SCREEN

        DEFINE FOREIGN LITERALS
```

Figure 2.14 This represents a list of a number of detailed activities from which to choose.

once completed. Note that all the variable fields are marked using a string of 'X' characters. The number of these characters actually corresponds to the length of each field or item.

The name field, for example, is in a completely free format. Twenty-Five characters have been allocated to the full employee name, meaning, last name, first name, then middle initial, if any. Some designers prefer to allocate three separate fields to the full name, rather than combining it into a single item. An additional field would also be allocated to prefixes and

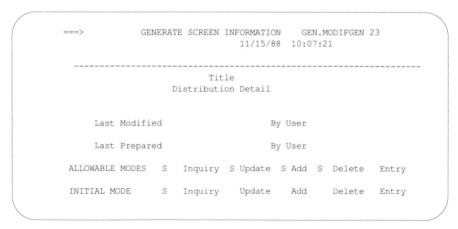

```
      ===>           GENERATE SCREEN INFORMATION    GEN.MODIFGEN 23
                          11/15/88  10:07:21

        ------------------------------------------------------------------
                            Title
                        Distribution Detail


        Last Modified                    By User

        Last Prepared                    By User

     ALLOWABLE MODES    S   Inquiry  S Update  S Add  S  Delete    Entry

     INITIAL MODE       S   Inquiry    Update    Add     Delete    Entry
```

Figure 2.15 This demonstrates allowable modes of data access.

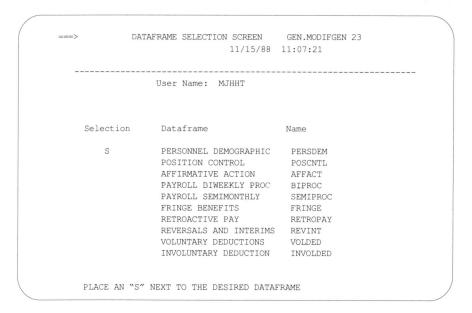

Figure 2.16 This screen demonstrates selecting the proper data frame for a new screen definition.

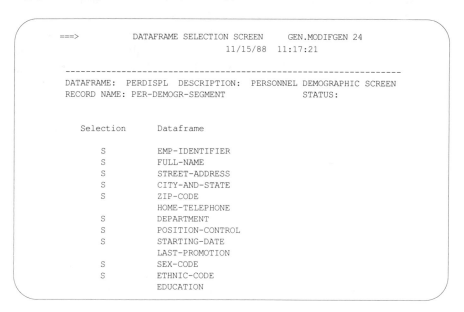

Figure 2.17 This screen demonstrates selecting the proper item(s) for a new screen definition.

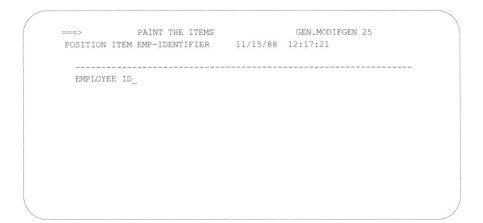

Figure 2.18 This is a paint the items blank screen, start painting your screen layout on the blank screen.

```
    ===>              PAINT THE ITEMS          GEN.MODIFGEN 25
    POSITION ITEM EMP-IDENTIFIER                  11/15/88  12:15:11

    ------------------------------------------------------------------
    EMPLOYEE ID     XXXXXX              DEPARTMENT XXXXX
    POSITION        XXX  SEX   X      ETHNIC    X
    NAME            XXXXXXXXXXXXXXXXXXXXXXXXXXXX
    STREET ADDRESS  XXXXXXXXXXXXXXX
    CITY/STATE ZIP  XXXXXXXXXXXXXXXXXXXX  XX  XXXXX
    STARTING DATE   XX/XX/XX
```

Figure 2.19 This demonstrates completing the screen painting process per item selection.

suffixes for certain qualifiers such as Dr for doctor, Jr for junior or Sr for senior, etc. Once the screen is laid out and designed, Information Expert requires that the above panel be "activated" for which a Prepare Screen Panel (Figure 2.20) is utilized.

The function of this panel is simply to advise the system that the above demographic screen has been completed (created) and is available for subsequent processing.

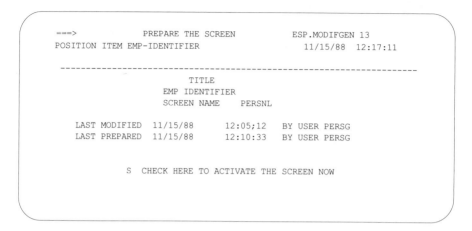

```
    ===>              PREPARE THE SCREEN            ESP.MODIFGEN 13
  POSITION ITEM EMP-IDENTIFIER                       11/15/88  12:17:11


    ----------------------------------------------------------------
                              TITLE
                         EMP IDENTIFIER
                         SCREEN NAME     PERSNL

       LAST MODIFIED  11/15/88        12:05;12   BY USER PERSG
       LAST PREPARED  11/15/88        12:10:33   BY USER PERSG


            S   CHECK HERE TO ACTIVATE THE SCREEN NOW
```

Figure 2.20 This represents a panel to prepare your screen through a selection process.

2.6   Reporting Systems

What is so different about reporting in a fourth generation environment? Unlike in most conventional surroundings, reporting here is not merely a data processing, but a user function, as well. In fact, apart from the standard reporting features, which only represent a relatively low percentage of the total picture, reporting, especially the ad hoc type, is rapidly becoming an end-user responsibility.

Much of this activity is due to an increased need for specialized information. Standardized reports, after all, are too generic, they offer little or no flexibility. What if a standard accounts payable report is sorted the "wrong way," listed by voucher numbers as opposed to a vendor identifier, the only way that particular report would make any sense to you? What if you need a particular report on a daily rather than on a weekly basis, the way it is currently available in the production environment? Or a biweekly in place of a monthly run? Actually, specialized user needs are not exactly new phenomena. They always existed. Unfortunately, not until recently have computer environments, both hardware and software, become sophisticated and powerful enough, to accommodate them.

In a conventional environment, of course, the source of the problem is simply that in order to generate a report, you need to write code, sometimes quite extensive, which is clearly outside the grasp of the average user. To overcome that situation, fourth generation reporting facilities allow you to "navigate" through sometimes a maze of logical steps and on-line delimiter definitions. Each panel invoked in the path outlines what to do, what information to fill in, and if there is still further question as to the proper response, you may yet invoke another building block in the system, which is purely tutorial, such as the Help functions. Figure 2.21 shows the first step in the I.E. menu-driven process.

```
ENTER NAME FOR YOUR REPORT SERIES  Comp-Sales-by-District _____

PRESS: ENTER Continue  PF1 Help   PF3  Previous Step
```

Figure 2.21   This screen shows the initial steps to generate your report.

```
DEFINE SELECTION CRITERIA FOR REPORT REP1

ENTER SELECTION VALUES BELOW FOR GL-ACCOUNT-ID


   FROM VALUE                      THRU VALUE


   midwest____                    _____
   southeast__                    _____
   western____                    _____
   southwest__                    _____
   canadian___                    _____
   _____                    _____
   _____                    _____
   _____                    _____
   _____                    _____
   _____                    _____


 PRESS:  ENTER Continue  PF1 Help  PF3  Previous Step  PF5 select data____
```

Figure 2.22   This represents a panel for defining selection criteria using the step-by-step method.

Steps 2 and 3 require the selection of one or a number of Data frames needed to be accessed, and subsequently, the item components of each of those data frames, a process previously described in the coverage on queries. Next, you need to define a set of selection criteria inherent in this process, as done in Figure 2.22.

Having done all that, you have to define to Information Expert the particular order of each report, that is how the report should be sorted in terms of control fields and for accumulating totals and subtotals. Two control fields are defined on the report which are the report identification number and the general ledger identifier (GL-CENTER-ID). Obviously, you want to sort on the report number first as the major sequence, to make sure you are not mixing two or a number of different reports in the same batch. What follows after this step is the "DEFINE CALCULATIONS FOR REP1", a panel explained earlier in Section 2.3 under Borderless Queries. When the system's report generator is used, unlike when you are querying, you have to define a number of additional requirements to Information Expert. To do just that, there are panels available to lay out the requirements: These are as follows:

```
    M S A    INFORMATION EXPERT  _____    VIEW REPORT
    SERIES: TOTAL SALES BY REGION     REPORT RPT1   PAGE 00001  LINE 001
    COMMAND INPUT ===>                              COLUMNS 026 104

              YEAR TO DATE SALES    (JANUARY - DECEMBER)
                    COMPARED TO PLAN

                                                     SALES
                     YEAR TO DATE    YEAR TO DATE   OVER OR UNDER
        REGION          SALES           PLAN           PLAN
        --------     -------------   -------------   -------------

        CANADIAN     $23,234,512.17  $21,450,000.00  $1,784,512.17
        MIDWEST       34,511,378.45   38,300,999.00   3,788,621.44-
        NORTHEAST     47,712,345.55   45,000,000.00   2,712.345.55
        SOUTHEAST     30,312,461.43   28,500,000.00     452,467.24
        WESTERN       35,675,557.67   34,700,000.00     975,557.67
                     ==============  ==============  ==============
                     $204,898,722.51 $200,950,000.00 $3,948,722.51

                      * END OF REPORT PRT1   *
        ACTION _____   PF3 End  PF6 Top  PF7 Pg Bwd  PF8 Pg Fwd  PF9 Bottom
```

Figure 2.23   This represents a user defined report using Information Expert reporting facilities

1. Building your page header for the above report,

2. Defining the position of each data element on that report, and

3. Describing totals, if any, for computation. The end product of these procedures are reflected in Figure 2.23.

Fourth generation reporting comes from cohesive modules, and the way they interface with each other. In reality, the above process heavily draws from the I.E.'s fourth generation language and from the data dictionary, both being transparent to the user.

Ironically, when implementing this extensive technology, efficient resource utilization is always a primary concern of a given data processing department. As a result, the issue sometimes becomes so critical that end users are denied access to the information they need, thereby negating one of the primary benefits of utilizing a fourth generation technology.

2.7 Up and Downloading to a Microcomputer

The 1980's saw a dramatic rise in the number of personal computers for large groups of users. There is no doubt that individual computing did improve with the advent of PC's. Personal computers substantially increase productivity, enhance operations, and yield a reasonable amount of return on investment. This is all fine in the beginning, but as PC's become more and more integrated into the general environment, the ability is needed to access from the reservoir of mainframe databases. To accommodate that, highly specialized software products were developed to provide a link between PC and mainframe environments, in order to "download" or "upload" information, as needed.

What is meant by the process of downloading and uploading information? Downloading is a method to transfer selected mainframe data to the microcomputer for inquiry or update. Uploading is simply the opposite, that is, when finished using the data, you simply need the ability to load it back to the mainframe.

In the Information Expert environment, one of the building blocks, which is part of the standard support system called EXPERTLINK, is the one that facilitates such communications between two, otherwise totally incompatible, computer systems. The first method in downloading information from the mainframe is referred to as a selective screen transfer method (SST). SST can draw certain pieces of data from a screen via a teleprocessing monitor. Through what MSA refers to as a "screen templating" process, you can pretty much choose what information to transfer, and where exactly that information should go on the microcomputer. This method is used primarily for low-volume data.

Selective screen transfer works as follows: assume one of your employees is ready for retirement and you need to calculate some of the fringe benefits, which is to be performed on a PC. By downloading the employee's database via a 3270 emulation mode, you can perform the necessary calculations on a microcomputer, then load it back to the mainframe where you can update the employee's original database, as needed.

A second method, called database sharing, on the other hand, is available for a high-volume transfer of information for the mainframe.

Database sharing works in conjunction with the I.E. dictionary (more on this in Chapter 9). Here, you may download entire payroll segments on a corporate level, for example, thousands of mainframe records to perform major payroll functions such as retroactive pay calculations, salary modeling, and a great deal more.

Most PC packages are compatible with popular PC products, such as LOTUS 1-2-3 and Symphony, Ashton Tate's dBase II and dBase III and software products using data interchange format (DIF). In the process of uploading, I.E. follows two basic methods. The first one is called real time uploading. You can use this method to transfer your data to the mainframe for real time updating. A second method has to do with high-volume mainframe processing triggered in the PC, or simply microcomputer environment.

What is great about this is the fact that although you are performing a bulk of your processing in a PC environment, never for a moment do you lose your security protection characteristic of mainframe computers.

Summary

Fourth generation support systems or environments were developed by application software companies with a vision. They are tools either to develop new systems from scratch or else to enhance and upgrade existing applications. The underlying philosophy is that such a support environment has to be created only once and then used as a primary source of reference for all subsequent systems.

This chapter dealt with a fourth generation model based on MSA's extended Information Expert environment. In this system the data dictionary is the very foundation of the I.E. extended architecture. In a fourth generation environment, databases are promptly integrated into an active data dictionary, which is the driving force.

The use of the data dictionary, thus is mandatory in this kind of environment, because it can reference just about any number of physical or logical databases through the above vehicle. Data dictionaries are made up of items, groups, records, and files called *data frames*.

A query provides you with the ability to retrieve information on-line. You can choose what you need to see and process in order to attain an up-to-the-minute response at the terminal.

The term "borderless" describes the fact that you can retrieve any number of participating systems that are defined to your data dictionary without a formal interface.

A fourth generation language merely represents a simple building block in the overall architecture of this fourth generation environment. Fourth generation languages are procedural and many aspects of them would be difficult to visualize or flow chart.

Screen painting is a tool in the hands of both the data processing technician as well as the user. Fourth generation screen painters are simplistic, yet powerful, and they expedite the process of designing and prototyping user requirements. They could also be looked upon as productivity tools to migrate from one specific environment to another.

Unlike in most conventional surroundings, reporting here is not merely a data processing function, but a user function as well. In fact, apart from the standard reporting features, which only represent relatively low percentage of the total picture, reporting, especially ad hoc type, is rapidly becoming an end-user responsibility.

Up and downloading between a mainframe and a microcomputer environment is another building block that now makes up this fourth generation support systems. In the I.E. architecture, for example, two methods of downloading are utilized. The first method is called a selective screen transfer method, which, as the terminology indicates, utilizes a number of selected records or data for concurrent processing. A second method called database sharing, on the other hand, is available for high-volume transfer of information for the mainframe.

Chapter 3

M&D's Millennium—Part I
What It Is, and How to Use it

3.1   Overview

Millennium was initially developed to provide an extensive support for all McCormack & Dodge applications. This product is not only a powerful fourth generation productivity tool, but also one that handles the interaction among a host of M&D designed application systems. In fact, it is so thoroughly integrated into a a given application, that it would be next to impossible to segregate components of the Millennium system from that of a given application.

Millennium does not function outside the immediate M&D line of products. So, if you need to integrate your own (in-house) payroll system into the vendor's general ledger system, for example, you need to approach the problem in a conventional way—that is, via an interface mechanism. External systems under the auspices of Millennium cannot be incorporated into the vendor's data dictionary without acquiring the more powerful System Development Tool (SDT) software, a topic to be extensively reviewed in Chapter 5.

The definition of external systems (and thus external files) simply means that while you can build conventional interfaces between M&D and non-M&D software, you cannot perform in a borderless fashion without any limits or restriction to your navigational capabilities. (This, by the way, is not a McCormack & Dodge deficiency, but a systems concept pretty much adhered to by MSA's fourth generation Information Expert environment, as well.)

The terms *borderless inquiry* or *design* refer to the system's ability to retrieve information, that is, to disseminate data in any location of a totally integrated multisystem environment.

A brief background on some of the specific capabilities of the Millennium product follows.

3.2   The Command Structure

3.2.1   Primary and Subcommands

Millennium relies extensively on two basic formats in executing a set of requirements. These are the "primary," and what the vendor refers to as "quick" commands.

Primary commands allow you to display records, execute queries, leave processing steps and so on. For efficiency, they are also thoroughly enhanced with a number of associated subcommands allowing you to refine every command in terms of adding, updating, replacing, deleting, moving, inserting, and displaying information without having to write code to achieve that. For example, assume you need to issue a command to read one of your files, and hold the information in memory (primary command) until such time you would specify a desired course of action. This may be a request to insert a record to a given Millennium database, clone it, or simply move it to another area in the system. These actions are normally triggered by a set of subcommands.

Millennium, overall, utilizes five types of primary commands which will be discussed in greater length throughout this chapter. These commands are as follows:

1. A DISPLAY command, which enables you to look at, but not change, a record. While you can use an update command to accomplish the same, technically, such commands are a great deal more expensive in terms of I/O resources, resulting in the degradation of your response time. (This has to do with sound systems design and not necessarily with the capabilities the Millennium system.)

2. An UPDATE command, which allows you to add, change, insert, replace, delete, or move a record within this fourth generation environment.

3. A QUERY command, through which you can execute stored queries, scroll through the results on an answer-set screen, and print a hard copy of a query answer set, if this is what you need.

4. A PROGRAM command, which is mainly designed for executing special Millennium programs.

5. A START-OVER command, allowing you to cancel or leave any processing step, or cancel link levels, and clear your terminal's memory buffer.

Quick commands are quite important as well, since they enable you to freely "navigate" across an array of M&D based applications while linking you to a particular database for your reference. To use quick commands efficiently, note that the vendor already provided you with a set of "canned" statements. If you need further breakdown or specification, you may create (and customize) your own line of QUICK commands.

When you issue a command in this Millennium environment, you must do so by using a specific format referred to as a command line, which may look something like this:

```
> GDA_____CITY,CHICAGO_____ON RLH01
```

where GDA is the actual (primary) command meaning to get a record for

```
>  E  RLH,VAR,FULLSCREEN                                        ON  CQUBR

_    DBID,  IDENT,  QUERY NAME   RLH VAR        FULLSCREEN

DISPLAY..
    *01          _____  _____  _____  _____

_____  _____  _____  _____  _____


WHERE...
            HILIMIT BT 100,000 150,000
            AND CITY EQ 'CHICAGO'
            AND STYLE = 'RANCH'

            _____
            _____
            _____
            _____
            _____
            _____

SORT...
     PRICE           _____  _____  _____  _____
SUB TOTAL -
SUMMARIZE  _    ASCENDING/DESCENDING A/D _  M: STATUS RANGE   _ _

                                08/15/88  11:01:12    M4LL DEV2 ___
```

```
GU  ___   RLH,VAR,FULLSCREEN                                    ON  CQUBR




        RECORDS SELECTED BY THIS QUERY -----     9

        ENTER GU, GD, IN COMMAND TO REVIEW

        OR HIT ENTER TO CANCEL AND RE-DISPLAY QUERY



                    08/15/88    11:01:15       M4LL DEV2 ____
```

Figure 3.1 - Part 1 This is a full screen definition and corresponding computations followed by the number of actual selections.

updating and apply such an update against the database using an alternate key. This is followed by the qualifier, CITY, which has a specific search value further enabling you to access all those records on the RLH database where the value for the CITY is equal to CHICAGO. Finally, the name of the screen RLH01 (the suffix 01 gets attached to the first panel associated

```
> GU    002 3000                                                    ON RLH01
                                                       LEVEL 01 LINK FROM CQUBR


                        ---HOUSE LISTING---


          AGENCY CODE> 002                 HOUSE CODE===> 3000
          STYLE======> RANCH               LIST REALTOR=> VARSEGI ASSOCIATES
          LOCATION===> CITY                LIST AGENT===> RICHARD OLTENDORF
          ROOMS======> 7                   STREET=======> 1072 WELLINGTON
          BEDROOMS===> 3                   CITY=========> CHICAGO
          BATHS======> 1.5                 STATE========> IL
          FLOORS=====> 1                   PRICE========> 123,000
          FIREPLACES=> 1                   TAXES=---===> 2,400
```

Figure 3.1 - Part 2   A house listing panel: first in the logical relationship.

with the RLH database) will be used to display the requested record. Figure 3.1 shows the position of the command line occupying the first line on your display panel.

Think of the Millennium system as a conglomerate of a number of databases, most of which are vendor created for a specific purpose. For example, a certain query command enables you to execute a query in its original format (or else in its modified form) stored on the CQU database. The actual search values for a record are stored on the CSF database and can be viewed on the corresponding CSFLS panel.

As you will soon see, both the CQU and the CSF databases are internally created files which you need to use, but remain transparent to you from a technical point of view. Figure 3.1 is made up of a series of three screens. The purpose of the first panel is to execute a conditional inquiry, the data being part of the RLH database. The command E (> E) tells Millennium that a query is to be executed against the RLH database that uses the search value 'VAR'. The term "FULLSCREEN" refers to a mode of display that is to be handled by the system one screen at a time.

Toward the middle of the panel I have specified some additional criteria on the CQUBR screen, which is in reference to a real estate database, a demo model created by the vendor. Here, it is stated that the user wanted to access all those records where the selling price of a particular house varies between $100,000 to $150,000 and the real estate is located in the Chicago area.

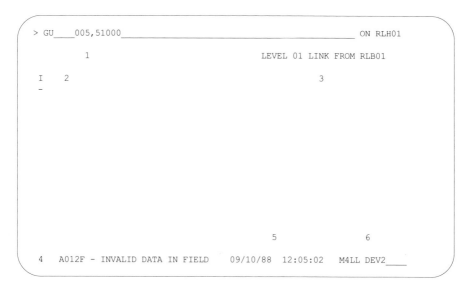

```
> GU____005,51000_____ ON RLH01

              1                            LEVEL 01 LINK FROM RLB01

    I    2                                          3
    _




                                        5             6
    4   A012F - INVALID DATA IN FIELD   09/10/88  12:05:02   M4LL DEV2____
```

Figure 3.2   This is a standard screen set up used by Millennium.

When the command is executed, Millennium displays an interim panel
to inform the user that the criteria specified earlier was successfully executed, and a number of records were selected, as the result. This is useful
information since Millennium, when operating in a FULLSCREEN mode,
can only display a single panel per inquiry.

To review the very first record on the RLH database using the RLH01
screen as a convenient media, the user entered the command GU (get a
record for update) and then pressed enter afterward. The result of this is
shown on the third sequential screen of Figure 3.1. There are two major
aspects of Millennium which will be expanded upon. The first one is the
organization of the screen, while the second pertains to the data structure of
this fourth generation environment. In Figure 3.2, the user took a standard
update screen and rearranged it into six functional areas, characteristic of
all Millennium driven panels. These are as follows:

1. The command line, which enables you to display, update, or place a
    query against any specific database in your application system using
    real time technology.

2. The subcommand line, which is where you can specify to the software
    just what it is exactly you need to do with the data (that is, insert a
    record into the database after you got hold of it, or whatever other
    alternative you have in mind).

3. A link level indicator, which enables you to develop screen relationships and screen paths. This is to say that you can exit your current screen, go to another part of the system to perform a different task, and then branch back to the original screen after successfully performing all those tasks.

4. A message area to provide you with proper diagnostics like the one presented in Figure 3.2. The message A012F, for example, shown on the bottom of the screen is a "fatal" message which needs to be corrected before processing can be resumed. (Note the character F in the fifth or last position of the message code.) Millennium utilizes additional suffixes in describing a potential problem: a "W", which is a warning message to flag an error condition (less severe than an F), and an "I", which is simply informational. (This will be discussed more extensively in subsequent chapters.)

5. Date- and Time-related information.

6. An action code normally to cancel or override an existing command.

Millennium constantly refers to a number of internally structured databases which may be in conflict with your own idea of a database, such as a DB2 type or the more conventional IMS. In the Millennium environment, *fields* are the smallest unit of information—the building blocks of a single record. Fields are extensively defined in the Millennium data directory, a term used by M&D in reference to the system's internal dictionary.

Physical records are next in this hierarchy, and they can be further classified into a physical database, which is exactly what needs to be pointed to in the inquiry.

The file is the largest focal point in the system that contains a number of physical databases. Actually, it is safe to think of a file as a logical entity in the sense that users are merely interested in a specific view or application window, which more frequently corresponds to a number of physical database structures (Figure 3.3).

3.2.2 Quick Commands

Quick commands are used to execute a task involving a set of logical relationships that exist between screens within the same database, between databases within an application or between a number of applications. As pointed out before, the vendor already created a standard set of commands; if you need something different, you can create your own commands.

To best understand what a quick command is, think about creating and storing a set of macro instructions which is normally made up of a number

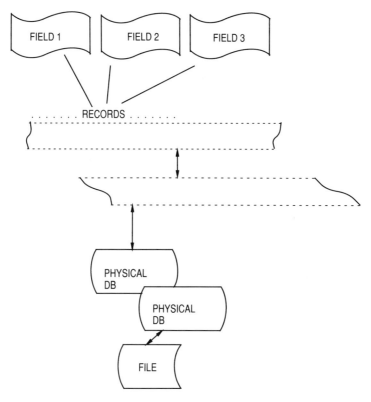

Figure 3.3   This flowchart represents Millennium-driven data structure.

of logical steps. In essence, a quick command can execute a number of instructions, executing them concurrently and with a great deal of speed. QUICK commands may be used when you need to link a specific screen on one database to another screen, or link to an altogether different database. There are other circumstances, as well, such as when processing multiple databases or when it is necessary to query information that is displayed on the screen. The real efficiency of these quick commands is simply the formulation of logical relationship among three components, such as your data, your respective database or bases and a set of screens on which such a logical relationship is initially defined. Thus, when executing a quick command, you need to have a starting point, a reference link, and a destination point.

A starting point is the source from which a quick command is executed. The reference link is the medium that provides you with a linkage between starting point and destination point regardless of the number of levels involved in the process. A destination point is simply the result of executing a quick command.

Certain quick commands, in addition to providing a linkage among this maze of databases and associated panels, also trigger specific utility type programs and display certain messages as the result.

The best way to illustrate this whole process is through a database created by the vendor initially, referred to as a "real estate" database. The following example will show how the owner of a real estate agency, The Varsegi Realtors (VAR), executes a set of quick commands to process the sale of a house by one of its agents, Charles Tomczak.

On July 15, 1988, the owner of the above house received a call from his agent that his property was sold to Jeff Anderson. In Figure 3.4, the realtor displays the sale of the house using the GUH command to gain access to the house record in update mode. (Get a record for update and hold.) Note that four lines of information are to be executed at this point. These are as follows:

1. An "R" in the sub command field (R stands for replacement or for record modification),

2. Date of sale, which is 07/15/88,

3. Varsegi Realtors, which happens to be the agency involved in the sale (and is also the list realtor), and

4. The buyer, Jeff Anderson.

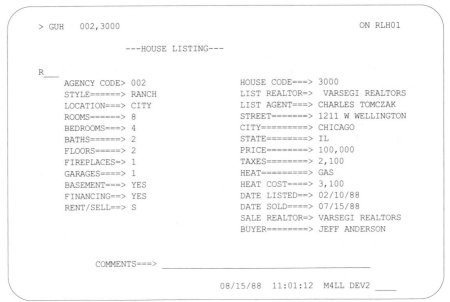

Figure 3.4 This house listing screen shows quick command relationship— step 1.

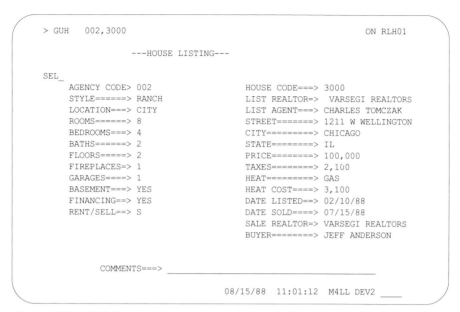

```
> GUH    002,3000                                              ON RLH01

                    ---HOUSE LISTING---

SEL_
        AGENCY CODE> 002                 HOUSE CODE===> 3000
        STYLE======> RANCH               LIST REALTOR=> VARSEGI REALTORS
        LOCATION===> CITY                LIST AGENT===> CHARLES TOMCZAK
        ROOMS======> 8                   STREET=======> 1211 W WELLINGTON
        BEDROOMS===> 4                   CITY=========> CHICAGO
        BATHS======> 2                   STATE========> IL
        FLOORS=====> 2                   PRICE========> 100,000
        FIREPLACES=> 1                   TAXES========> 2,100
        GARAGES====> 1                   HEAT=========> GAS
        BASEMENT===> YES                 HEAT COST====> 3,100
        FINANCING==> YES                 DATE LISTED==> 02/10/88
        RENT/SELL==> S                   DATE SOLD====> 07/15/88
                                         SALE REALTOR=> VARSEGI REALTORS
                                         BUYER========> JEFF ANDERSON


        COMMENTS===> _____

                        08/15/88  11:01:12  M4LL DEV2 ____
```

Figure 3.5   This house listing screen shows quick command relationship—step 2.

After the house listing database was updated, the realtor linked Jeff Anderson's, or the buyer's record, to the "base" screen that was triggered simply by executing a "SEL" quick command (Figure 3.5). SEL will establish the reference link between the two databases (RLH and the RLB databases) by utilizing the value in the buyer's field (Jeff Anderson) to access the customer information database via the name field (Figure 3.6).

Since the purchase is now complete and the house is off the market, the real estate agency (Varsegi Realtors) can go ahead and change Jeff Anderson's account status to inactive. To do just that, the realtor needs to go back up one link level to the RLH01 panel which is depicted in Figure 3.7.

So far, you have updated both the house and the buyer databases and you are ready to post commission for the sale on Charles Tomczak's record. To accomplish this, you need to execute a PST quick command: observe the messages on the bottom of the screen indicating the sale, and that the commission has been posted.

The PST quick command executes a special program that takes the price of the house from the RLH record, multiplies it by the commission percent field on the RLS record, and then updates the sale-to-date and the

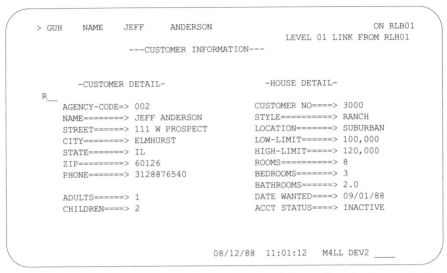

```
> GUH    NAME    JEFF    ANDERSON                                ON RLB01
                                              LEVEL 01 LINK FROM RLH01
                    ---CUSTOMER INFORMATION---


          -CUSTOMER DETAIL-                    -HOUSE DETAIL-
  R__
        AGENCY-CODE=> 002              CUSTOMER NO====> 3000
        NAME========> JEFF ANDERSON    STYLE==========> RANCH
        STREET======> 111 W PROSPECT   LOCATION=======> SUBURBAN
        CITY========> ELMHURST         LOW-LIMIT======> 100,000
        STATE=======> IL               HIGH-LIMIT=====> 120,000
        ZIP=========> 60126            ROOMS==========> 8
        PHONE=======> 3128876540       BEDROOMS=======> 3
                                       BATHROOMS======> 2.0
        ADULTS======> 1                DATE WANTED====> 09/01/88
        CHILDREN====> 2                ACCT STATUS====> INACTIVE



                        08/12/88   11:01:12    M4LL DEV2 ____
```

Figure 3.6   This shows the updated customer information database via the RLB01 screen—step 3.

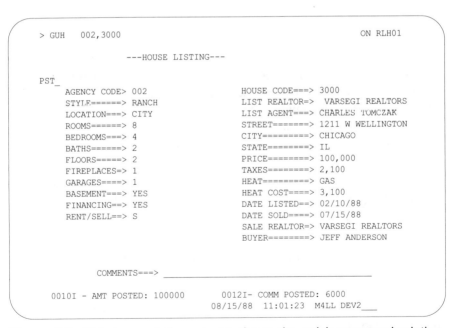

```
> GUH    002,3000                                        ON RLH01

                    ---HOUSE LISTING---

  PST_
        AGENCY CODE> 002              HOUSE CODE===> 3000
        STYLE======> RANCH            LIST REALTOR=>  VARSEGI REALTORS
        LOCATION===> CITY             LIST AGENT===> CHARLES TOMCZAK
        ROOMS======> 8                STREET=======> 1211 W WELLINGTON
        BEDROOMS===> 4                CITY=========> CHICAGO
        BATHS======> 2                STATE========> IL
        FLOORS=====> 2                PRICE========> 100,000
        FIREPLACES=> 1                TAXES========> 2,100
        GARAGES====> 1                HEAT=========> GAS
        BASEMENT===> YES              HEAT COST====> 3,100
        FINANCING==> YES              DATE LISTED==> 02/10/88
        RENT/SELL==> S                DATE SOLD====> 07/15/88
                                      SALE REALTOR=> VARSEGI REALTORS
                                      BUYER========> JEFF ANDERSON


            COMMENTS===> _____

     0010I - AMT POSTED: 100000        0012I- COMM POSTED: 6000
                              08/15/88  11:01:23  M4LL DEV2___
```

Figure 3.7   This house listing screen shows the quick command relationship— step 4.

commission-to-date fields on the RLS database. The program also preloads the correct command in the command qualifier field at the top of the screen, so the user can link to the RLS01 screen to verify the transaction.

To make sure that the commission has been posted correctly, the realtor presses enter to link directly to the agent's record on the RLS01 screen. The value in the list agent field establishes the reference link to the RLS01 screen. Since this is Charles Tomczak's first sale of the year, the sale to date field reflects the value of the house just sold for $100,000. Similarly, the commission to date field reflects the six percent commission for that sale (Figure 3.8).

3.3   Data Manipulation

As you can see, primary commands are used by Millennium to retrieve records and display them on the screen. Subcommands, on the other hand, enable you to manipulate the data: more specifically, they allow you to add, revise and delete records from a particular database.

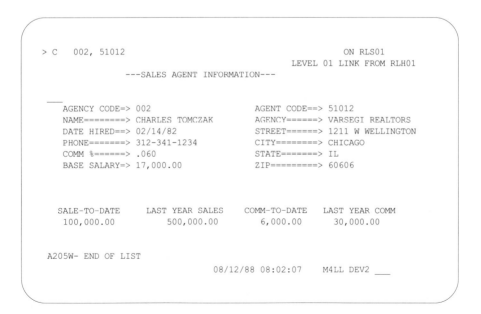

```
> C   002, 51012                                        ON RLS01
                                              LEVEL 01 LINK FROM RLH01
                    ---SALES AGENT INFORMATION---


  ____
      AGENCY CODE=> 002              AGENT CODE==> 51012
      NAME========> CHARLES TOMCZAK  AGENCY======> VARSEGI REALTORS
      DATE HIRED==> 02/14/82         STREET======> 1211 W WELLINGTON
      PHONE=======> 312-341-1234     CITY========> CHICAGO
      COMM %======> .060             STATE=======> IL
      BASE SALARY=> 17,000.00        ZIP=========> 60606



    SALE-TO-DATE     LAST YEAR SALES    COMM-TO-DATE    LAST YEAR COMM
     100,000.00          500,000.00       6,000.00        30,000.00


  A205W- END OF LIST

                              08/12/88 08:02:07    M4LL DEV2 ___
```

Figure 3.8   Posting the commision is the final step using the RLS01 screen.

The "INSERT" subcommand is used to add a new record to a database. The term "insert" (rather than "add") is used by the vendor to denote a number of different methods in which you can add data to an existing database. The first method is called the "mask screen method." When you insert a record via this method, you need to fill in each required field on the screen leaving the command qualifier blank as follows:

```
> GU _____    ON RLH01 __
```

Note that you will also have to enter an "I" in the subcommand field to describe to Millennium the type of operation requested. Since all required data elements (including those pertaining to the record key structure) must be entered on the screen, Millennium can easily identify where that particular record fits into such a database. If you did not fill in the proper key fields (remember, as in add mode, you cannot have a duplicate set of keys using the INSERT subcommand), you will receive a system message: "CANNOT INS/ADD SAME KEY." When this happens, fill in the key fields or simply change the key values.

A second method of adding or inserting is referred to as the "clone method." The clone method is essentially a time saver since you can simply copy an existing panel, then make some minor changes to come up with the required screen format. To copy a screen in this manner you need to:

1. Decide on the database to clone such a "From" screen,
2. Physically retrieve the screen which is "close" to what is needed in the given situation,
3. Enter an "I" (Insert) in the subcommand field on the screen, and
4. Change or customize the record to "create" the desired panel.

When using the clone method, the entire command line needs to be "fixed up" as follows:

```
> GU _____002,VARSEGI_____    ON RLH01 ____
```

or, in plain English, get the record you want to copy into the desired database using the GU command. The GU command enables you to update and hold a record until you're through modifying it. (See Figure 3.9 for more detail.) In order to do that the key field, 002, must have the search value "VARSEGI". Once the information is retrieved, it should be displayed on the RLH01 screen which is aligned with the RLH database.

Another term used by M&D to manipulate a record is the subcommand Replace (R), which is pretty much like changing a field, or a number of fields on a record. As with the revision technique, you cannot modify an existing key. To do that you need to perform a delete and subsequently an add to the designated database.

Function	Primary Command	Subcommand	Purpose
DISPLAY	G, GD		Get record for display
	GA, GDA		Get record for display with an alternate key
	GG		Get Global Records
		(AAA)*	Quick Commands can be executed from the subcommand field, if the screen has been set up to accommodate them.
UPDATE	GU		Get record for update
	GUH		Get record for update and hold
	GUA		Get record for update with an alternate key
		I	Insert new record
		R	Replace an existing record
		D	Delete an existing record
		M	Move or change a key to a record
		(AAA)*	Quick commands can be executed from the subcommand field if the screen has been set up to accommodate them
QUERY	E		Execute a query
	.T		Return to the top of a query answer set
	.B		Go to the bottom of a query answer set
	+NN		Scroll forward (nn) lines
	-NN		Scroll back (nn) lines
	PRINT		Print a query answer set
		V	Verify a query prior to execution.
PROGRAM	GEX		Execute a special Millennium program Quit the current processing step and return to a blank command line
	C		Cancel the current processing step and return one link level
	CC		Cancel the current processing step and return two link levels
	CLEAR		Clear the terminal's memory buffer

(AAA)* represents a three-character quick command name

Figure 3.9 This shows primary and secondary commands used by Millennium.

So if you want to replace a record, you have to consider the following:

1. Which record is to be replaced,

2. Define to Millennium the command line requirements as follows:

......command　　　　　..........command qualifier　.............screen name
any "get for update"　key to an existing record　the "model" data
statement　　　　　　　　　　　　　　　　　　　used to make the
　　　　　　　　　　　　　　　　　　　　　　　change

3. Enter an "R" in the subcommand field for replacement, and

4. When you change a record, Millennium assumes that the record is already in existence. If not, a message will be displayed on the screen: "CANNOT REP/UPD DIFFERENT KEY".

Millennium also relies on the "move" subcommand, which has two components to it: first of all, it allows you to move a record to one of the databases and, secondly, it lets you change the key itself without deleting and readding the contents of the same record. So, MOVE is a real time saver, unavailable in a conventional environment. The following needs to be determined when moving a record:

1. What specific record or records you intend to move

2. What is the existing record key which will be used in the process

Once the Above is determined, place the character "M" (M meaning move) in the subcommand field on the screen, and change the existing to a new record key to be replaced in this fashion.

When the system processes the MOVE subcommand, a new record is created and the old one is deleted automatically, the result is the creation of an identical record with a new key.

Last is the DELETE subcommand that enables you to delete a record from the database. To delete a record, all you have to do is to define to Millennium the particular record and "flag" it using the character "D" (Delete) in the subcommand field. The command line at this point can utilize any get for update command, an existing record key, and a corresponding data base/screen identifier.

3.4　Manipulating Multiple Records

A brief explanation follows of "manipulating," or processing a number of records using a single screen or conversely using a number of screens for processing a single database record.

When you look at this situation from a practical point of view, in the majority of cases you will have to extract data from a number of databases to produce a single screen. When you prepare certain general ledger reports, which is an accounting focal point for various transactions, you need to draw information from the accounts payable module, from the accounts receivable module, from budget, payroll, inventory, and, depending on the nature of the business, from a half a dozen other accounting modules, as well. On a single screen, you can only display or process a maximum of 1,920 characters (80 characters by 24 lines), but you would normally want to see a lot less to be practical about it. On a standard Millennium screen, or any other kind of screen, you will seldom find a design that calls for all 1920 characters due to certain conventions. You will need to dedicate a substantial portion of your screen for system messages, command line requirements, titles and header information and embedded spacing that will make the panel legible. The chances are good that you will not be able to fit all the requirements on a single screen. Likewise, to create a single (composite) screen, you need to draw certain selected fields from a number of records to provide for the necessary information.

A multiple screen contains a list of records with keys matching the entry in the qualifier. When the records appear on the panel, Millennium will display the key of the last record which was entered in the qualifier field. Every record that satisfies the given criteria will be listed followed by an END-OF-LIST message. Millennium also preloads the character "C" in the command field (see Figure 3.9) to terminate the operation. (C stands for "completion.")

Records are always displayed in an update mode (that is, GU). Figure 3.10 shows how to perform different functions on each of the displayed records merely by specifying them in the subcommand field.

As previously indicated, this fourth generation environment enables you to utilize alternate keys or indices to retrieve your records.

Another situation is where a particular record, to be accessed and displayed in its entirety, requires a multiple-screen media. This is to say, you will need two or several panels to display and disseminate a group of logically related information.

3.5   Querying with Millennium

So far a comprehensive command line concept has been discussed which enables you to specify to this fourth generation support environment what needs to be performed. Also discussed was Millennium's ability to maintain

```
  > C     002,10007                                        ON RLSAA

                 ---CURRENT AGENT STATUS REPORT---

  AGENCY==> VARSEGI REALTORS           CODE==> 002

        NUMBER    AGENT NAME              SALES TO DATE    COMMISSION

    D   10002    ALEX KOWALSKI            $234,998.00      23,499.80

    I   10003    GEORGE GREGORY           $654,112.00      72,456.00

    _   10004    JOHN TANNENBAUM          $112,909.00      11,290.00

    R   10005    BETTY SMITH              $290,000.00      31,567.00

    M   10007    MARY KESSLER             $309,700.00      32,765.00


    _   ____     _____          _____       _____

    _   ____     _____          _____       _____


    A205W-END OF LIST
                                  08/19/88   11:09:18  M4LL DEV2 ____
```

Figure 3.10 This shows a multiple screen record using different sub-command instructions.

a set of internally developed databases in a thoroughly real time environment. These are significant breakthroughs in design. To achieve these abilities in an otherwise conventional system, you would need to develop a comprehensive file-maintenance mechanism which could be costly and time consuming.

A third function to be addressed is a set of vendor's supplied facilities to query—that is the ability to selectively retrieve and display information using real time technology. McCormack & Dodge has developed a number of query-related databases over the years to support the user in utilizing standard, as well as special query functions. An extensive list of these features is summarized in Figure 3.11. Standard queries allow you to retrieve and display information residing in the application database using the CQUBR panel.

Figure 3.14 charts out the entire Standard Query mechanism, which happens to be a rather complex apparatus. Refer to this chart throughout the discussion on standard queries and how they operate internally.

Standard queries have four basic elements. These are: a query name, a display block, a where block, and a sort block. Figure 3.14 depicts this structure.

DBID	Database name	Function
CDD	Data Dictionary	Contains records defining each field in your application and control file databases
CDM	Data Macro	Contains data macros that can be used in the display and sort blocks of the CQUBR screen
CFP	Print Profile	Contains print profiles that allow you to print a hard copy of a system generated answer set
CH1	Hierarchy	Contains records defining the hierarchical reporting structure used in queries
C02	Filter Criteria	Defines the physical attributes of the application source files processed in the Batch Extractor Program.
CQU	Query	Contains query records and allows you to create, store, modify and execute queries.
CQQ	Query Question	Contains a list of predefined records that are questions linked to a standard query on the CQU database
CSF	Search Field	Contains records that define the name of the field on which you want to query.
CSS	Stop Values	Contains search field values for a specific search field that will not have indexes built during the batch extraction run.
NDX	Index	Contains indexed values associated with the search fields in your application databases

Figure 3.11   This list describes query-related databases.

The query name, as depicted in Figure 3.14, is made up of three components: the database identifier (DBID), a user-defined second component which is the identifier (IDENT), and a query name.

The display block on the CQUBR panel is responsible for the result of the query process. This block has the ability to accommodate a number of values, such as the CDD field names, $$COUNT module, data macros and a number of screen identifiers.

The CDD field is the data dictionary drives Millennium and contains all the necessary field names for reference, including specific edit rules and other important definitions. To enter display fields correctly, you need to know each field name as it appears on the data dictionary database (CDD).

To digress for a second, it is important to point out something quite practical. The easiest way to keep track of the data elements is to keep the most current copy of data dictionary at hand, for reference. This needs to be done constantly. Millennium, of course can also do it interactively, but then every time you need a specific piece of information, you will have to make an entry on the command line such as:

```
> GD _____  (DBID) _____ ON CDDLS
```

Millennium will then respond by going down a link level to display the required field names, it returns afterwards to the previous screen that triggered this second level display. If you were on a query screen, you could position your cursor over the display field before activating PF4 and, then, use the "sticky cursor" (PF6) to bring the correct field name back to the display screen.

The sticky cursor is a neat concept. It simply means that while you are looking at a certain screen, you will be able to set it aside as you require additional information elsewhere, within or outside the current application environment. Thus, you can trigger a related screen through the positioning of the cursor and by pressing PF Key 6. This will take you to the specific data while allowing you to access and "transport" an image of that data field back from where the original request was issued. You can achieve all that with cursor action and by pressing a PF key.

$$COUNT works in conjunction with the sort block, which is an optional feature on the CQUBR screen. Sort allows you to display the result of a query according to the value of a CDD field or the Data Macro. (If a sort sequence is not specified to Millennium, the result will be a primary key display.)

Data macros, the third component, under the display block concept also has an extensive role in manipulating the data stored in your application and in displaying the sorted result of a query. Data macros, allow you to manipulate such data in memory or in other storage areas, perform special statistical commands like averaging, totaling and formatting through the use of special command words. Their special versatility also allows one to reformat a particular data field, or simply to concatenate a number of them to retrieve values from memory.

The fourth component of the display block is the screen identifier. The screen identifier entered in the display field can be any screen ID within the database being queried. As probably noted by now, Millennium combines the screen ID with the database identifier (DBID) of the query name to determine the screen name of the target (or receiving) screen. When you execute a query, an intermediate screen will display informing you just how many records were selected by the query.

The where block (Figure 3.12) appears on the CQUBR screen and determines what specific record or records are to be selected by the query process. It contains one or a number of search expression, which are then evaluated against each record.

A search expression, such as the one shown in Figure 3.12, is made up of the following components: a search field name, a relational operator and

```
> GUH   RLS,COMMISSION,4THQUARTER                          ON CQUBR

   DBID, IDENT, QUERY NAME   RLS COMMISSION 4THQUARTER
   _
DISPLAY..
      AGENCYCDE     AGENTLSNAM    SALESTODTE/U    SALETODTE,4    #4THCOMM
      $$COUNT       _____    _____      _____     _____

WHERE...
         (AGENCYCDE EQ '001' OR '002')
         AND SALESTODTE GT 700,000

         _____
         _____
         _____
         _____
         _____


SORT.....
      AGENCYCDE      AGENTLSNAM     _____   _____   _____
SUB TOTAL   Y           _                  _                           _
SUMMARIZE   _   ASCENDING/DESCENDING  A/D  _  M: STATUS RANGE  _ _

                           08/12/88  12:08:32        M4LL DEV2 ____
```

Figure 3.12   This is a query panel in reference to the where block.

a search value. Search fields, such as the AGENCYCDE, have to be defined on the CSF database.

Relational operators enable you to establish a relationship between a search field and its value to form a search expression such as "equal," or "not equal," "less than," "greater than," etc. Take a quick look at Figure 3.13, which gives an inventory of the relational operators used by Millennium. It is surprising how effectively these Boolean operators perform as you begin combining them into cohesive statements for selecting, excluding, computing, etc. For example:

```
SALARY BT 29,000 AND 35,000 AND STARTDT LE 01/01/75 OR
SALARY GT 35,000 AND CLASSCD EQ '12387' OR '12007'...
```

The above statement can be translated into the following: Select all those employees whose annual salary is between $29,000 and $35,000 and who started with the company prior to January 1, 1975. Also, select that category of employees whose annual salary is greater than $35,000 a year in job classification 12387 or 12007.

The above illustration contains both relational operators (that is, GT, LE, NGE), and search field values. Imagine the amount of effort you would need if you were to code the above criteria using a conventional language interactively.

Operator	Function
EQ, NEQ	Determine if the search field/value combination in the query is equal to or not equal to the corresponding field and its value on the record.
GT, NGT	Determines if the search field/value combination in the query is greater than or not greater than the value of the corresponding field on the record.
GE, NGE	Determines if the search field/value combination in the query is greater than or or not greater then or equal to the value of the corresponding field on the record.
LE, NLE	Determines if the search field/value combination in the query is less then or equal to or not less than or equal to the value of the corresponding field on the record.
BT, NBT	Determines if the value of the field on the record is between or not between the two search field values indicated in the query.
SW, NSW	Determines if the value of an alphanumeric field on the record starts with or does not start with the value indicated in the search field of the query.
WI	Determines if the value of a field on a record falls within the framework of the hierarchy set up of the CH1 database. This relational operator is used only with search fields that have been defined as part of a hierarchy.

Figure 3.13 This list describes Millennium relational operators.

Millennium, overall employs the following search field values:

1. Alphanumeric search field—these must be enclosed in single quotes such as '12387'.

2. Numeric field values, which should be entered according to the amount format field on the CSFBR screen (including commas, signs, and decimal points) such as 29,000.00.

3. Date search field values, which should be entered according to the date edit mask. For example, if the date edit mask for the search field is MM/DD/YY (month, day, and year with slashes) and the value of the search field is January 1, 1975, enter the search field value as 01/01/75.

The sort block is the fourth component part of the standard queries structure, which is an optional feature on the CQUBR screen. Essentially, it allows you to display the result of a query according to the value of a CDD field or the data macro. As already pointed out in the preceding text, if you do not specify a sort sequence to Millennium, your result will be a primary key order display.

Millennium has five 15 character sort fields on the CQUBR screen that enables you to sort a query up to five levels. Figure 3.12 shows these sort control fields such as AGENCYCDE and AGENTLSNAM. Millennium interprets sort fields using a sequence in which they are entered on the screen that is from left to right, so that the first sort break will be the rightmost sort field on the CQUBR screen.

Note that there are also five subtotal fields in the system corresponding to each sort field so that you can specify that a subtotal be taken on a sort break by entering a 'y' in the subtotal field directly underneath each sort delimiter. To carry this a bit further, you can also summarize your answer if you specified subtotaling for a sort field. The summarization process allows you to display only the total lines that take place at each sort break and a final or grand total. As the result, the detail records within each sort break are not displayed.

Two additional features are available in conjunction with the sort.

1. The system performs a sort either in ascending or in descending order.
2. The extensive SORT field Help can be used when you need clarification for a given procedure.

Sort field Help is based on the value entered in the sort field and the position of the cursor. When you request Help, you need to be aware of one of four situations.

1. If the sort field is blank, link down to the THPBR screen displaying the vendor's Help for the sort field.
2. If the cursor is positioned over the first character of a valid CDD name, link down to the CDDLS panel and display the data dictionary record for that sort field
3. If the cursor is positioned over the first character of a data macro, you need to link down to the data macro on the CDMBR panel. (A particular data macro entry results in the selection of a number of such entries...)
4. If you want a complete list of all valid sort fields for the particular database being queried, enter a question mark or an asterisk in the first position of the sort field and press PF1. At that point Millennium will link you to the CDDLS panel and display a list of the CDD fields.

Figure 3.14 is a brief overview of the entire standard queries processing mechanism.

3.6   Millennium Driven Screens

Millennium based screens are no different from your own design in the sense that they are used to display, retrieve, and maintain data according to your specifications. Actually, Millennium, as long as you stay within M&D

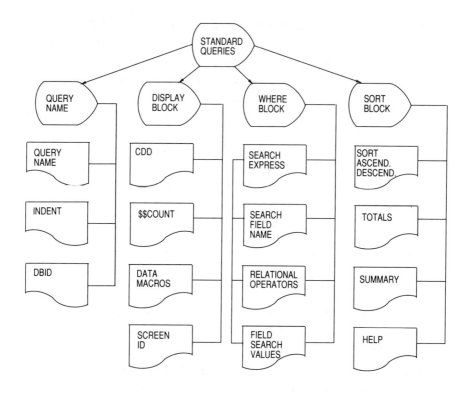

Figure 3.14 This flowchart presents an overview of the standard queries processing mechanism.

applications (if not, you will need SDT, which is a topic of Chapter 5) allows you to create your own screens, or simply customize the vendor's original product.

There are two methods available to modify your screens: the first one is through the screen designer and a second one which is done through screen maintenance. When you use the Screen Designer method, you can easily modify an existing panel, or to create a new one. You should use the screen designer facilities when you are in the process of making extensive changes to your screen such as rearranging them, or moving the location of certain fields from one area of your screen to another. Screen maintenance, on the other hand is best used when you need to modify an existing screen via standard file maintenance. This method is normally used for less extensive changes—mostly cosmetic in nature.

3.6.1   The Screen Designer Technique

The screen designer can be invoked through menu selection or simply through the use of the command line. If you are a beginner, take time to learn to handle this method via a set of menus. Only after you have gained some efficiency with the system should you try entering an instruction directly into the command line. When you use the screen designer, make a copy of a particular screen before modifying it. User screens are denoted by the character "U" in the fourth position of your screen identifier such as RLHU2.

In order to display the screen designer menu, invoke the command line and press enter afterwards. The result is shown in Figure 3.15.

The reason for copying a screen and using the copied version of it is purely security, and the vendor, for that obvious reason will not allow you to modify an existing panel with a "production" status. So, to copy the above RLHMD screen: position the cursor over the enter cmd qualifier (Figure 3.15) and type RLHMD. (Also enter an "X" in the sub-command

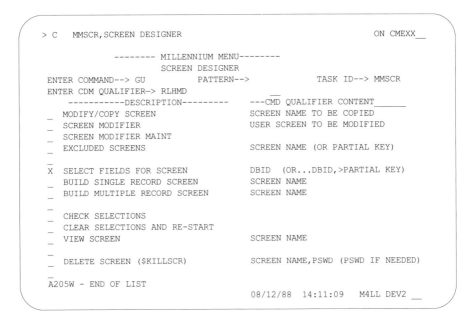

```
> C   MMSCR,SCREEN DESIGNER                               ON CMEXX__

              -------- MILLENNIUM MENU--------
                     SCREEN DESIGNER
   ENTER COMMAND--> GU         PATTERN-->              TASK ID--> MMSCR
   ENTER CDM QUALIFIER-> RLHMD                __
      -----------DESCRIPTION---------    ---CMD QUALIFIER CONTENT_____
   _  MODIFY/COPY SCREEN              SCREEN NAME TO BE COPIED
   _  SCREEN MODIFIER                 USER SCREEN TO BE MODIFIED
   _  SCREEN MODIFIER MAINT
   _  EXCLUDED SCREENS                SCREEN NAME (OR PARTIAL KEY)

   X  SELECT FIELDS FOR SCREEN        DBID  (OR...DBID,>PARTIAL KEY)
   _  BUILD SINGLE RECORD SCREEN      SCREEN NAME
   _  BUILD MULTIPLE RECORD SCREEN    SCREEN NAME

   _
   _  CHECK SELECTIONS
   _  CLEAR SELECTIONS AND RE-START
   _  VIEW SCREEN                     SCREEN NAME

   _
   _  DELETE SCREEN ($KILLSCR)        SCREEN NAME,PSWD (PSWD IF NEEDED)

   _
   A205W - END OF LIST
                                      08/12/88  14:11:09   M4LL DEV2 __
```

Figure 3.15   This is a screen designer menu to handle all systems-related functions.

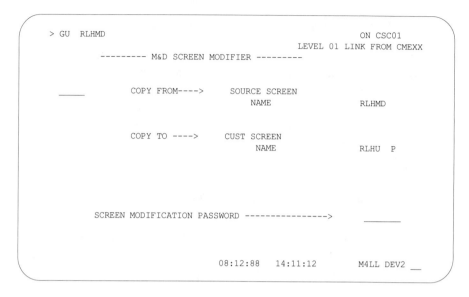

```
  > GU   RLHMD                                                  ON CSC01
                                               LEVEL 01 LINK FROM CMEXX
                  --------- M&D SCREEN MODIFIER ---------


                          COPY FROM---->      SOURCE SCREEN
                  _____                            NAME            RLHMD


                          COPY TO ---->       CUST SCREEN
                                                   NAME            RLHU  P




                  SCREEN MODIFICATION PASSWORD --------------->      _____



                                    08:12:88   14:11:12        M4LL DEV2  __
```

Figure 3.16 This is an example of the M&D Screen Modifier submenu.

field for the selection and press enter.) The result is shown in Figure 3.16, which is M&D's Screen Modifier panel. The CS01 screen indicates the name of the screen being copied in the copy field which now contains the first four characters of your new screen name. Note the character "P" in the rightmost position of the copy field: "RLHU P". This will actually become the fifth character of your screen identifier to be consolidated with the previous ID such as RLHUP to further differentiate an existing panel from your modified one. For added security, note also that the vendor provides you with password protection. This is more or less an optional situation, although, if you assign a password to a screen, it must be entered after the screen name when you are in update or delete Mode.

A brief exercise follows to show you how to "clone," modify, or simply develop your own panel via the screen designer process. In Figure 3.17, a screen was simply copied from an existing one for the purpose of customizing it. The "Employee Address" screen shows five variable fields, each one corresponding to a title header, such as the "EMPLOYEE:ID", the "EMPLOYEE:NAME", etc. Note two initial field designators in the variable portion of the "EMPLOYEE:ADDRESS" panel. These are the pound signs (#) and the dollar signs ($). As you can see, a "$" sign represents one character of an alphanumeric string. So, a 13-position long field, such as

```
 > GUH RLHUP                                          ON SCREEN CSCRN
                                            LINK LEVEL 01 FROM CMEXX

                1    2          EMPLOYEE:ADDRESS

     ------
     :
     $$$       3
     ------

     EMPLOYEE:ID              #######
     EMPLOYEE:NAME            $$$$$$$$$$$$$$$$$$$$$$$$$$$$$
     EMPLOYEE:DEPT            #####
     EMPLOYEE:STREET:ADDRESS  $$$$$$$$$$$$$$$$$$$$$$
     EMPLOYEE:CITY:STATE:ZIP  $$$$$$$$$$$$$$$$ $$   #####


                              08/12/88  11:12:01  M4LL DEV2___
```

Figure 3.17   This is a copy of an M&D "production screen" to be modified.

the "EMPLOYEE:NAME" would be represented by a string of dollar signs such as $$$$$$$$$$$$$$. A pound sign, on the other hand denotes a single character of a numeric field. You are advised to define a numeric field only when you need to perform some form of computation within the field. A percent sign (%) represents one character of a date field. All you need to do is to define an eight-position-long date field such as %%%%%%%, which will result in a field display format of __/__/__ or, to use an example, 11/12/88. The percent sign actually represents both the date field and the date delimiter with a colon (:) denoting embedded space or spaces in a literal.

In reviewing Figure 3.17, you need to start out with three basic premises.

1. You want to place the character "D" next to the title header as done in Figure 3.18. The character "D" (also refers to Figure 3.20), will delete the screen title.

2. You need to replace the main title of the current panel with another header such as "EMPLOYEE DEMOGRAPHIC".

3. You also want to add a whole blank line in order to separate the "EMPLOYEE:ID" constant from the six dashes that appear underneath the dollar sign. You are not through yet with modifying the RLHUP panel, You want to continue the customization process of that screen with two additional objectives in mind. These are as follows:

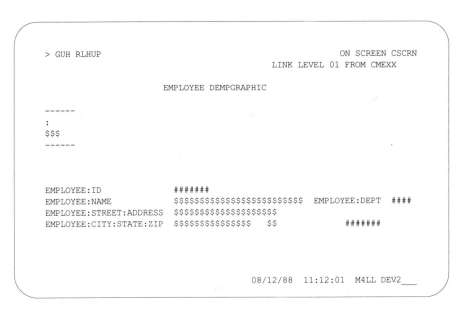

```
> GUH RLHUP                                      ON  SCREEN CSCRN
                                         LINK LEVEL 01 FROM CMEXX


          1   2        DEMPLOYEE:ADDRESS


  ------
  :
  $$$        3
  ------

  INSERTB
  EMPLOYEE:NAME              $$$$$$$$$$$$$$$$$$$$$$$$$$$$$$      =
 -EMPLOYEE:DEPT             #####--------------------->   4
  EMPLOYEE:STREET:ADDRESS   $$$$$$$$$$$$$$$$$$$$$$$$
  EMPLOYEE:CITY:STATE:ZIP   $$$$$$$$$$$$$$$   $$    >>>>>#####      5



                           08/12/88  11:12:01  M4LL DEV2___
```

Figure 3.18   This is an example of implementing changes on the copied screen.

```
> GUH RLHUP                                      ON  SCREEN CSCRN
                                         LINK LEVEL 01 FROM CMEXX

                    EMPLOYEE DEMPGRAPHIC


  ------
  :
  $$$
  ------



  EMPLOYEE:ID               #######
  EMPLOYEE:NAME             $$$$$$$$$$$$$$$$$$$$$$$$$$$$$$  EMPLOYEE:DEPT  ####
  EMPLOYEE:STREET:ADDRESS   $$$$$$$$$$$$$$$$$$$$$$$$
  EMPLOYEE:CITY:STATE:ZIP   $$$$$$$$$$$$$$$   $$              #######



                           08/12/88  11:12:01  M4LL DEV2___
```

Figure 3.19   This is the revised screen, now "EMPLOYEE DEMOGRAPHIC" reflecting changes shown in Fig 3.18.

Command	Function
>	Shift a screen title, field name or field to the right. Enter this command to the immediate right of the field you want to move. Enter one greater than sign for each space you want the field to move.
<	Shift a screen title, field name or field to the left. Enter this command to the immediate left of the field you want to move. Enter one less than sign for each space you want the field to move.
'	Add a screen title or field name by enclosing it in single quotation marks.
"	Duplicate the line above the line it's entered on. Enter two single quotation marks at the beginning of a blank line under the line you want to duplicate. This command works only on a blank line.
+	Add a new fields to a screen. Fields that you add to a screen are for display only. This command can only be used on screens that you create from scratch. Enter this command to the immediate left of the field you want to add/ To change an existing field, you must first delete it using the "D" command and then reenter it using this command.
-,=	Move a screen title, field, or field name from one place on a screen to another. Place a dash in front of the field you want to move and the equal sign where you want to move it to. You can only move one field at a time. Also, a field can only be moved to another place within its original screen block.
*	Link down to the control record for either field names or fields. Enter this command to the immediate left of the field you want to prompt. Multiple entries are permitted. However,, Screen Designer displays only one control record each time you press enter.
/	Split a description field. This command allows you to split certain field with special CSV names into nine sub-fields. When you split a field, it is recommended that you split it from left to right. For example, if the CSV name of a field is desc or comment, you can split the field.
D	Delete a screen title, field name or field. Enter this command to the immediate left of the field you want to delete.
DELETE	Delete a blank line. Enter this command in the first position of the blank line you want to delete.
INSERT	Insert a blank line below the line it's entered on. Enter this command starting in the first position of the blank line. If the line isn't blank, press the EOF key to temporarily erase the line
INSERTB	Insert a blank line above the line you enter the command on. Enter this command starting in the first position of a blank line. If the line isn't blank, press the EOF key to temporarily erase the line before you press enter.

Figure 3.20   Screen designer commands

4. To place a dash (or a minus sign) in front of the "EMPLOYEE:DEPT" field and an equal (=) sign following the "EMPLOYEE:NAME" field. This means that you intend to move the entire "EMPLOYEE:DEPT" field a line up so that it would appear next to the equal sign. Note that the characters '-' and '=' go pretty much hand in hand.

5. Finally, you are going to move the zip code field to the right by five positions for added clarity.

Once all these changes are in place, press enter and the result will be shown in Figure 3.19. Figure 3.20 reveals that the vendor has a powerful screen painter within the Millennium system which enables you to utilize a dozen or so major commands for enhancing, modifying and editing a screen. (This discussion will be enhanced in Chapter 5 with regards to the System Development Tool or SDT environment.)

3.6.2   The Screen Maintenance Technique

Every screen in the Millennium environment is made up of a number of control records that are stored on a set of corresponding databases. To change the format of a screen, all you need to do is modify the database via standard file maintenance procedures. If you were to change one of the title headings at the top of the screen, for example, you do not need to flag it by using the character "D". Simply display the screen in update mode, make the necessary changes and then press enter to update the data associated with the screen. In the Millennium system every database has a pointer set up which keeps the panels in sync with its corresponding database.

There are four screen databases within this fourth generation Millennium system. These are the so-called screen parameter database or CSP, the screen literal database or CSL, a screen variable database or CSV, and the optimized screen database, or COS. The screen parameter database defines the framework or the parameter of a given panel with regard to format, spacing, or overall screen layout. The screen literal database, as the title reveals, stores the literal portion of the data that appears on the screen that makes up the "mask." This database, which is technically referred to as the CSL database, contains headings, titles, and field names and other constant information. To gain access to it, you need to rely on the corresponding CSLLS panel. In fact, the CSLLS panel enables you to define and store the various forms of literals and provides you with positional values of these literals (such as the rows and the columns of each field). The CSLLS screen also provides you with certain attributes such as normal or high-intensity display of your literals and so on.

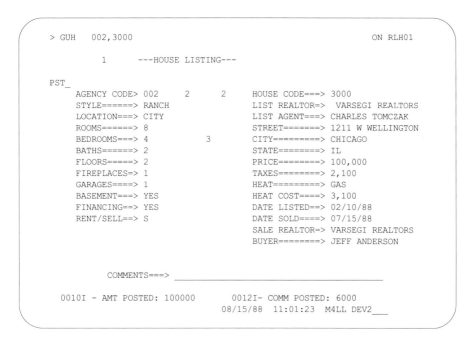

```
 > GUH    002,3000                                          ON RLH01


            1         ---HOUSE LISTING---

 PST_
        AGENCY CODE> 002        2        2     HOUSE CODE===> 3000
        STYLE======> RANCH                    LIST REALTOR=>  VARSEGI REALTORS
        LOCATION===> CITY                     LIST AGENT===> CHARLES TOMCZAK
        ROOMS======> 8                        STREET=======> 1211 W WELLINGTON
        BEDROOMS===> 4                  3     CITY=========> CHICAGO
        BATHS======> 2                        STATE========> IL
        FLOORS=====> 2                        PRICE========> 100,000
        FIREPLACES=> 1                        TAXES========> 2,100
        GARAGES====> 1                        HEAT=========> GAS
        BASEMENT===> YES                      HEAT COST====> 3,100
        FINANCING==> YES                      DATE LISTED==> 02/10/88
        RENT/SELL==> S                        DATE SOLD====> 07/15/88
                                              SALE REALTOR=> VARSEGI REALTORS
                                              BUYER========> JEFF ANDERSON


            COMMENTS===>  _____

     0010I - AMT POSTED: 100000       0012I- COMM POSTED: 6000
                                      08/15/88  11:01:23  M4LL DEV2___
```

Figure 3.21   This screen shows the three major blocks in the Millennium system; (1) represents the header block, (2) represents the two global fields, and (3) denotes the literal/variable blocks.

The variable part of the screen, on the other hand is accommodated on the CVS database, or the screen variable database. This is information directly retrieved from data entry or from a file.

Each panel to be utilized in your system contains a CSV record. In fact, there is a corresponding record for each variable field that appears on the CSVLS screen. There are also security levels attached to the CSVLS screen responsible for defining who has access to what, as well as the mode of access, that is, update mode versus browse or inquiry. The optimized screen database or COS stores the optimized version of the screen. The term "optimization" or "optimized screen" denotes the system's internal processing mechanism where all the control features that make up a screen are summarized on a single record.

To explain the screen maintenance apparatus, an explanation of the concept of screen blocks is needed. Screen blocks always appear in a particular sequence such as a heading and global blocks followed by the literal and variable blocks. (Note that a similar explanation of this infrastructure is given under SDT.)

The heading block, which is an optional feature, contains title information that explains the function of a screen. It appears only at the top of the screen, even on multiple record screens. The header occupies the first row following the command line and the line the link level indicator utilizes.

The global block contains optional fields of both literals and variables. Global literals define field names that apply to everything that has a key value. In Figure 3.21, the employee identification number and the department number are both literals. Should your panel contain globals, they will come immediately after the heading block, although, as mentioned previously, you can omit them if you wish.

The literal/variable block contains all the fields and field names that are not classified as headings or globals on the rest of the screen. The easiest way to think about a literal/variable field is as a piece of data entered by the user as part of an on-line transaction. (In batch mode this type of information would be entered through a file update.)

3.7   How To Create a Screen Via the Millennium System

When you use the screen designer mechanism, you may create a set of new display screens, but not have the ability to update them. When you "clone" a screen, on the other hand, Millennium will allow you to copy the control record of an existing screen. Afterwards, you can modify such a panel to suit your particular need. Since creating a screen requires some systems analysis or investigative work, you will need to decide on the kind of information that will be displayed on this screen in terms of data elements or data fields. The best approach for you to take would be to review your data dictionary to make sure that the fields are spelled correctly and to verify their length, disposition, and other viable attributes.

To invoke the dictionary simply issue the following statement on the command line:

```
> GD ____ (DBID) _____ ON CDDLS _____
```

A record for this example has been created containing the following fields from the RLH database:

```
EMPADD
EMPCITY
EMPCLAS
```

```
        ROW              -1-                      -2-

         1             EMPID                   EMPDEPT

         2             LEAVE BLANK
                         -1-                      -2-
         3             EMPNAME                 EMPCLAS
                         -1-
         4             EMPADD
                         -1-                      -2-
         5             EMPCITY                 EMPSTA
                         -1-                      -2-
         6             EMPZIP                  EMPPHON
```

Figure 3.22 This is a sample rough draft of a screen layout used in this case study.

```
EMPDEPT
EMPID
EMPNAME
EMPPHON
EMPSTA
EMPZIP
```

First of all, you want to draw a rough draft of the previous layout that is presented in Figure 3.22. Note that the numbers above each field reference their relative position on the screen: simply -1- displays on the left side of the panel whereas -2- appears on the right side.

EMPID and EMPDEPT are key fields. Millennium stores all key fields with a value of 'K' or 'A' in the key audit field on the CDDLS screens. These values are called command qualifiers or "Comquals" for short.

Once you have completed the rough draft, display the screen designer menu, which, as mentioned earlier, can be invoked via the command line in the following manner:

```
> GD _____MMSCR _____ ON  CMEXX _____
```

The result is shown in Figure 3.23. Here, the DB identifier "RLH" has been entered as the CMD qualifier. The cursor has been positioned next to the SELECT FIELDS FOR SCREEN, placing an 'X' adjacent to it. Afterward, enter was pressed, triggering the field selection panel presented in Figure 3.24. Note that the fields are displayed in alphabetical order. For that reason, you may not be able to select all the required fields on the same "page." In order to display the rest of the fields, keep pressing enter until an "END OF LIST" message appears.

The CDDSC screen enables you to define the field's relative row (RR), and position within that row (##). Based on this rough draft, nine fields

```
> C   MMSCR,SCREEN DESIGNER                              ON CMEXX__

            -------- MILLENNIUM MENU--------
                     SCREEN DESIGNER
    ENTER COMMAND--> GU         PATTERN-->            TASK ID--> MMSCR
    ENTER CDM QUALIFIER-> RLHMD                __
        ----------DESCRIPTION---------      --------CMD QUALIFIER CONTENT_____
    _   MODIFY/COPY SCREEN                  SCREEN NAME TO BE COPIED
    _   SCREEN MODIFIER                     USER SCREEN TO BE MODIFIED
    _   SCREEN MODIFIER MAINT
    _   EXCLUDED SCREENS                    SCREEN NAME (OR PARTIAL KEY)
    _
    X   SELECT FIELDS FOR SCREEN            DBID  (OR...DBID,>PARTIAL KEY)
    _   BUILD SINGLE RECORD SCREEN          SCREEN NAME
    _   BUILD MULTIPLE RECORD SCREEN        SCREEN NAME
    _
    _   CHECK SELECTIONS
    _   CLEAR SELECTIONS AND RE-START
    _   VIEW SCREEN                         SCREEN NAME
    _
    _   DELETE SCREEN ($KILLSCR)            SCREEN NAME,PSWD (PSWD IF NEEDED)
    _
    A205W - END OF LIST
                                    08/12/88  14:11:09   M4LL DEV2 __
```

Figure 3.23 This is a screen designer menu screen (also shown in Figure 3.15) to select certain data fields.

Copyright © 1988 McCormack & Dodge Corporation. Used by permission.

```
> GU  RLH,FNAME                                        ON CDDSC
                                        LEVEL 01 LINK FROM CMEXX
            ----- MILLENNIUM NEW SCREEN GENERATOR -----
                   ----- FIELD SELECTION -----
    DATABASE--> RLH

    RR  ##---NAME---K ------DEFAULT LITERAL--------- --OPTIONAL LITERAL--
    __  __  EMPADD     ADDRESS                       _____
    __  __  EMPCLAS    CLASSIFICATION                _____
    __  __  EMPCITY    CITY                          _____
    __  __  EMPDEF     DEFERRED COMP.                _____
    __  __  EMPDEPT  K DEPARTMENT                    _____
    __  __  EMPGROS    GROSS PAY                     _____
    __  __  EMPID    K IDENTIFIER                    _____
    __  __  EMPLIF     LIFE INSURANCE                _____
    __  __  EMPNAME    NAME                          _____
    __  __  EMPNET     NET EARNINGS                  _____
    __  __  EMPPHON    PHONE                         _____
    __  __  EMPSTA     STATE                         _____
    __  __  EMPTSA     TAX SHELTERED ANNUITIES       _____
    __  __  EMPUN      UNION DUES                    _____
    __  __  EMPZIP     ZIP CODE                      _____
                        08/17/88  09:12:03      M4LL DEV2 _____
```

Figure 3.24 This is the field selection menu screen showing data fields alphabetically.

Copyright © 1988 McCormack & Dodge Corporation. Used by permission.

```
> GU   RLH,FNAME                                              ON CDDSC
                                                LEVEL 01 LINK FROM CMEXX
              ----- MILLENNIUM NEW SCREEN GENERATOR -----
                     ----- FIELD SELECTION -----
   DATABASE—> RLH


   RR   ##---NAME---K -------DEFAULT LITERAL--------- --OPTIONAL LITERAL--
   _4   _1 EMPADD      ADDRESS                        _____
   _3   _2 EMPCLAS     CLASSIFICATION                 _____
   _5   _1 EMPCITY     CITY                           _____
   __   __ EMPDEF      DEFERRED COMP.                 _____
   _1   _2 EMPDEPT  K  DEPARTMENT                     _____
   __   __ EMPGROS     GROSS PAY                      _____
   _1   _1 EMPID    K  IDENTIFIER                     _____
   __   __ EMPLIF      LIFE INSURANCE                 _____
   _3   _1 EMPNAME     NAME                           _____
   __   __ EMPNET      NET EARNINGS                   _____
   _7   _1 EMPPHON     PHONE                          _____
   _5   _2 EMPSTA      STATE                          _____
   __   __ EMPTSA      TAX SHELTERED ANNUITIES        _____
   __   __ EMPUN       UNION DUES                     _____
   _6   _2 EMPZIP      ZIP CODE                       _____

                            08/17/88  09:12:03         M4LL DEV2  ____
```

Figure 3.25   This is the field selection menu screen following the selection.

need to be extracted from the data dictionary, which was accomplished interactively as shown in Figure 3.25.

Once field selection is completed and the information is processed, the Screen Designer Menu is reinvoked for the second time so that you can provide a screen name for the newly created dataset. The first four characters of the identifier, as mentioned earlier, will be "RLHU", since you are utilizing the RLH database and the last character designates that it is a user-defined panel. The fifth position will contain an additional identifier you picked (see Figure 3.16 where the character "P" was used at random) so that the five-character screen identifier will be RLHUP.

As part of the standard process, verify that the screen, which was defined, is not already in existence. You do this simply by entering the following command:

```
> GD _____ RLHU _____ON COSLS _____
```

Afterward, press function key 4. To continue the new record building process, enter an "X" next to the "BUILD SINGLE RECORD SCREEN" on the Screen Designer Menu, then press enter. The result is shown in Figure 3.26.

```
  > GD  1234567,12117                                    ON RLHUP

                    EMPLOYEE NAME AND ADDRESS

    ___   EMPLOYEE ID 1234567 DEPARTMENT 12117
  NAME GEORGE W STONE
  ADDRESS 127 W PARK AVENUE
  CITY ELMHURST STATE IL
  ZIP CODE 60126
  PHONE (312) 833-5674




                    08/12/88  11:12:08  M2LL  DEV2  ___
```

Figure 3.26 This is what you see when you display the first "automatic" layout by screen designer.

The problem with this layout is that it looks sort of cramped since the screen designer mechanism only gives you a single space between each data field. To make your layout a lot more legible, you need to rely on some sort of an editing character (or characters). These were highlighted earlier in Figure 3.20 (Parts I & II). For example, once you have selected the SCREEN MODIFIER FUNCTION on the screen designer menu screen, all you have to do is to apply some of the characters to further clarify your layout. To reedit line five:

CITY>>>>>>>>>>>>ELMHURST>>>>>>>>>STATE>>>>>IL

With some relatively minor cosmetic changes, your panel could very well look like the one presented in Figure 3.27. Once you have completed the definition of your panel, verify the command qualifiers (COMQUAL), as well. To achieve that, position your cursor over the subcommand field and type "COMQ", then press enter. This will trigger the COMQUAL definition panel for your verification.

Summary

Millennium was initially developed to provide extensive support for all McCormack & Dodge vendor products. This product is not only a powerful

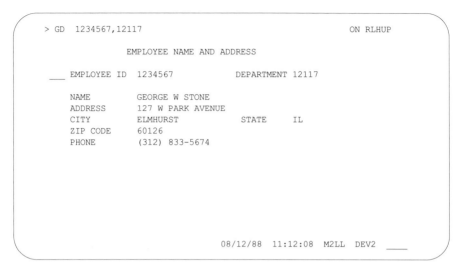

```
  > GD  1234567,12117                                ON RLHUP

                    EMPLOYEE NAME AND ADDRESS

  ___  EMPLOYEE ID  1234567           DEPARTMENT 12117

       NAME         GEORGE W STONE
       ADDRESS      127 W PARK AVENUE
       CITY         ELMHURST          STATE    IL
       ZIP CODE     60126
       PHONE        (312) 833-5674




                              08/12/88  11:12:08  M2LL  DEV2  ___
```

Figure 3.27   This represents the employee name and address screen after editing and adjustments.

fourth generation productivity tool, but also one that handles the interaction among a host of M&D designed applications. In fact, it is so thoroughly integrated into a a given application, that it would be next to impossible to segregate components of the Millennium system from that of a given application.

Millennium only works with M&D file structures. If you need to consolidate your own file structure or those of other vendor's into Millennium, you need to utilize M&D's system development tool product which communicates with all other external systems. The term "borderless" inquiry or design refers to the system's ability to retrieve information, that is to disseminate data in any location of a totally integrated multisystem environment.

Millennium relies extensively on two basic formats in executing a set of requirements. These are the primary and what the vendor refers to as "quick" commands.

Primary commands allow you to display records, execute queries, leave processing steps, and so on. For efficiency, they are also thoroughly enhanced with a number of associated subcommands which allows you to refine every command in terms of adding, updating, replacing, deleting, moving, inserting, and displaying information without having to write code to accomplish that.

Overall, Millennium utilizes five types of primary commands. These commands are as follows:

1. A DISPLAY command, which enables you to look at, but not change, a record. While you can use an update command to accomplish the same, technically, such commands are a great deal more expensive in terms of I/O resources, resulting in the degradation of system's response time. (This has to do with sound systems engineering and not with the capabilities of the Millennium system.)

2. An UPDATE command, so you can add, change, insert, replace, delete, or move a record within this fourth generation environment.

3. A QUERY command, through which you can execute stored queries, scroll through the results on an answer-set screen, and print a hard copy of a query answer set, if this is what you need.

4. A PROGRAM command, which is for executing special Millennium programs.

5. A START-OVER command, allowing you to cancel or leave any processing step, or cancel Link Levels, and clear your terminal's memory buffer.

Quick commands are very important because they allow you to freely "navigate" across an array of M&D based applications while giving you linkage to a particular database.

Primary commands are used by Millennium to retrieve records and display them on the screen. Subcommands, on the other hand allow you to manipulate the data: more specifically, they allow you to add, revise, and delete records from a particular database. Standard queries are deployed to retrieve and display information residing on your application database using the CQUBR panel.

Standard queries have four basic elements. These are: a query name, a display block, a where block and a sort block. The query name, as depicted in Figure 3.14, is made up of three components: the database identifier or DBID, a user-defined second component which is the identifier (IDENT), and a query name.

It is the display block on the CQUBR panel that is responsible for the result of the query process. This block has the ability to accommodate a number of values, such as the CDD field names, $$COUNT module, data macros and a number of screen identifiers. The CDD field is the data dictionary which drives Millennium and contains all the necessary field names for reference including specific edit rules and other important definitions. To enter display fields correctly, you need to know each field name as it appears on the data dictionary database (CDD).

The sticky cursor simply means that while you are looking at a certain screen, you can set it aside as you require additional information elsewhere, within or outside the current application environment. Thus, you can trigger a related screen through the positioning of the cursor and by pressing PF Key 6. This will take you to the specific data while allowing you to access and "transport" an image of that data field back from where the original request was issued. All of that can be accomplished with cursor action and by pressing a PF key.

$$COUNT works in conjunction with the sort block. Data macros, the third component, under the display block concept also plays an extensive role in manipulating the data stored in your application. Data macros overall, enable you to do calculations on such stored data, perform special statistical commands, like averaging, totaling through the use of key words. Their special versatility gives you the ability to reformat a particular data field, or simply to concatenate a number of them in order to retrieve values from memory.

A fourth aspect of the display block is the screen identifier. The screen identifier entered in the display field can be any screen ID within the database being queried. When you execute a query, an intermediate screen will display informing you just how many records were selected by the query process. Relational operators enable you to establish a relationship between a search field and its value to form a search expression such as "equal," or "not equal," "less than," "greater than," etc.

Millennium-based screens are no different from your own design in the sense that they are used to display, retrieve, and maintain data according to your specifications. Actually, Millennium, as long as you stay within M&D applications (if not, you will need SDT, which is a topic of Chapter 5) allows you to create your own screens, or simply customize the vendor's original product.

There are two methods available to you in modifying your screens: the first one is through the screen designer and a second one through screen maintenance. When you use the screen designer method, you can easily modify an existing panel, or develop a new one, as well. You should use the screen designer facilities when you are in the process of making extensive changes to your screens such as rearranging them, or moving the location of certain fields from one area on your screen to another. Screen maintenance, on the other hand is best used when you need to modify an existing screen via standard file maintenance. This method is normally used for less extensive changes, mostly cosmetic in nature.

Chapter 4

M&D's Millennium—Part II

4.1   Building and Using Menu Screens

In a fourth generation environment, it is quite important not only to have the ability to utilize menu screens, but also the ability to build them from scratch. After all, these screens give you the ability to find your way through a maze of complex procedures, while providing you with a great deal of tutorial facilities.

Probably one of the more significant aspects of using menu screens is that they tend to simplify a system for you that would otherwise be overwhelming from a procedural point of view. The terminal operator who handles only a narrow segment of the total features can do so with a great deal of efficiency without having to understand the nuts and bolts of the complete environment.

Interestingly enough, looking at this concept from a machine viewpoint rather than from the viewpoint of human resources, the use of menus can be a great deal more demanding on the computer than its human counterpart. This means longer CPU cycles, as well as response time. The trade-off, however, is unquestionably in favor of simplicity of operation. Thus it is designed to work efficiently with people rather than prioritizing on hardware considerations alone. In the Millennium system, you can by-pass the menu selection process and still maintain a desired level of procedural simplicity just by using the command line for both selecting and executing a particular task.

Menu screens, and thus the concept of a menu driven system, are quite important in the Millennium environment for a number of reasons. Suppose you need to add one or a number of tasks to an existing application that will be handled by a new user group. Or suppose you need to develop a module dealing with some statistical analysis of the company's hiring practices, which entails a set of new screens, reports, and maintenance procedures. You may need this module to be incorporated into the payroll system, since it utilizes information provided by the payroll/personnel database. The new user who will be operating this recently incorporated subsystem is assumed to have no previous payroll experience and will only be using perhaps a tiny fraction of the system, a total of 2 to 3 percent of the overall application software.

This new enhancement is best handled through a set of menu screens (both main and submenus) rather than entering data directly through the command line. A command line, although it is a fast way of getting things done, may not be best suited for beginners. When requesting an action via the command line, you need to know the particular database or databases you want to access and some of the search fields associated with them.

For our new user group, we will need to give explicit instructions. We need to give them the choices, the procedures available, and how those procedures should be utilized. So for them, we will have to develop a new module using Millennium generated menu screens. Millennium stores all the control records necessary for building and retrieving a menu screen for the systems designer on the CME database.

This definition of a database has to do with M&D's approach to systems engineering in the Millennium environment. McCormack & Dodge uses dozens of internally created (and Monitored) databases to address tasks and functional areas. Thus, the CME database gives you the ability to create new, or simply maintain existing menu screens. All viable functions that are mandatory in reference to a data dictionary, for example, are "locked into" the CDD database. These would include format and field attributes, disposition, field lengths, edit criteria, and on a higher level, some proto-typing facilities.

M&D databases are transparent to the user. They do not require you to have a clear understanding of the table of normalization process, aliases, and synonyms. All you need to remember the M&D databases are the three-letter acronyms, and what they mean.

Overall, there are three screens that work in conjunction with the CME database. These are as follows: CMENU, which is what the vendor refers to as the first basic menu screen. This, in turn will trigger the secondary CMEXX panel. A third screen which is available to build physically a new menu or maintain an existing one is called the CMELS panel.

Databases in the Millennium environment are associated with specific panels. Information which is available on the CME database can be accessed via the CMELS, the CMENU and the CMEXX screens. Like-wise the data dictionary database is available either through the CDDBR panel, or through the CDDLS panel. How can you remember all this? Actually, it is relatively easy. The first three characters of a database and its associated panel are identical. The two extra characters attached to such acronym denote a screen function (such as BR for browse, etc.).

First, a discussion of the CMENU screen. The CMENU, or Menu Definition Screen is the initial menu in the system, which, by the way, is only available in display mode, and which enables you to select from among a set of secondary (CMEXX) functions. For example, if your primary function is defined as payroll processing, then your secondary functions could very well be made up of a set of tasks such as: retroactive pay, W2 processing, quarterly statements, special payroll requests, file maintenance, interface, and a host of others. In order to invoke the CMENU, enter the following information on the command line:

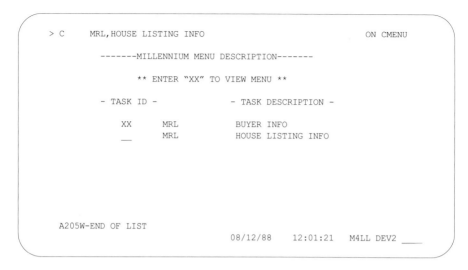

```
> C      MRL,HOUSE LISTING INFO                        ON CMENU


        -------MILLENNIUM MENU DESCRIPTION-------

           ** ENTER "XX" TO VIEW MENU **

        - TASK ID -              - TASK DESCRIPTION -

          XX      MRL           BUYER INFO
          __      MRL           HOUSE LISTING INFO




  A205W-END OF LIST
                            08/12/88    12:01:21    M4LL DEV2 ____
```

Figure 4.1 This Screen displays the CMENU format using the vendor "Real Estate Database."

```
> GG _____ (task ID) _____ ON CMENU
```

Note that the task ID is the key field, in this situation, responsible for relating a set of logical menus. Task ID is essentially a global field, recalling the term from the previous chapter, meaning that it applies to all CME related panels. (The CME function will be discussed shortly.) Because of this global nature of the field, you will have to use the "GG", or Get Global command to have access to the CMENU. Figure 4.1 shows the layout of the CMENU, which is also referred to as the Millennium Menu Description screen. The selection process using the CMENU is in no way different from utilizing a main menu to invoke one or a set of submenus in response. To select, simply place "XX" in the subcommand field and press enter.

The CMEXX Menu Screen displays a number of tasks associated with the CMENU, except that these tasks are now further magnified or "detailed" showing a number of operations-oriented activities. If you want to invoke the CMEXX menu screen directly through the command line (rather than through a menu selection process), use the following set of code:

```
> GD ____ (Task ID),(Task Description) _____ ON CMEXX _____
```

Figure 4.2 displays the layout of the CMEXX secondary menu screen.

Note the following terms on the CMEXX panel:

An asterisk (*) in the CMD qualifier appears automatically. It tells Millennium to retrieve all records whose database identifier is requested on

```
   > C    MRL,HOUSE LISTING INFO                        ON CMEXX

                    -------MILLENNIUM MENU-------
                       HOUSE LISTING INFO
   ENTER COMMAND--> GU             PATTERN-->   __        Task ID-->MRL
   ENTER CMD QUALIFIER    *
        ----------DESCRIPTION-----------    ----CMD QUALIFIER CONTENT------
   _  INSERT A NEW HOUSE LISTING            BLANK OUT ASTERISK
   _  CHANGE AN EXISTING HOUSE LISTING       AGENCY CODE, HOUSE CODE
   _  CONDOMINIUMS FOR SALE
   _  HOUSE LISTING BY STYLE                STYLE
   _  HOME FOR LESS THAN $200,000




   A205W-END OF LIST
                                08/12/88    12:01:21   M4LL DEV2 ____
```

Figure 4.2   This screen displays the CMEXX format using the vendor "Real Estate Database."

the screen. This may be too much or too unspecific for you, so it may be preferable to enter a partial key instead, or a question mark wild card.

A partial key (also known as a generic key) will match the contents of a corresponding screen as it exists on the database. The more complete the generic key, the more specific the search will be, and therefore, the quicker the response. Thus, if you were to look for the value 'HOUSE', and your key is defined as 'H', then, every word in the dictionary that starts with an 'H' will qualify. A question mark (wild card) in the position of a value will match the criteria of a specific character or characters as defined by the key. (Chapter 5 explains the wild card concept in more detail.)

You may also enter a pattern number that is tied to your specific application running under the Millennium environment. The term Task ID describes the current processing step as required by the system, which is further clarified by a description identifier.

To select a step on the CMEXX screen, enter your selection (*), in the subcommand field (another form of a wild card definition) shown in Figure 4.2. This selection will take you down to the initial application screen.

As previously mentioned, you have to be careful in setting up your menu screens. Purely from the designer's point of view, you need to be knowledgeable about the specific idiosyncrasies of the system—you should understand intimately how the various modules relate to one another. In building your menu screen, you will utilize the CMELS panel. Any time you need to implement some changes on the above panel, those changes will also be reflected on the CMENU and CMEXX menu screens respectively. You may access the CMELS panel via the CMENU by entering LS in the subcommand field, or simply through the command line.

Figure 4.3 shows the layout for the Millennium menu definition screen or CMELS. Note that this screen is subdivided into two areas: a task (1) and a step (2) area. Data from the task fields relate to the CMENU screen. Data from both the task and step areas display on the CMEXX panel. Figure 4.4 reveals the relationship among the three previous screens (CMELS, CMENU, and CMEXX).

When building your own menus, the first position of the task ID must contain a "U", (the character U stands for user created), and the rest may contain any alphanumeric characters. Since the display takes place in a sorted manner, you may want to use qualifiers or sequence numbers for the display of each task, such as: task ID1, task ID2, task ID3, and so on. The SCRNM contains a five-position screen name of the particular application to which you want to link. This is what is called a physical pointer. Enter this field only when it involves branching to a particular screen.

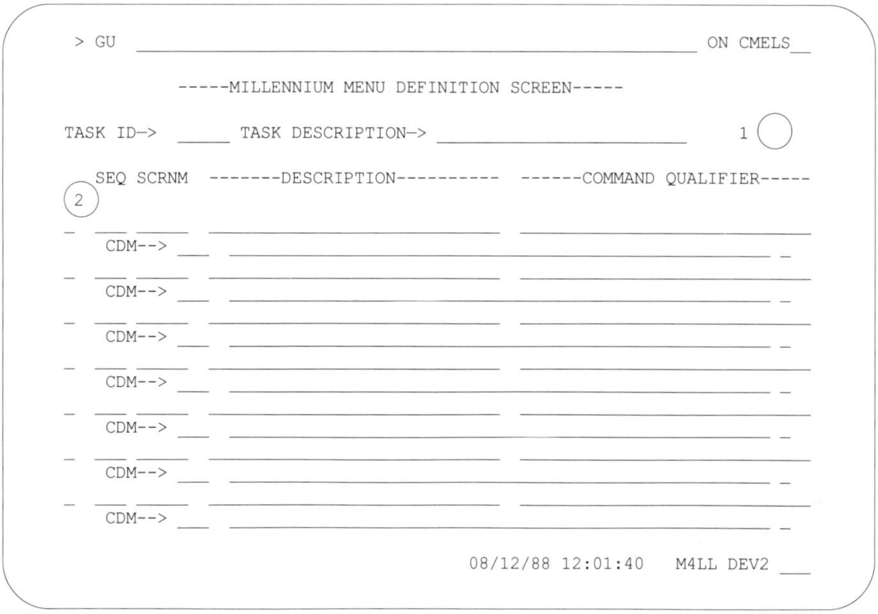

Figure 4.3   This screen shows the format for the CMELS panel.

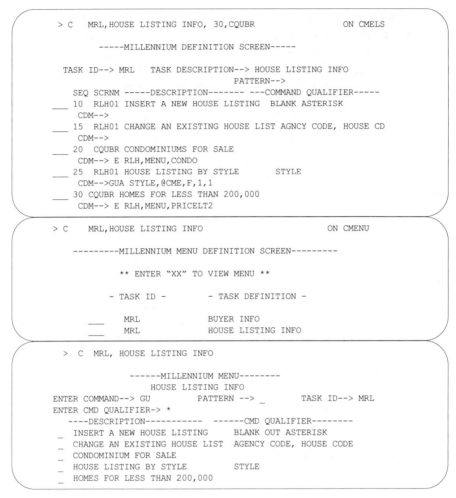

```
    > C    MRL,HOUSE LISTING INFO, 30,CQUBR                    ON CMELS


            -----MILLENNIUM DEFINITION SCREEN-----

      TASK ID--> MRL    TASK DESCRIPTION--> HOUSE LISTING INFO
                                   PATTERN-->
        SEQ SCRNM -----DESCRIPTION------- ---COMMAND QUALIFIER-----
  ____  10  RLH01 INSERT A NEW HOUSE LISTING  BLANK ASTERISK
        CDM-->
  ____  15  RLH01 CHANGE AN EXISTING HOUSE LIST AGNCY CODE, HOUSE CD
        CDM-->
  ____  20  CQUBR CONDOMINIUMS FOR SALE
        CDM--> E RLH,MENU,CONDO
  ____  25  RLH01 HOUSE LISTING BY STYLE        STYLE
        CDM-->GUA STYLE,@CME,F,1,1
        30 CQUBR HOMES FOR LESS THAN 200,000
        CDM--> E RLH,MENU,PRICELT2
```

```
    > C    MRL,HOUSE LISTING INFO                        ON CMENU

          ---------MILLENNIUM MENU DEFINITION SCREEN---------

                ** ENTER "XX" TO VIEW MENU **

           - TASK ID -        - TASK DEFINITION -

   ____      MRL              BUYER INFO
   ____      MRL              HOUSE LISTING INFO
```

```
    > C  MRL, HOUSE LISTING INFO

                  ------MILLENNIUM MENU--------
                     HOUSE LISTING INFO
  ENTER COMMAND--> GU        PATTERN --> _       TASK ID--> MRL
  ENTER CMD QUALIFIER-> *
     ----DESCRIPTION----------- ------CMD QUALIFIER--------
   _  INSERT A NEW HOUSE LISTING    BLANK OUT ASTERISK
   _  CHANGE AN EXISTING HOUSE LIST  AGENCY CODE, HOUSE CODE
   _  CONDOMINIUM FOR SALE
   _  HOUSE LISTING BY STYLE        STYLE
   _  HOMES FOR LESS THAN 200,000
```

Figure 4.4 These screens show the relationship among the three menu builder screens: CMELS, CMENU and CMEXX.

In the Millennium environment, you will seldom, if ever, need to develop screen layouts from scratch. You can just "cut and paste" them, so to speak. That means you can copy existing panels and customize them in minutes. You can accomplish what otherwise would require substantial time if you were to handle it the conventional way. The "conventional way," of course would mean substantial coding in basic assembler, which is a machine- and programmer-oriented tool.

4.2   The Batch Extraction Process

It is important to discuss the batch extraction process to further highlight some background information on queries which were discussed briefly in Chapter 3. However, this chapter will be a bit more specific and supply some additional technology to build, modify, and execute your queries. Strictly from an operational point of view, you will not need a very thorough understanding of how queries are triggered, as long as they are triggered by Millennium the way you want them to be. However, the more you understand fourth generation technology, the more efficiently you will be in designing or customizing procedures.

The process for making data in your Millennium environment available for query is called the batch extraction process. This is a series of programs to achieve two functions:

1. to build indexes for your records so that the system can locate the specific data in the where block of the query.
2. to make those indexes available for your inquiry as efficiently as possible so you will not have to search through the entire file every time you issue an inquiry.

Technically speaking, this whole process of query preparation depends on the following processes: an extraction process, a so-called "filter" process, which is accomplished through a number of "filter" programs, and an external file access process, which deals with non-Millennium file structures.

"Extraction Process," or more precisely "Batch Extraction Process," refers to your ability to select data from your Millennium based application file and organize it so that it can be queried. To perform this process, you must provide information to Millennium and then execute the batch extraction run. The batch extraction run is a series of programs that select or filter the application records you wish to query.

The batch extraction process accomplishes two objectives:

1. it enables you to access data by building indexes to it. Indexes arrange values from your application database so that the system can find the data specified in the where block of a query.
2. it enables you to select only those records you need to query since you may not want to query all of the data on your existing file.

The batch extraction is illustrated in Figure 4.5. As As you can see, the whole process entails additional and specific databases.

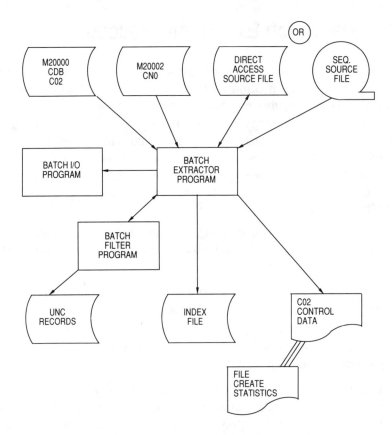

Figure 4.5   This flowchart demonstrates the batch extraction process.

Input to the batch extraction programs (M2X500 and MNN526) is made up by a number of files. Figure 4.5 shows this configuration. The CDB Control Database which represents a summary of all other databases during the extraction run describes all the physical characteristics of each database used during the extraction run.

A second database required to build your indexes through the batch extraction run is your data dictionary database. The data dictionary database (CDD) defines every data field and query definitions that has to do with your application. A sample screen of the data dictionary database is shown in Figure 4.6. A third database in this process is the optimized search field database or CNO. This optimized search field database is the one that enables you to access your source file via search indexes. Last, there is the filter information database or CO2, which you may reference in conjunction with non-M&D data files for the purposes of downloading information to a PC link module. The actual record selection process is done through the execution of the batch extraction run using a number of internal programs. A more comprehensive review of the above will be presented to you later in Chapter 5 under the SDT (System Development Tool) module.

4.3   The M&D Help Environment

One of the more significant aspects of fourth generation business systems is its ability to respond to specific problems and to communicate such problems back to the user. This type of communication is normally achieved via message displays and by tracing the error to the particular piece of data involved.

In a conventional systems design, error messages can only provide some limited facilities that are structured to accommodate generic situations. For example, if you should have multiple error occurrences on your screen, it would be nearly impossible to explain the nature of every error with regards to a specific transaction especially when restricted to a single line, or perhaps to a few lines.

What is needed is an entire mechanism to explain to the user the type of error that needs to be corrected, and more significantly, what can be done to resolve them. This mechanism, or apparatus, is referred to as a

```
  >  GU    RLS,DEMOGR                                          ON CDDLS

                 ------MILLENNIUM DATA DICTIONARY------

     DBID--> RLS


           FIELD    NO                    EDIT  KEY/   SEC       AUX    FIELD
         ---NAME---  OC  DISP  LEN  F Q  MASK  AUDIT   D U   TOT FLD  HEADING
    ____  EMPADD     __  100   25   A _  _____   _     5 5   ___ ___  ADDRESS
    ____  EMPCLAS    __   82    5   A _  _____   _     5 5   ___ ___  CLASS
    ____  EMPCITY    __   10   15   A _  _____   _     5 5   ___ ___  CITY
    ____  EMPDEPART  __   30    5   A _  _____   K     5 5   ___ ___  DEPART
    ____  EMPID      __   36    7   A _  _____   K     5 5   ___ ___  EMPID
    ____  EMPNAME    __   45   25   A _  _____   _     5 5   ___ ___  NAMED
    ____  EMPPHONE   __  172   10   A _  _____   _     5 5   ___ ___  PHONE
    ____  EMPSTA     __  192    2   A _  _____   _     5 5   ___ ___  STATE
    ____  EMPUN      __  205    1   A _  _____   _     5 5   ___ ___  UNION
    ____  EMPZIP     __  195    5   A _  _____   _     5 5   ___ ___  ZIP CODE


                           08/12/88  10:01:22  M2LL ACTION___
```

Figure 4.6   This is a display screen for the data dictionary database (CDD).

"Help subsystem" which is thoroughly integrated into the vendor's fourth generation environment. Figure 4.7 illustrates a simple problem-solving technique using such a Help module.

Assume you entered the wrong department code on the "employee demographic" screen while you were adding or modifying a record. You will note, there are two error conditions shown on this panel. The message, which is displayed on the bottom of each screen, is not specific enough to describe multiple occurrences of error—at best, it will say "INVALID

```
              EMPLOYEE DEMOGRAPHIC PROFILE                W125 SYS:PAY2D

      EMPLOYEE ID          123677822
      EMPLOYEE NAME        ALEX VARSEGI
      DEPARTMENT NUMBER    112354 =================>   1
      DEPARTMENT DESCRIPT
      CURRENT JOB NUMBER   3321
      CURRENT TITLE        SR PROJECT MANAGER
      HOME ADDRESS         11123 CHANDLER
      CITY/STATE/ZIP       ELMHURST,    IL.    60126
      TELEPHONE            (312) 833-4577
      START DATE           02/14/79
      LAST DATE PROMOTED   09/12/87
      PREVIOUS JOB NUMBER  3320 ====================>   2
      PREVIOUS TITLE
      CURR. ANNUAL SALARY  54,219.09
      PREV. ANNUAL SALARY  49,750.99

   TWO FIELDS ARE IN ERROR - RESUBMIT
   PF1 HELP SCREEN  PF2  RETURN TO MENU
```

```
         HELP    W125 SYS:PAY2D                    LEVEL 1

DEPARTMENT
NUMBER    :   112354
              THE ABOVE CONTROL NUMBER IS INVALID AND UNIDENTIFIED ON
              THE DEPARTMENT CONTROL TABLE.
              PLEASE VERIFY YOUR DATA BEFORE RESUBMITING.
              IF YOU WISH TO REVIEW THE CONTENTS OF THE DEPARTMENT
              TABLE, PLEASE PRESS PF3.
              ANY ADDITIONAL ENTRY ON THE DEPARTMENT TABLE NEEDS TO
              BE DONE IN A SEPARATE STEP AND IS SUBJECT TO PASSWORD
              PROTECTION.

              SUGGESTION:
              ----------
              THE EMPLOYEE'S CURRENT JOB NUMBER - 3321 - SUGGESTS
              THAT THE CORRECT DEPARTMENT NUMBER SHOULD BE  - 112364
              WHICH IS INFORMATION SYSTEMS!
       ***PRESS ENTER TO RETURN TO THE SOURCE SCREEN***
       ***NO SECOND PAGE EXPLANATION IS AVAILABLE ON THIS SCREEN***
```

Figure 4.7 This is a maintenance panel prompting a Help screen for clarification.

FIELDS—RESUBMIT!" If you were to highlight the department number and the previous job number, in addition to the above standard error message, you would still only be guessing at the nature of those errors, even if the specific field or fields are intensified. In the Millennium-based Help subsystem, all you need to do is to position the cursor over to the first character of the actual department number and press function key 1 (PF1). This maneuver will invoke a first level Help screen for your review. As you can see, you will find a rather lengthy explanation of the kind of problem there.

A Help screen can be made up of one or a number of logically related "pages" depending on the length of the explanation required. Once you understand the problem, you need to return to the initial source screen (employee demographic profile) and continue your processing.

Note that the second problem or error requiring clarification is the employee's previous job number, which also happens to be invalid. To resolve it, again press function key 1 to invoke a second set of Help screens.

As you can see, in a full blown Help environment every data field can be magnified. This would aid the user in thoroughly describing all automated procedures, why certain data elements were entered incorrectly and what can be done to correct them.

With this brief background in mind, a review of some of the mechanics of M&D's on-line, real time Help environment follows. Millennium offers two types of Help functions that can be utilized in your application. These are, a set of Help procedures set up by the vendor and your own Help scheme. The vendor's Help module generally covers all data fields that are referenced in his or her application including messages reflecting system related problems and inconsistencies. When you rely on the vendor's Help mechanism, you can expect a brief explanation of the field's purpose, its values, and some of the edit rules associated with it.

User Help serves the same purpose as the vendor's own mechanism, however you can design it to handle highly customized situations that are specific to your business. Thus, user messages give you additional flexibility in the form of specialized information. What you need to keep in mind is the effort such a task would take you to develop on your own.

Help modules, of course, may not totally be functional in a conventional environment due to the lack of an all-encompassing data dictionary and the unjustifiable development cost associated with it. (As you recall, conventional environments refer to a third generation "conventional" system, which was briefly described in Chapter 1.) As previously mentioned, Millennium gives you two types of Help environments: one which is fairly standardized, and another one which can be customized as if you developed an expensive subsystem on your own.

The vendor's Help procedures are stored on the THP database, which is associated with the THPBR display screen. To display a particular set of information, position the cursor over the field or message that requires clarification and press PF1 to invoke the screen.

The second set of Help procedures that are not part of the original package, is stored on the THU database and is associated with the THUBR display screen. To invoke this particular Help function, all you need to do is press PF key 2. Thus, if you were to design a little subsystem and incorporate it into one of your Millennium-based applications, you would need to rely on the THU database for tracking and explaining your errors.

What are some of the conceptual merits of providing the user with two different databases for single Help functions? This question is contingent upon the vendor's periodic "releases." If you set up "personalized" messages on the THP database to accommodate your own procedures then, all those messages would be deleted at the implementation of a new release. This situation would be quite different if you were to store your message on the more permanent THU database.

Briefly, this database remains at the disposal of the systems designer subject to his or her own maintenance apparatus. As you can see, you also trigger a highly specialized panel, such as the THUBR screen to display data resident on the THU database. Likewise, the THPBR screen is dedicated to the vendor's own Help messages via the THP database.

The Millennium fourth generation support environment is made up of three levels of Help functions that were briefly discussed before. These are field level, message level, and system level functions. (Please note that these functions will be periodically reiterated during the explanation of the Systems Development Tool package, or SDT, and also during the discussion of an SDT derivative Fourth Generation Language called Procedural Development Language, or PDL.)

1. field level Help is designed to provide you with information with regards to a given data field or element. If you were to enter your employee identifier using other than, for example, numeric characters, or if such an entry has no matching record on a corresponding master file, Millennium will inform you of the problem; all you have to do is ask for it.

2. millennium also enables you to obtain information on a particular message. Due to the versatility of these messages, M&D classifies them into three major categories, such as fatal messages (F), informational messages (I) and warning messages (W). Let me explain what each of these messages means to you. When you get a fatal message, it indicates that an error occurred from which you can only recover if you

correct the problem, and thus resubmit the entire transaction. For example, you have failed to include the employee's mandatory department code which happens to be part of his or her concatenated record key.

Warning messages are less restrictive. They will indicate one or a number of potential problems to be resolved. They are only displayed once, however, and if you do nothing about them, they will go away the second time you hit enter. (You may get a warning message on a missing employee's starting date during a payroll run, for example, since a number of fringe benefit reporting modules may be affected by it. However, that will not stop you from writing a check or reconciling your outstanding balance.)

last, but not least, there are informational messages that indicate the status of the system even though they do not interrupt your processing activities.

3. system level Help is the third kind of assistance by the vendor. It provides you with a list of valid commands. In addition, it offers command qualifier Help, screen name Help, action field Help, sub-command Help and so forth. As mentioned earlier, the Millennium system is essentially made up by two Help databases: the THP and the THU databases. These two sets are almost identical in format with the exception of the record key identifier. The THP database contains Help records for every field and system message in your application. To retrieve a record from this database, position the cursor over the field or message you want Help on and then press PF1. At that point the system will drop down a link level (see coverage on Menus), and display the requested information on the THPBR panel. Figure 4.8 is an overview of a Help screen.

Let me elaborate on some of the variable data presented here. The DBID or database identifier contains the field identifier of a particular record. In the above situation "RLH" refers to an M&D built "Real Estate" database. This field is actually the first component of a concatenated key that drives the Help record. It only appears where the screen (THPBR) is in update mode.

The term "Screen" or Screen ID refers to the second component of the concatenated record key used in the display process. "Field" is the variable element in this Help environment which is retrieved and classified on an on-demand basis. Because of the way M&D structures its database records, you might want to think about the field as part of the combined data making up the total key value for the record.

DBID	Database name	Screen
CAE	ON LINE INDEX FATAL LOG	CAELS
CAT	AUDITRACK	N/A
CBC	BTP CONTROL	CBCBR
CBO	BATCH OPTIMIZED RECORDS	CBOLS
CBP	BATCH PARAMETERS	CBPLS
CBV	BATCH VARIABLES	CBVLS
CDB	CONTROL	CDBBR
CDD	DATA DICTIONARY	CDDBR
		CDDLS
CDM	DATA MACRO	CDMBR
		CDMLS
CFI	FIX INCLUSION	CFIDS
		CFILS
CFP	FILE PRINT OUTPUT PROFILE	CFPBR
CFX	FIX	CFXDS
		CFXEX
		CFXLS
CGI	PDL INCLUDE SOURCE	CGILS
CGD	PDL DIRECTORY	CGOOO
CGS	PDL SOURCE	CGSLS
CHI	HIERARCHY	CHIBR
		CHILS
CH2	HIERARCHY/STRING	CH2LS
CME	MENU	CMELS
		CMENU
		CMEXX
CMS	MASK RECORD	CAELS
COS	OPTIMIZED SCREEN	COSLS
CQQ	QUERY QUESTION	CQQBR
		CQQLS
CQU	QUERY	CQUBR
		CQULS
CSC, CSD	SCREEN DESIGNER	CSCRN
CSF	SEARCH FIELD	CBCBR
		CSFLS
CSL	SCREEN LITERAL	CSLBR
		CSLLS
		CSLSD
CSP	SCREEN PARAMETER	CSPBR
CSS	STOP VALUES	CSSLS
CST	TABLE STATISTICS	CSTAT
		CSTA2
CSV	SCREEN VARIABLE	CSVBR
		CSVLS
		CSVSD
CTA	RECORD TABLE/KEYS	CTABL
CTP	CTP UTILITY	CTPBC
		CTPER
CTW	TRANSITION WORK	CTWLS
CUC	QUICK COMMANDS	CUCBR
		CUCLS
CO1	DUMP/RESTORE	CO1BR
		CO1O2
CO2	FILTER CRITERIA	CO2BR
CO3	INQUIRY PARAMETER	CO3BR
CO4	AUDIT TRIAL	CO4BR
		CHIILS
CO5	BTP CONTROL DATA	CO5BR
LGL	PDL LISTING	LGLBR
LTR	MILLENNIUM TRACE	LTRLS
NDX	INDEX	NDXLS
TER	ERROR TEST	TERAT
		TERBR
THP	HELP DATABASE	THPBR
THU	USER HELP	THUBR
UCN	MILLENNIUM INDEX CONTROL	UCNBR
XER*	BTP ERROR RECYCLE	XERBR

Figure 4.8   This list shows Millennium control files databases and screens.

The last key component of the Help record is the page number. This refers to any number of pages in the display sequences if you should need to rely on more than a single page. A screen literal is the field that has the actual name or message number of that piece of data you are requesting.

A field name contains either the name on the CVS database or a systems message part of the TER database. (For a comprehensive review of Millennium databases, please refer to Figure 4.8).

Finally, the pause field has a switch you need in order to initiate a redirection process. This switch can be set to a 'Y', if you require redirection, or an 'N' if that is to be by-passed. (The process of "redirection" will be highlighted.)

Help screens come in two basic formats: a single-page screen and a multiple-page screen. Single page Help screens are a great deal more common.

Multiple Help screens are normally used when a particular data element or message requires a lengthy explanation with different values and edit rules (that is a list of values for the two-position state identifier—50 of them altogether).

There are two ways to recognize a single page Help panel. First, a warning message will pop up on the bottom of the screen (such as: A205W END OF LIST [Figure 4.9].)

```
> C  RLH, RLH,EMPNO,     1                                      ON THPBR
                                              LEVEL 01 LINK FROM RLH01
             ---MILLENNIUM HELP FOR DATA FIELDS---
                                                  PAGE-> 001


   SCREEN LITERAL-> EMPLOYEE ID
   FIELD NAME-----> RLH,ENMNO
   DOC REFERENCE-->
   COMMAND:          PAUSE->
   >                                                        ON

   THIS IS A NINE POSITION NUMERIC FIELD REPRESENTING THE EMPLOYEE'S
   IDENTIFICATION NUMBER ON BOTH THE PAYROLL AND PERSONNEL DATABASES.

   IT MUST BE ENTERED AS A NUMERIC NUMBER. WHEN ADDING A NEW RECORD TO
   THE FILES, THIS KEY FIELD CANNOT BE LEFT BLANK.

   VALUES STARTING WITH 999-9 - ARE RESERVED FOR SPECIAL CASES WHEN
   EMPLOYEES ARE ASSIGNED TEMPORARY POSITIONS NOT EXCEEDING A WEEK IN
   DURATION.


   A205W-END OF LIST
                         08/02/88  11:09:11   M4LL DEV2 ___
```

Figure 4.9   This screen shows a single page Help screen.

Second, and equally characteristic, the system will preload the character "C" in the command field (meaning cancel the current processing step and return to the original link level.)

Multiple Help screens are structured differently. In place of the warning message (END OF LIST), it usually indicates "MORE" and the command line on the top of the first screen will show the command GD (get a record for display). If more than two Help screens are required for a display, a table of contents will appear on the first page of the Help screen.

There are also two methods of paging multiple Help screens. Browsing is one of them. To invoke the first panel, simply press enter. Then, keep hitting enter until the last page finally displays the END OF LIST warning message along with the message number, as above, and with the character "C" preloaded into the command field. At that point, you may press enter one more time or PF3 to return to the original panel, from which your Help was issued.

The second method of multipaging is called "direct access." This method enables you to invoke any particular screen in the multipage environment randomly. It is relatively easy to use this technology since each Help screen and its corresponding page number is listed in a table of contents that appears on the first page of the Help screen.

To refine direct access paging further, M&D breaks it down into the following methodologies:

1. position your cursor over the page number you need to look at and press PF1 afterwards, which will cause the system to drop down a link level (see Menus) to display the requested screen.

2. another way to accomplish direct access paging is by moving the cursor over to the page portion of the concatenated key and then press enter.

There are also some other features that will enable you to obtain additional information on the field on which you need Help. Through a technique referred to as "redirection," you can access an application screen from a Help panel that has more information about that particular data, thus redirecting your Help. If a Help function relies on redirection, a message appears on the bottom of the screen as follows:

```
A351I - HIT PF1/PF2 FOR HELP REDIRECTION
```

The importance of this sort of fourth generation technology is that you can utilize a wealth of information already on file or stored in the system without spending a lot of time or effort in locating it. Help redirection requires a special command line. It will be helpful to walk through an actual redirection process.

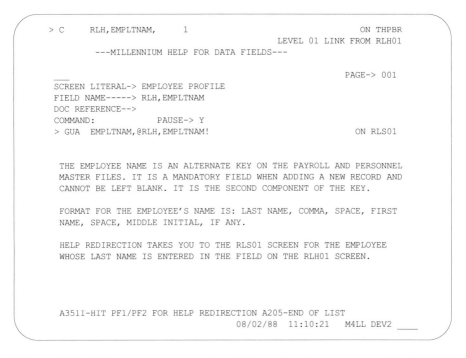

```
   > C    RLH,EMPLTNAM,     1                                    ON THPBR
                                              LEVEL 01 LINK FROM RLH01
              ---MILLENNIUM HELP FOR DATA FIELDS---


      ___                                              PAGE-> 001
   SCREEN LITERAL-> EMPLOYEE PROFILE
   FIELD NAME-----> RLH,EMPLTNAM
   DOC REFERENCE-->
   COMMAND:            PAUSE-> Y
   > GUA  EMPLTNAM,@RLH,EMPLTNAM!                        ON RLS01


   THE EMPLOYEE NAME IS AN ALTERNATE KEY ON THE PAYROLL AND PERSONNEL
   MASTER FILES. IT IS A MANDATORY FIELD WHEN ADDING A NEW RECORD AND
   CANNOT BE LEFT BLANK. IT IS THE SECOND COMPONENT OF THE KEY.

   FORMAT FOR THE EMPLOYEE'S NAME IS: LAST NAME, COMMA, SPACE, FIRST
   NAME, SPACE, MIDDLE INITIAL, IF ANY.

   HELP REDIRECTION TAKES YOU TO THE RLS01 SCREEN FOR THE EMPLOYEE
   WHOSE LAST NAME IS ENTERED IN THE FIELD ON THE RLH01 SCREEN.



   A351I-HIT PF1/PF2 FOR HELP REDIRECTION A205-END OF LIST
                              08/02/88  11:10:21   M4LL DEV2 ____
```

Figure 4.10   This screen represents a Help redirection screen on the THPBR panel.

As mentioned earlier, the pause field controls the execution of the redirection command line and the display of the associated Help screen. A "Y" indicates redirection. An "N" simply by-passes the entire mechanism. Figure 4.10 shows the required screen, which is a spin off of the THPBR database. Here is the command:

```
   > GUA_____EMPLTNAM,@EMPLTNAM!_____ON RLS01____
```

The GUA command was used simply because there was a need to display a record on the RLS database using an alternate rather than a primary key. An alternate key refers to a data set which is organized by using a different key or sort sequence. Actually, the sort sequence is very much the same, except that the alternate, or secondary pointers, are set up in a different collating sequence. For example, you may have a payroll master file which is organized by the employee identifier, but you may also need to access that database via the employee name.

The EMPLTNAM, as you can see, is already defined as an alternate key on the RLS database (consider the demographic information shown in Figure 4.7 as part of the RLS database). Assume that it also has indexes

built on the NDX database. The indexes keep track of the required relationship, as well as the CSF database that contains or monitors the value of the
search field (See Figure 4.8). These databases are available in the Millennium environment and you may refer to them as needed.

There are two methods for coding redirection: through hard coding or
through symbolics.

When you hardcode a redirection command, you can enter either the
partial or the full key as part of the command qualifier. Symbolics, as the
name suggests, means that you must enter a delimiter which will have the
value of that key just as soon as the command is executed. The first part of
the command qualifier EMPLTNAM is a valid search field on the CSF

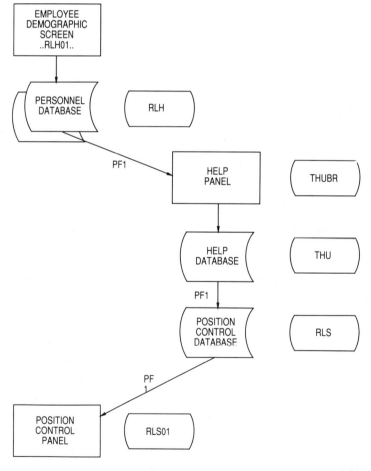

Figure 4.11 This flowchart represents the redirection process between
two application screens and databases (RLH01, RLS01) via the Help
(THUBR) panel.

database. Millennium encounters the second component of the command @RLH,EMPLTNAM! and retrieves the associated value of that field from the RLH database. Then use the search field/value combination, to find the correct employee on the RLSD01 panel. This process is briefly summarized in Figure 4.11. (Symbolics, as used by M&D will also be expanded on in Chapter 6 in reference to the PDL fourth generation language.) Why use symbolics in the redirection process? You can use symbolics simply, to retrieve the value of a field from memory. This process is more efficient and it requires less intermediate steps.

4.4   The Sticky Cursor

The following scenario is an example of what the sticky cursor business is all about. The payroll clerk is in process of reviewing the gross-to-net register before running it with the actual check generation. Half-way through the process, the clerk needs to check on an address change (which would normally require an exit from the current procedures). This means the clerk must go back to a sublevel menu and invoke another part of the system which has to do with the employee's demographic profile. At this point the clerk needs to make a note of the address to be verified and "transported" and then finally exit the "target" procedures to continue the review of the current gross to net register.

This is a lot of work, which can be error prone and time consuming, this is where M&D's sticky cursor comes in handy. The sticky cursor allows you to copy a string of data from one screen and insert it into a field of another. This eliminates the need to memorize the value on one screen, jot it down, go back to the initial screen to fill in the value and then check to be sure that the value is right.

At first, you will probably want to use this feature to retrieve data from one of the vendor or Help screens and to insert them on a specific application screen. There are very few restrictions on the use of the sticky cursor. For example, if you have more than one application and are proficient in using the Millennium software, you may use it to carry data back and forth between application screens. If you go back to any screen from which you pulled data, you'll find the data intact.

Sticky cursor deals with two types of screens; the screen you want to put data on and the screen from which you want to retrieve them. Always start the screen you want to put data on. Most likely, you'll be filling in a screen and will need to know the acceptable values for the field. Position the cursor over the first position of the field in which you want the data entered. The way you access the screen to retrieve data depends largely on the location of the data. The simplest case is to pull data from a Help screen. Here you would press PF Key 1 or PF Key 2 in order to get the Help screen. You can also use PF Key 4. Complete the command line to request the record that contains the data; then, press PF Key 4 to go down a link level.

You can take any data string from the second screen; numbers, field names, or even screen titles. Starting at a character over which the cursor is placed, the sticky cursor will take every character up to the length of the field that you are trying to fill including spaces. For example, if the field on the the original screen has a maximum length of ten characters and the data string you want to copy has thirteen, the sticky cursor will only copy the first ten characters.

4.5   Millennium-Driven Applications

We begin this section with a brief review of a typical M&D application, such as a credit management system using the Millennium environment. Although, this is not a case study, some of the techniques we discussed earlier in conjunction with the above support environment can be applied beginning with picking and talking about M&D's credit management system in general terms.

Actually, the credit management system is one of the two building blocks that makes up the M&D accounts receivable system. The other one, of course, is the actual Receivable portion of the system. The term M:AR is an acronym for the above: M means Millennium-based and AR denotes the accounts receivable application system. In a fourth generation environment the application system cannot be segregated from the powerful support environment which in this instance is Millennium based upon. The following gives you some background for this review.

The McCormack & Dodge Credit Management System or M:AR, includes the process of assembling timely information about your customer, analyzing and evaluating the risk involved in selling to him or her, and monitoring his or her performance after the sale is made. This means that you want to be sure that payments are received promptly and that problem accounts are highlighted before they become simply unmanageable.

Credit management is essentially made up of three functions. These are as follows:

1.   maintaining the different types of customer information or database,

2. evaluating the credit risk and monitoring performance, and

3. managing slow or delinquent accounts.

Overall, the system maintains a number of levels of customer information that range from basic demographic type data (such as the customer name and address) to more complex data (such as pay habits). The information to build such a database comes from various sources from day-to-day receivable processing, correspondence, phone conversation with customers, and a number of other contacts and communications.

Along with the basic data and rules, the credit management system closely monitors transactions and payments. Millennium-driven databases can operate in an on-line real time environment, which means that your customer receivable balance is up-to-the-minute at all times. For example, if the customer calls with a question about his receivable balance, not only can you display his current balance, but, using Millennium commands, you can check the individual's open items and when receivables were paid. You'll also be able to see any invoices that are in process or payments that are not yet posted to the account.

Figure 4.12 shows the customer credit status panel. This screen displays all fundamental credit information including current and past-due

```
> C  004, CR0012                                    ON TLK1

          ---- AR:M - CUSTOMER CREDIT STATUS ----

004 CR0012  VARSEGI MEN'S CLOTHES   CREDIT/SALES REP> HTF  AMV TERM> FOL3
CHICAGO        IL, 60601            PAY FROM--------> 004   CR0012
ALEX C PERKINS   312 867-8876       CHGO ACCOUNT----> 004   CR0012

BALANCE-->      79,936.00  *   CR LIM-->  75,000    ( 107   %) 121187
   PAST DUE-->  28,504.30       REM-->   4,936-     (   7-  %)
   ON-ACCT--->  10,868.80-     HI BAL--->    79,936.00EN--> 060188

      ---AGING SUMMARY---      ---PAYHABITS---       ---CREDIT STATUS---
UNAGD->  .26  +30--> .04    PAYINDEX---> 60 122087  COLLECT-->     030788
DISP-->  .33  +60-->        CUR 6  MO-> SLOW 45     DISPUTE-->     000000
-60--->       +90--> .31    PR1 6  MO-> SLOW 30     CR HOLD-->     000000
-30--->       +120->  .     AVG DSO---> 31.4        NSF------>     040488
CURR-->  .04  +150->        DYS LATE--> 27.3        D&B RAT->3C1   122687
+1--     .01  +180->        LASTPMT---> 031488      RISK-CD--> A   042688

       --- DUNNING ---                    -FIN -    --- STATEMENT ---
  LST/CUR LVL: 5   5  082587   NXT: 000000 H: 012988 MTH: STD LST: 012988 H:
     COMMENT-> CALLED ABOUT THE NACM REPORT. THEY HAVE A BACKLOG  061788
                          06/23/88  11:09:05      M2LL ACTION ____
```

Figure 4.12   This screen demonstrates an M&D Customer Credit Summary.

balances, breakdown by aging, percent of credit remaining and most recent comments on the account. The highlighted asterisk next to the balance indicates that an in-process payment exists with the account.

Another feature, which is part of the M:AR credit management system, is your ability to select essential history. You can select just what information you would like to display on the customer screens, decide if some of that information would be more significant as a comment or as a label as opposed to some numeric values.

As seen in Figure 4.13, you can display logical labels or comments on a piece of historical data in place of a conventional numeric value. This allows you to highlight certain information by displaying a comment instead of a number. In Figure 4.13, M:AR uses both a logical label and numeric data. Here, the pay habits label (—slow 45—), may replace the average date late calculation of 49.8 days. Logical labels are useful to describe pay habits. M:AR enables you to define pay habit categories and assign a meaningful label to each category, instead of limiting your choice to "slow 30," "slow 60," and so forth, the system displays whatever label you define.

```
 > G        21                                          ON   TLK1

              ---- AR:M - SELECTED HISTORY ELEMENT DISPLAY ----

    CORP--> 004    CUSTOMER--> CR0012          BALANCE--->    79,936.00

       ---- FIELD DESCRIPTION ---         --- FIELD VALUE ---

       HIGHEST BALANCE            -->          79,936.00
       HIGHEST PAST DUE BALANCE   -->          63,904.30
       DSO CURRENT SIX MONTHS     -->              31.39
       ON ACCOUNT BALANCE         -->          10,868.80
       TOTAL WRITE OFFS THIS YEAR -->             145.00
       AVG DAYS LATE              -->              49.80
       PAYHABITS                  -->          --SLOW 45--
       LAST SALE AMOUNT           -->           1,405.00
       PAST DUE RECEIVABLES       -->          28,504.30
       AGING UNAGED               -->          21,131.70
       AGING - DISPUTES           -->          26,950.00
       AGING - (CURR)             -->           3,200.00
       AGING - (+30)              -->           1,405.00
       AGING - (+60)              -->           3,290.00

                           06/23/88   11:59:38   M2LL ACTION ____
```

Figure 4.13 This screen represents an M&D User Defined History Display Panel.

The Millennium system also has a very extensive reporting module to support its fourth generation environment. This is quite important, because it provides the package with a great deal of flexibility over and above the set of standard reports. The Millennium M:AR system, for example contains the following (partial) standard reports:

1. standard credit reports: which Millennium enables you to produce on summary or detail level,

2. aged trial balances,

3. credit snapshots,

4. cash forecasting reports, and

5. customer correspondence such as dunning letters, customer statements, chargeback invoices, financial statement follow up letters, finance charge invoices, etc.

If, however, these reports are not specific enough for you, you can use M:AR's report writer facilities to design your own reports, sort them, perform the necessary calculations and display or print such information. (Briefly, every Millennium application package has its own report writer facilities (that is, M:AP, or accounts payable Report writer, etc.).

To develop a new report, define from which particular database you will be retrieving the information and describe all the secondary databases from where all additional data will be forthcoming (assuming that they are available on different databases in the Millennium system). Through the M:AR report writer, you can define to Millennium the format of that report, the headings, literals, page breaks and computations, total accumulations, etc.

In practice, you will see that unless your requirements are quite unique, you will be able to copy or clone an existing standard M&D report and modify it according to your needs. Designing a report in the Millennium fourth generation system is an on-line process, that is, you can run a test and correct all subsequent problems interactively. You or your respective user may review a report on the screen before it is printed and abort it if you find that it requires additional customizing. Aborting a report on the screen is quite efficient, especially if you are dealing with an 800-900 page long personnel or payroll printout where the final totals are out of balance, and thus the whole process will probably have to be reinitiated from scratch. Another function to touch on briefly has to do with a dunning method.

This method entails a series of letters that you send to your customers who are either tardy paying their bills or not paying them at all. Each stage of delinquency is normally followed by a harsher tone of notification to the delinquent party until the account is turned over to a collection agency. (Most large companies have their own internal collection agencies.)

This continuously rising tone or severity level is reflected in Figure 4.14. where the specific level is incorporated into PAYHAR1, PAYHAR2, PAYHAR3, etc. The result of this screen is shown in Figure 4.15 under the statement of account panel. A standard dunning letter may only consist of three levels. When an item on an account is, for example, 30 days past due, the customer could receive a reminder that his account should be brought back to a current status. When the account is 60 days past due, a more demanding letter is to be generated, and, as previously mentioned, a 90 day past due account may be turned over to a collection agency.

What happens, however, when the customer pays off part or most of the outstanding balance? Certainly, you would not want to threaten the customer with collection procedures. This is where this Millennium-based application allows you to exercise a great degree of flexibility. You may utilize or develop an option through the Millennium system to exempt an account temporarily if the balance of that account falls below a certain minimum, thus stop sending out dunning letters at that point. Also to prevent "run away" dunning letters, Millennium, allows you to specify conditions under which dunning letters will be canceled.

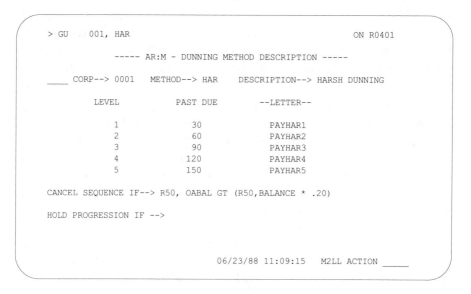

```
  > GU      001, HAR                                          ON R0401

                ----- AR:M - DUNNING METHOD DESCRIPTION -----

  _____  CORP--> 0001    METHOD--> HAR    DESCRIPTION--> HARSH DUNNING

             LEVEL            PAST DUE          --LETTER--

               1               30              PAYHAR1
               2               60              PAYHAR2
               3               90              PAYHAR3
               4              120              PAYHAR4
               5              150              PAYHAR5

  CANCEL SEQUENCE IF--> R50, OABAL GT (R50,BALANCE * .20)

  HOLD PROGRESSION IF -->


                          06/23/88 11:09:15   M2LL ACTION _____
```

Figure 4.14 This screen shows dunning methods using severity layers through Millennium AR:M.

```
                    STATEMENT OF ACCOUNT

ALEX C. PERKINS                          REMIT PAYMENT TO
VARSEGI MEN'S CLOTHING                   FIRST NATIONAL BANK OF CHICAGO
234 W ELMHURST ROAD                      FIRST NATIONAL PLAZA
ELMHURST, IL, 60126                      CHICAGO, IL, 60605


ACCOUNT NUMBER: 004    CR0012

THIS STATEMENT REFLECTS TRANSACTIONS POSTED AS OF 06/23/88. PLEASE
RETURN THIS STATEMENT WITH YOUR PAYMENT.
------------------------------------------------------------------
   TR DT      ITEM #    PURCHASE ORDER NO  TR CD   AMOUNT    DUE
   -----      ------    -----------------  -----   ------    ---
   031288     C-32          F-22                   450.00-  000000
   010188     DD-11                          1    1,575.00  022888
   ******** THIS STATEMENT IS SEVERELY PAST DUE, PLEASE REMIT **********
   030788     DED-000000003                  1    3,800.00  000000
   031288     K-90          1 D88            1    1,350.00  041588

        TOTAL FOR 004  CR0012                     6,275.00

 0-30 DAYS   31-60 DAYS  61-90 DAYS   91-120 DAYS   OVER 120 DAYS
 ---------   ----------  ----------   -----------   -------------
     450.00-    5150.00                  1575.00
```

Figure 4.15   This screen represents a customer statement with specialized dunning message.

Summary

In a fourth generation environment, it is quite important not only to have the ability to utilize menu screens, but also the ability to build them from scratch. After all, these screens give you the ability to find your way through a maze of complex procedures, while providing you with a great deal of tutorial facilities.

One of the more significant aspects of using menu screens is that they tend to simplify a system for you that would otherwise be overwhelming from a procedural point of view. The terminal operator who only handles a narrow segment of the total features can do so with a great deal of efficiency without having to understand the nuts and bolts of the complete environment.

In the Millennium system, you can by-pass the menu selection process and still maintain a desired level of procedural simplicity just by using the command line for both selecting and executing a particular task.

Overall, there are three screens that work in conjunction with the CME database. These are as follows: CMENU, which is what the vendor refers to as the first basic menu screen. This in turn will trigger the secondary CMEXX panel. A third screen which is available to physically build a new menu or maintain existing one is called the CMELS panel.

The process to make data in your Millennium environment available for query is called the batch extraction process, which is a series of programs to achieve two functions:

1. to build indexes for your records so that the system can locate the specific data in the where block of the query, and

2. to make those indexes available for your inquiry as efficiently as possible so you will not have to search through the entire file every time you issue an inquiry.

Technically speaking, this whole process of query preparation depends on the following processes: An extraction process, a so-called "filter" process, which is accomplished through a number of "filter" programs, and an external file access process, which deals with non-Millennium file structures.

You will need the CDB control database which defines all other databases during the extraction run. What you really want to understand about the CDB database is that it has a single control record for each database and that these records essentially describe all the physical characteristics of that database (such as the number of records on them, their block size, record length, and so on). A second database required to build your indexes through the batch extraction run is your data dictionary database. The data dictionary database (CDD) defines every data field and query definition that have to do with your application.

One of the more significant aspects of fourth generation business systems is its ability to respond to specific problems and to communicate such problems back to the user. This type of communication is normally achieved via message displays and by tracing the error to the particular piece of data involved.

In a conventional systems design, error messages can only provide some limited facilities that are structured to accommodate generic situations. For example, if you should have multiple error occurrences on your screen, it would be nearly impossible to explain the nature of every error with regards to a specific transaction when you are restricted to a single or perhaps to a few lines.

What is needed is an entire mechanism to explain to the user the type of error that needs to be corrected and, more significantly, what can be done to resolve them. This mechanism, or apparatus is referred to as a "Help subsystem" A Help screen can be made up of one or a number of logically related "pages" depending on the length of the explanation required.

Millennium offers two types of Help functions that can be utilized in your application. These are, a set of Help procedures set up by the vendor and your own Help scheme. The vendor's Help module generally covers all data fields that are referenced in his or her application including messages reflecting system-related problems and inconsistencies.

When you rely on the vendor's Help mechanism, you can expect a brief explanation of the field's purpose, its values, and some of the edit rules associated with it.

User Help serves the same purpose as the vendor's own mechanism, however, you can design it to handle highly customized situations that are specific to your business.

The sticky cursor concept is a creative idea that lets you retrieve a piece of information from one screen and insert it into another, as the need arises.

Chapter 5

SDT: A Fourth Generation Design Tool by M&D

5.1   Overview

SDT or Systems Development Tool was developed by the McCormack & Dodge Corporation based on a number of creative ideas.

The first one of these ideas has to do with designing your own systems and not having to worry about the mechanics involved in creating your databases in the conventional sense. All you need to do is to define your data elements as they would appear on a physical record, that is length, disposition, format, and other important attributes. Developing a database is purely a system function, since once you have defined your logical and your physical databases, SDT will do the rest. It will set up your physical pointers, your keys, and relate the various tables and data elements the way you have defined them earlier on your control records.

A second idea, as was briefly discussed in Chapters 2 and 3, deals with your ability to design, quickly and efficiently, a specialized set of screens via a fourth generation screen painter, which is exactly what this Millennium-based product will do for you. SDT, which is a systems-oriented package of many facets, enables you to go outside the restricted boundaries of a vendor package, while providing you with the advanced architecture of a proprietary system. Thus, SDT can indeed consolidate not only M&D based systems, but applications, some of which are in-house and some that are the product of competing vendors. Is this a big deal? Sure it is. This means that the screen you have just painted can draw information from any "foreign" databases and place it on your own panel. In the SDT environment, screen painting has a great deal of power. It relies on a set of programs that can access and process, for example, an in-house payroll module, an MSA position control database coupled with a GLOBAL software, neither of which happens to be a Millennium-based system.

(Note that SDT is a subset of Millennium, which was discussed extensively in Chapters 3 and 4) Millennium, however, is restricted to M&D applications alone, and it is not intended to support any other file structure designed externally.

A third idea revolves around SDT's ability to query any given database in the system. This is a further refinement of the prior idea. When you query, you can, in fact, draw information not just from one, but from a number of different databases defined in the SDT "family." Thus, in addition to your "programmable" smart screens, you have the ability to query an employee's salary, which is carried on the Payroll Master. His job classification is part of the Position Control database. All that may be further enhanced through the employee's brief demographic profile retrieved from the personnel system, showing the accout out of which the employee is paid, which may be closely associated with one of the general ledger data-bases or simply with the budget.

A fourth idea has to do with SDT's fourth generation language, referred to as PDL, an acronym for Procedure Definition Language. Fourth genera-tion languages are employed for a variety of reasons. You may be able to perform all your programming needs using such a language or develop it to support a report writer subsystem, which most business environments are now trying desperately to curtail.

Since most of the SDT System's attributes relate to the idea of consoli-dating a number of different environments, the question that comes to one's mind is why not simply build interfaces between the various systems and not worry about SDT?

The answer is that, with SDT, you will have full access to all the fourth generation features of a powerful support environment, not just a language, giving you a borderless and technically sound advantages over status quo. SDT will interface and disseminate data in a single step, while creating a set of logical databases from which you may draw.

Another aspect of SDT has to do with enhancing your existing system which may have limited facilities. Suppose you have an in-house payroll system that was designed and developed in the mid-seventies. Historically, it still performs the basic functions, that is, calculates taxes and wages, prints and reconciles checks, generates a set of corresponding registers, and does all that rather flawlessly. The problem, however, has to do with the external volatility of the system caused by new local, state, and government legislations, corporate mergers, and dozens of other controlling events. To revamp constantly a thirteen-year-old system may be a difficult task for a number of reasons. You may not have any space left on your current files, which now require the redefinition of every permanent and temporary data set being utilized in the system.

Changes, especially those affecting querying and special reporting, re-quire substantial reprogramming in a conventional setting, apart from the major procedural changes. If there are new data elements to be added to the current files, you will have to review the various interfaces to make sure that all intersystem dependencies with regard to the new data elements are satisfied. If the above payroll system is strictly a batch module, it will lack any querying facilities. This means that you will not be able to respond to any emergency situation dictated by a dynamic business environment.

Figure 5.1 is an overview of the SDT systems cycle. Unlike a fourth-generation programming language which only resolves programming is-sues. SDT encompasses several stages of a project beyond the program-ming activities. Among these are SDT's ability to prototype during the

Systems Documetation

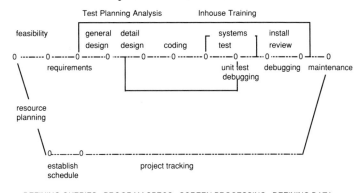

Figure 5.1   This chart represents a systems development life cycle (SDLC).

requirements study cycle, screen painting, and some of the basic procedural definitions during the general systems analysis, querying, and reporting—all that without generating a single line of code.

5.2   Defining Your Database

In order to define your data to Millennium, you need to group your respective data fields and record keys into physical databases. Physical databases (as opposed to logical ones) require that you clearly define to SDT the physical characteristics of a file, record keys, data elements, what does (and does not) need to be cross-referenced with other physical files in this transparent environment. These definitions are centrally defined through a data dictionary (CDD) which is the focal point of all SDT activities.

Designing a physical database is not purely an SDT function. This will be discussed more extensively later on. You might want to make a decision at this point regarding the utilization of a single database versus multiple databases. The governing factors in the decision process are as follows:

- Is there a need to link to another database repeatedly or only for a particular function?

- What is the relative importance of maintaining your data on separate databases?

Strictly from the processing point of view, you can save yourself a great deal of processing requirements (not to mention processing time) by storing information on a single database. This will reduce I/O usage while conserving expensive systems resources. A multiple database application, on the other hand, may require linked queries to access certain data or I/O routines in order to update all databases involved.

So in designing your system under SDT, you need to consider how such information is clustered: simply how that information is used, disseminated.

SDT essentially utilizes three basic "modes" or formats in defining physical file types, thus databases. Before reviewing the mechanics of these steps, it is necessary to explain the difference between a logical and a physical database.

A physical database will tell you just what is on that particular database in terms of data elements, physical pointers, keys, etc. For example, a payroll database is likely to contain everything that relates to payroll processing: employee information with regards to taxes, deductions, fringe benefits, retroactive pay scale, and so on. The problem, however, is that from a practical point of view there may be too much or too little information on such a physical database to satisfy the requirements of a particular user. If you are a personnel officer, for example, you only need a fraction of that database for your reference, but, in addition, you also need to extract data from another database to satisfy your particular inquiry. Thus, out of those two physical sets, you need an all-together different database which will contain that information in a consolidated manner. This "view" then, is your logical database, or window, which concisely represents what you need to see and access in the overall system.

In reality, one physical database may be represented by a number of logical databases, and, likewise, a logical database can be easily part of a half-a-dozen different physical database environments.

The first format is designed to access a sequential file such as an ESDS source file. (ESDS means "Entry Sequenced" and is one of the VSAM type file structures.) Thus, the first format or mode 1 database is part of what M&D refers to as a "UR" file.

The primary function of the UR database is to locate records queried on more quickly. Each source file in your system, that you query has a UR and an index file associated with it, which is created either through a batch extraction run or simply when you need to add new records to a database. A UR record is there, containing all the physical features required by a query.

Database	Explanation
STEP 1 - Defining Data	
Data Base Control (CDB)	Describes the physical attributes and standard operating capabilities of each database in your application. You specify one CDB record per Database.
Data Dictionary (CDD)	Contains a definition for every field in your application data base that you want to access
Mask Record (CMS)	Reflects an image of the record, as defined on the CDB and CDD databases, the occurrence, length, and displacement of each field. In this way, all on the application database will be initialized to process the proper data characteristics (default values).
STEP 2 - Defining Screens	
Screen Parameter (CSP)	Defines the parameters, or framework of a screen
Screen Literal (CSL)	Defines the literals, such as titles and field names that appear on the screen
Screen Variable (CSV)	Defines areas of a screen where data from individual records will be placed
Optimized Screen (COS)	Contains listing of all optimized screens in your system.
User HELP (THU)	Allows you to define HELP for your new system
STEP 3 - Defining PDL Programs	
PDL Source (CGS)	Enables you to create and store PDL programs
PDL Include Source (CGI)	Allows you to create and store frequently used blocks of PDL code that can be accessed by a PDL program during compilation
PDL Directory (CGO)	Contains the optimized code of a PDL program
PDL LIsting (LGL)	Enables you to view the compile listing of a PDL program
Error Message and Attributes (TER)	Contains M&D supplied systems messages and any user defined messages.
STEP 4 - Defining Queries	
Optional - Search Field (CSF)	Enables you to establish which CDD fields you will use as search fields in the search expressions of queries.
Queries (CQU)	Allows you to create and store queries so that you can analyze data in your new application.
Query Question (CQQ)	Enables you to set up queries so that you can execute them by answering questions.
Filter Information (CO2)	Allows you to establish selection criteria and other parameter information that will be read by the Filter Program during the batch extraction run.
Optimized Search Field (CNO)	Contains optimized search fields
Index (NDX)	Contains index values for search fields and the record numbers that contain those values for your application databases
UR Record (UR)	Contains UR records which either point to or contain the data that you want to access for a query.

Figure 5.2   This chart explains design steps and associated controlfile databases.

In Figure 5.2, I listed the processing steps associated with building your control file databases.

Control file databases are used by SDT to perform certain functions through a number of control mechanisms. To define each and every data field in your data dictionary, for example, you need to do it on the CDD database, which is the facility in the SDT structure for that purpose. If you want to store a PDL fourth generation program (for additional information see Chapter 6 on this topic), you need to do it on the CGS source database. SDT, as you can see by now, is an environment primarily driven by control databases or files and is thoroughly menu driven. Mode, or Format 1 type databases are used by SDT to create direct access images of a sequential file. You need this mechanism to transform a particular batch portion of your system to a set of on-line procedures. In viewing this first format (which is depicted in Figure 5.3), note that the key to such a database is made up by the UR database identifier, a record number, and a source DB identifier. A strong argument for using this mode is that there is less I/O processing during a query. Since the system does not have to find data on the source record (refer to Figure 5.3 and its associated narrative) during the execution of such a query, this eliminates a processing step, which can be time consuming.

One of the practical uses for a Mode 2 database is to store header and detail type records on a single file. To put it in more formal terms: when a particular set of data is dependent on other data which must be consolidated for you to view.

Mode 2 databases are key sequenced and randomly accessed files, that, unlike the first model, utilize a unique key. It is important to remember that here, records are not necessarily grouped by the Data Base Identifier (DBID) on the physical file. Rather, they are interspersed, and the system must read records off other databases to process your request.

Mode 3 databases are probably the most common databases. You use them when you need to have more than one logical database per physical file. These databases are key sequenced (truly KSDS) random access files.

The third mode and how it is utilized by SDT needs to be examined. First of all, to accomplish certain objectives using the SDT architecture, you are restricted to specific formats. In addition to such a set of restrictions, mode 3 databases are also quite efficient when performing both sequential and random processing. Here the system reads the records of the given database based on keys rather than reading the entire file. The efficiency comes into play as the system ends the read at the end of the logical database and not at the end of the physical file, which can be a great deal more voluminous.

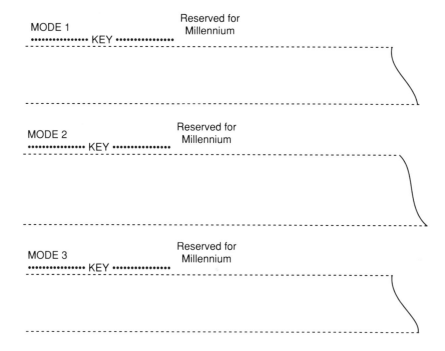

Figure 5.3 This chart shows UR records for Mode 1, 2, and 3.

As briefly touched upon in the discussion of the organization of the M&D databases under Millennium (Chapter 3), such a central repository is made up of records, which serve as building blocks of the system. However, these records must contain certain control fields to be processable to SDT: such as a record number, a source database identifier, the date and time of the last I/O (input/output) operation—the latter to prevent the user from simultaneously accessing and updating a database.

Actually, SDT allows you to place these control fields just about anywhere on the record, although, logically, they should immediately follow the key. Once the data portion of your record is designed, that is laid out in the desirable format, all you have to do is to define the incoming data to SDT.

Start with the CDD control record, which was briefly described in Figure 5.2 (Parts 1 and 2). Visualize this: every database is made up of data elements, and, for every data element, you need to define a CDD control

```
 > GU   GLD,M2LL                                           ON CDBBR

         ———— MILLENNIUM DATA BASE CONTROL ————

              DBID,  TRANS, DESCRIPTION -> GLD M2LL DETAIL REPORTING
  _ CALL SEQ, VERSION MODE (1-5), E/R DBID -> 04 2 1 ____
     READ LIMIT,  INDEX READ LIMIT, DBMS  -> 100    100
                       UR REC LEN   -> 179  _
     UR EXP/COMP  (Y/N), START EXP/COMP   -> N _____

  - - - THE FOLLOWING FIELDS APPLY TO SOURCE DATA BASE ONLY - - -
  DATASET ID, FIXED/VAR/UNDEF, MAX RECLEN -> M2204U __ V 179
  KEY: LENGTH, DISP TO START, BACKGROUND ——> 10 1 _____
  IF V DISP TO LENGTH AND FORMAT TYPE (P/B/C)-> 12___ P
  BLKSIZE, CARRIAGE CNTL, EXTRNL ACCESS IND -> _____ _____
  DISP TO: QUERY CONTROL FLDS, DATA/TIME ——>  _____  15___
  DISP TO: MILL STATUS IND. SECURITY ——————>  _____ _____
  EXP/COMP IND, DISP TO E/C, USER E/C PGM IND->  N
     TABLE INCLUSION IND, MAINTENANCE IND ——>    N
     AUDIT CHANGES, RETENTION ACCT TYPE NAME->  N
       DATE AND TIME OF LAST UPDATE ———> 07/22/88  12:12:20
```

```
  ...VSAM CLUSTER...                    ...FCT TABLE...

  DEFINE CLUSTER   -          M2204U  DFHFCT  TYPE=DATASET,
      (NAME,(VEND.SDT.FLE.M220FU)  -          DATASET=M220FU,
      VOL(VSAM21) -                           ACCMETH=(VSAM,
      CYL(1,1) -                              KSDS),
      SPEED -                                 SERVREQ=(GET,PUT,
      IXD -                                   UPDATE,BROWSE,
      REPLICATE -                             NEWREC,DELETE),
      NOIMBED -                               RECFORM=(VARIABLE,
      RECSZ (179,179) -                       BLOCKED),
      FSPC (10,10) -                          OPEN=INITIAL,
      KEYS (10,0) -                           BUFNO=2,
      REUSE -                                 BUFNI=1,
      ) -                                     STRNO =2

  DATA..........
        INDEX...........
```

Figure 5.4 This screen shows user-supplied information on the CDBBR screen as it relates to a VSAM cluster and a file control table definition.

record. For example, if you were to enter a department I.D. field into your data dictionary, you would have to define a number of descriptive attributes to the system. These may go as follows: a Department I.D. is a five-position numeric field. The upper limit of the field is 88888, and it cannot be zero or left blank. Then, you need to define certain edit criteria and decide whether the standard messages generated by SDT upon failing to meet such criteria would suffice. Last, but not least, you want to relate the data dictionary to all database definitions (where used) referred to in your system. The SDT data dictionary is no different from other automated directories in the sense that each field carries a "long" name and a "short" name for reference. A long name is normally used in a full-blown application program, which, in this instance would be the vendor's fourth generation PDL module. The short name (acronym) is normally used during the execution of a query.

In addition to the CDD database, SDT also relies on a CDB control record, which describes all the physical attributes and the standard operating capabilities of each database referenced in the system.

You also need a third type of control record which is the CMS "Mask" record, and its use pertains to initializing every single data field on the dictionary with the proper default values. (Figure 5.2)

In Figure 5.4, a screen is laid out that corresponds to creating the Database Control Record or CDB. Technically, this parameter relates to the file control table (a CICS telecommunications function) and to the VSAM cluster.

Note that the last qualifier of the name parameter in the VSAM cluster and the data set name under the file control table are user supplied. So are the variable record format, the physical length of the record, as well as its keys. (This also points to the fact that SDT is a technical environment requiring specialized expertise, rather than a user-oriented software.) Since SDT is a fourth generation productivity tool that is geared to the analyst, you need to have a fair technical background to implement your project. (Note that the vendor offers a week-long seminar of the SDT, architecture that has a long list of technical prerequisites.)

Purely from the design point of view, it is practical to use a data dictionary for a number of reasons. First, it lets you to centralize your data. This always simplifies design and systems analysis, while it eliminates the need to develop complex maintenance programs. It also cuts down on redundancies that can cause synchronization problems in the way you store, and often display, required information.

For example, one file in the personnel area may show an employee's hourly rate being $17.281. However, a corresponding payroll record reflects the new rate, which is now set at $17.812 per hour (not to mention some of the other changes affecting the employee's classification and home department). Another advantage of such a dictionary is that you can simply eliminate erroneous definitions with regard to a single data field. I have seen instances where an employee's status indicator was coded as a four-position alphanumeric field in one set of records, while it showed up as a three-position signed numeric field in another. This is an intolerable situation.

5.3   Screen Processing

Let me give you some historical background on screen processing techniques. Among the earliest, and probably the least efficient ways of creating a screen (or map, if you will), was the one where you had no way of visualizing the physical layout of your design until your map had assembled, processed, and was invoked by an on-line transaction. You started by coding such a map on a field-by-field basis, defining the actual length, the horizontal and the vertical coordinates of every element on it, its attributes, its disposition, and so on. If your layout was off, you certainly would not know it until the map was displayed: then, and only then, via an on-line transaction would you be able to determine whether your product was satisfactory or had to be reassembled one more time. Here, you were really developing part of your specifications in batch mode, even though most of it entailed real time, state-of-the-art technology. Closely associated with this concept is an old IBM product called BMS, which is an acronym for basic mapping support.

A second generation technique in developing a screen layout is where you have the ability to do it on-line, so that you can continuously monitor what your map may look like—whether you are "off" or not, so that you can efficiently correct the flaw. In addition, this method has a relatively simple scheme. IBM's Screen Development Facility package or (SDF), comes the closest to this sort of interactive technology, which is a superior product when compared to BMS.

A third generation concept in screen painting techniques has to do with the idea of prototyping. Here you can design your own panel, lay it out interactively, and, through a data dictionary, you can also perform functions previously program driven. I don't mean real difficult functions, only simple ones, like checking a field for a numeric value, checking the presence or the absence of a particular field, simulating a number of logical paths between a number of panels, and so forth. This kind of screen painting can be done through some of the productivity tools currently available on the market or through procedural languages.

Finally, a fourth generation screen processing environment, which is one of the components of the SDT support system, will be discussed. (Please note that the term "fourth generation screen processing environment" is this author's own definition in reference to some of the conceptual changes taking place in interactive screen painting. This term bears no relationship to fourth generation languages, or even to systems design as used by the vendor.)

What is so vastly different about this concept? In a fourth generation processing environment, every individual screen has the ability to access, display, and maintain one or a number of databases concurrently. It is also possible for such a "smart" screen to carry enough logic that would enable the user to perform a substantial portion of the file maintenance without developing a single line of code; all of that logic would be fed into the process through the data dictionary and via the control records.

In a conventional data processing environment, you will develop files and record layouts; you will define and create query facilities, and write code to maintain your database. In a conventional environment, a screen is nothing but a shell which may or may not interact with such a central data directory. If it does, it can pick up some limited logic from it, but it will never have its own set of command structures to minimize substantially or, to a certain degree, eliminate programming efforts. Designing a screen in the SDT support environment actually requires a new set of considerations. In order to accommodate the flow of your application, you need to know whether your screen will contain a single or multiple records. This means you have to know quite intimately who is going to use a given screen and in what manner, for reasons of efficiency and security. Obviously the more records are being displayed and interspersed on a single screen, the more elaborate is the security scheme and the more complex the design. Generally speaking, a multiple-record screen allows you to enter your data quickly, although you may not be able to accommodate all the necessary detail required to do file maintenance, for example. For one thing you are restricted to 1920 positions on most standard display terminals.

Yet, most of the design considerations in an SDT environment are no different from the "conventional" design approach. Overall, you need to create easy-to-use, concise, uncluttered screens. The way you lay out your data should be self-explanatory, and some of the ambiguity may be clarified through the Millennium-supplied Help functions.

Additionally, if you are entering your data from a standard form, make sure your panel is laid out in a manner that closely corresponds to that form. When you create a screen under SDT, you must concern yourself with a fundamental design feature referred to as "screen blocks." The reason you need to incorporate "screen blocks" into your design is to provide conformity for your users, a set of standards, if you will. Note that in Figure 5.5 "A" designates the screen heading block, a constant that only appears once on the top of the screen, even when such a screen contains multiple records. The letter "B" corresponding to the department field is a global screen block, simply because it contains data that is associated with a number of other screens, thus used globally. A global screen block, pretty much like the screen heading block, is only displayed once.

```
 >  C                                                      ON RLSAA
                          "A"
              — EMPLOYEE DEMOGRAPHIC INFORMATION —

       DEPARTMENT: 12785
          "B"


       EMPLOYEE ID      —EMPLOYEE NAME—      CLASS    STATUS

       123-45-7683      GEORGE, J. KOWALSKI      Y32      A
       138-76-1547      ALEX QUITTNER            Y38      A
       380-12-5807      CARL L. SIMPSON          289      A
       391-01-7614      DENNIS O. JACKSON        100      A      "C"
       401-92-5087      LEO A. ARTHUR            101      A
       403-08-6604      SHIRLEY O'CONNOR         074      N
       471-12-1537      KAREN LENETZKI           511      A


                        09/12/88   10:10:52      M2LL ACTION ____
```

Figure 5.5   This is a screen design showing M&D defined "Screen Blocks."

A third component of this SDT screen architecture is the literal/ variable block, which normally represents information that is directly entered into the system by the user. The significance of this concept is that it provides a set of standards (which help organize a particular screen) for the analyst to follow throughout the design. Your SDT software comes with two separate designer subsystems: the first one is the standard Millennium screen package, the second one is a special screen painter developed for SDT. Out of the two software products available to you, SDT has more powerful screen processing features due to the fact that it has the ability to encompass any "foreign" files not part of the vendor's proprietary environment. This provides tremendous flexibility.

You can access SDT's screen designer in two ways: either via a set of menu screens or simply through the command line, a concept I discussed in Chapters 3 and 4. In the beginning, and until you have a fair amount of experience with the SDT system, it is recommended that you use the available menus to navigate through the software. (Ironically, the first menu screen also needs to be invoked through the command line...) It is further recommended that, when you decide to alter an existing screen, you use a copy of that screen, since all changes made, for example, to a production version will replace an actual "live" member. Thus should there be any problem with the new screen, it will be necessary for you to have it backed up using the previous version you have stored in your library.

```
>  C  CSD, SCREEN DESIGNER                               ON CMEXX

          ———————— MILLENNIUM MENU ————————
                        SCREEN DESIGN
    ENTER COMMAND —> GU        PATTERN —>         TASK ID—> SCD
    ENTER CDM QUALIFIER —> RLHMD,RLHRW
         —— DESCRIPTION ——    —— CHD QUALIFIER CONTENT ——

    ___  CREATE/MAINTAIN SCREEN              SCREEN NAME

    ___  SAVE SCREEN                         SCREEN NAME

    ___  RESTORE PREVIOUSLY SAVED SCREEN     SCREEN NAME

    ___  RESEQUENCE SCREEN SPECS             SCREEN NAME, INCREMENT
    ___  SCREEN DIRECTORY                    PARTIAL SCREEN NAME
    ___  OPTIMIZE SCREEN                     SCREEN NAME
         COPY SCREEN                         'FROM' SCREEN 'TO' SCREEN
         $KILLSCR                            SCREEN NAME


    ___

    A205W-END OF LIST           02/23/88  22:01:01    M2LL  ACTION _____
```

Figure 5.6   This is the SDT menu screen to issue a copy procedure.

Both Figure 5.6 and Figure 5.7 show the SDT designer menu screen. In Figure 5.6, and next to the qualifier, two delimiters are displayed. The first one (RLHMD) is the currently utilized screen name, while the second delimiter (RLHRW) refers to the copied version, that is, a copy of the RLHMD screen represented under RLHRW. An "X" in the Copy Screen field designates a "cloning" operation. In Figure 5.7, and following the successful outcome of the copy operation, you can now update the newly created RLHRW screen simply by placing an 'X' next to the create/maintain screen field.

The CSD, screen design (in the upper-left-hand corner of both Figure 5.6 and Figure 5.7) refers to SDT's special screen designer panel, which then creates a blank screen for you to design your respective layouts. Suppose you want to create a screen that looks like the one presented in Figure 5.8. How do you tell SDT to paint such a screen layout for you?

First, design your own screen using what the vendor refers to as a CSDBR panel. The SDT screen designer will let you utilize the various commands offered by the system and a set of special characters which will be explained shortly. Once you have completed your design, the quit command, will allow you to optimize your screen. Optimization in this

```
 >   C   CSD, SCREEN DESIGNER                              ON CMEXX

           ──────── MILLENNIUM MENU ────────
                         SCREEN DESIGN
  ENTER COMMAND ─> GU          PATTERN ──>          TASK ID─> SCD
  ENTER CDM QUALIFIER ─> RLHMD,RLHRW
        ── DESCRIPTION ──        ── CHD QUALIFIER CONTENT ──

  X    CREATE/MAINTAIN SCREEN              SCREEN NAME
  ____
  ____ SAVE SCREEN                         SCREEN NAME
  ____
  ____ RESTORE PREVIOUSLY SAVED SCREEN     SCREEN NAME
  ____
  ____ RESEQUENCE SCREEN SPECS             SCREEN NAME, INCREMENT
  ____ SCREEN DIRECTORY                    PARTIAL SCREEN NAME
  ____ OPTIMIZE SCREEN                     SCREEN NAME
  ____ COPY SCREEN                         'FROM' SCREEN 'TO' SCREEN
       $KILLSCR                            SCREEN NAME

  ____

   A205W-END OF LIST            02/23/88  22:01:01    M2LL  ACTION ____
```

Figure 5.7   This is the SDT menu screen used to create a new screen.

```
                      EMPLOYEE:ADDRESS:SCREEN

  EMPLOYEE NAME       XXXXXXXXXXXXXXXXXXXXXXXXXXX
  STREET ADDRESS      XXXXXXXXXXXXXXX
  CITY & ZIP CODE     XXXXXXXXXXXXXXX       XXXXX
  TELEPHONE #         XXXXXXXXXX
  DEPARTMENT          XXXXX
  STATUS              X    XXXXXXXXXXXXXXXXXXXXXXX
```

Figure 5.8   This shows a screen layout to translate to SDT.

particular instance means that you have finished putting in all of your changes and that those changes are to be reflected on subsequent screen displays. (If you modify an existing screen, but forget to optimize it, your recent changes will not be reflected.) It is somewhat like updating your file on your library before calling it quits.

Finally, you want to fine-tune your screen by adding a Help function to each and every field. The Help function will enable you to utilize the

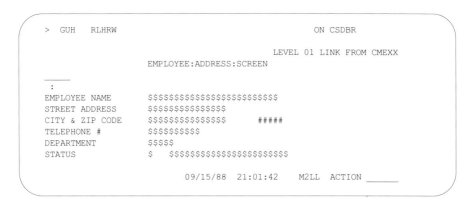

```
 >  GUH    RLHRW                                    ON CSDBR

                                        LEVEL 01 LINK FROM CMEXX
                       EMPLOYEE:ADDRESS:SCREEN


    ___
     :
    EMPLOYEE NAME         $$$$$$$$$$$$$$$$$$$$$$$$$$$$
    STREET ADDRESS        $$$$$$$$$$$$$$$
    CITY & ZIP CODE       $$$$$$$$$$$$$$$        #####
    TELEPHONE #           $$$$$$$$$$
    DEPARTMENT            $$$$$
    STATUS                $    $$$$$$$$$$$$$$$$$$$$$$$$$$

                          09/15/88  21:01:42    M2LL   ACTION _____
```

Figure 5.9 This shows the previous employee address screen transcribed to the SDT screen designer.

system's definition of problem handling and what courses of action you might take to get out of it. Can you imagine the amount of programming you would have to incorporate into your system for such extensive diagnostic facilities? Figure 5.9 shows the previous screen layout as translated to the SDT screen designer.

Note the following conventions used in conjunction with the special characters:

'$'   represents a single position of an alphanumeric field.

'#'   stands for a single numeric character on your screen.

':'   denotes an embedded space in the literal, while

'%'   is used to designate a single character of a data field.

The colon between the header (EMPLOYEE:ADDRESS:SCREEN) and the detail section represents an entire blank line for clarity. Look at some of the already familiar features in Figure 5.9. The GUH acronym is simply a Millennium command (Chapter 5), meaning that you want to get a specific record and hold it for update. The RLHRW is the name of the screen you recently copied, and now you need to use the CSDBR screen designer to develop your layout. This screen is considered Level 01, since it has been derived from the CMEXX source which is now considered Level 00. The real beauty of the SDT screen designer is in its full-blown command capabilities, which will be briefly highlighted, including some examples. Figure 5.10 summarizes all related SDT commands.

Command	Command Function
DELETE	Delete a blank line
D	Delete a field or a field name or a screen title
INSERT	Insert a blank line below your command
INSERTB	Insert a blank line above your command
/	Split a description screen
*	Prompt a field
+	Add a new field. (If you want to change an existing field, you'll have to delete it first
- =	Move a field or a field name on the screen "-" designates the move to area while "=" represents the move from area
"	Duplicate the line above the command (this only applies to blank screens)
>	Shift a screen title, field name or field to the right
<	Shift a screen title, field name or field to the left

Figure 5.10 This is a set of commands used by SDT's screen designer facilities.

Although the SDT screen designer is capable of automatically generating the required screen control records, you need to customize these records to help refine your application flow. Each screen you utilize in your system has a Screen Parameter or CPS record which, in fact, provides a framework for your screen: information such as the name of the screen, spacing and formatting, the type of screen about to be processed, etc. In addition, the CPS database contains all the pre- and post-screen processing programs in reference to your particular screen, which is essentially what the SDT screen designer is all about.

During the prescreen phase screen processing programs have the ability to edit your data, perform whatever computations need to be performed, or simply access a specific database bringing it into memory. Since prescreen processing occurs before a field is displayed, you can rely on some of the automatic functions of the prescreen programs to perform the necessary calculations before displaying such a panel. For example, you can add up

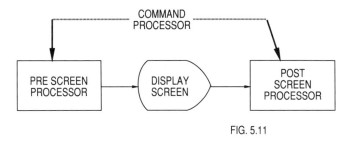

FIG. 5.11

Figure 5.11 This flowchart demonstrates the pre- and post-screen processing mechanism.

all of an employee's voluntary deductions and display the resulting totals on the screen. The postscreen program, on the other hand, works with the data entered on the screen. The logic inherent in this process can check and edit your data entered on that screen and respond to you via a message on a specific error condition. What is nice about these programs is that they allow the respective screen to be either in an inquiry mode or simply in a file-maintenance mode—whatever is necessary at the time. A brief over-view of this concept is presented in Figure 5.11. Think of the CPS control record as a required framework for the entire screen processing environment. A second such control mechanism, which is the CSL or literal record, contains all the field names and field titles associated with the screen in your particular application. A third record, the so-called screen variable data record or CSV, on the other hand, contains all the variable records you need to refer to in your system. Therefore, each screen in your application has a CVS record for each and every variable that shows up on the screen. (Variable simply refers to the data being entered on the screen by the terminal operator as opposed to a constant such as a title heading.)

The idea is to set up those automatic Help facilities to show people how to use the system and to show a way out of an error situation. If the users have questions about certain fields, they can simply press PF2/14 to invoke such a Help module. What you want to remember is that SDT also allows you to set up your own Help functions, if you need to customize that aspect of your system, apart from what is already available through Millennium.

In Chapter 4, I mentioned that you should always rely on the THU database in developing a set of customized Help functions. The above discussion pertains not only to the basic Millennium product, but the SDT environment which is functional only under the umbrella of Millennium.

Suppose, in designing your own Help procedures, you also need to formulate some highly customized error messages, customized (tutorial) instructions as well as tutorial narratives. Since these messages have little, if anything to do with the vendor's own conventions, it is important that they be kept on a separate database. If you were to mix the standard and customized tutorial conventions by placing them on the common THR database, you would be running the risk of having your own enhancements blown away during the vendor's periodic maintenance procedures (referred to as releases).

5.4   Setting up Queries

SDT's querying facilities are purely on-line real time inquiries. PDL, a fourth generation Millennium-driven language is more of a maintenance and design tool and does not replace SDT's inquiry functions as such. Why talk about queries? Better yet, why do you need to build queries into your design?

First of all, you need to create query facilities for an existing system that has no such interactive facilities to respond to emergency situations that are part of a typical business environment. When you utilize SDT's query module to design a new system, you can accomplish this with little or no coding effort on your part. This gives the user full-blown capabilities to real time technology.

Why do you need query facilities in the first place?

Queries enable you to find an individual or an item in a system, regardless of which one of the databases you need to reference. So queries are meant to be useful to you in the global sense. Ideally, a piece of data that was created in the payroll module, for example, can be used elsewhere in the same system or in an altogether different system which is referenced via the present one.

Queries normally carry enough logic to respond to your immediate needs, especially when you are under the gun. From time to time, management has the tendency to utilize the system's report generator rather than its query facilities, because advanced software packages such as the Millennium product allows you to create a desired report on-line using a fourth generation language, that is, PDL, or simply relying on some of the conventional techniques such as SAS or Easytrieve. The trouble is that while most report generators do function in an on-line environment, they are the product of batch, rather than real-time technology. Also, queries are user-oriented tools because of their relative simplicity. On-line report generators are a great deal more cumbersome to develop, and, although they are purely procedural, you will need to have some familiarity with coding conventions, I/O structures, and a set of standardized criteria. You are a great deal better off using query facilities when you need information fast and up to the minute. Most vendors charge a hefty price for such a subsystem and it is normally not part of the standard package.

The first aspect about setting up your queries is that you need to define certain search fields, which are the primary components of a search expression on the CQUBR screen. The CQUBR screen is a derivative of one of a number of databases SDT utilizes to perform query functions. The CQU database in this particular instance contains stored queries and allows you to create, store, and execute queries against a database. Obviously, you could search through every data field on file, if you wished, but from an efficiency point of view it is not practical. Search fields require that an entire database be scanned, from top to bottom, with the selection criteria thoroughly analyzed. SDT allows you to concatenate up to five search fields. In order to make such a concatenation work, you need to rely on the CSF "search field" database, which will contain all those selected records with the proper search values.

A comprehensive list of the system's databases used in conjunction with the querying process is listed in Figure 5.12. If you have two fields in the data dictionary, one called DIV (short for "division"), and another DEPT ("department" abbreviated) you may combine the two fields into DIVDEPT for a valid search argument.

Standardized queries are expensive due to their high dependency on real time resources. This is why you need to be careful about setting up queries which will become standard routines in the future. To simplify query evaluation, do the following: review your data dictionary for every field in the system. Afterwards, make a list of all the search possibilities, to make sure that that is indeed how a query should be set up. Only then do you want to create a CSF database for each search field to be utilized via the CSFBR screen.

What are considered search fields in the SDT environment? Search fields normally refer to indexes, upgrading indexes and UR records. Index records contain search field names and their associated values as well as pointers to the UR file. When you use an index, you essentially eliminate the need for a sequential "browse," that is, scanning your file, record by record, which is time consuming and thus expensive. Instead of reading an entire record, you merely want to look at the index portion of it since that is only a small physical part of your total record.

DBID	Database name	Function
CDD	DATA DICTIONARY	Contains records that describe every field in your application and control file databases
CDM	DATA MACRO	Contains data macros that can be used in the display and sort blocks of the CQUBR screen
CFP	PRINT PROFILE	Contains print profiles that allow you to print hard copy of system generated answer set.
CH1	HIERARCHY	Contains record defining the hierarchical structure used in queries
CNO	OPTIMIZED SEARCH FIELD	Contains optimized search fields
CQU	QUERY	Contains stored queries and allows you to create, store and execute queries against a database
CQQ	QUERY QUESTIONS	Contains query records
CSF	Search Fields	Contains records defining each field name you want to query on
CSS	STOP VALUES	Contains search field values for specific search field that will not have indexes built during the batch execution run
CO2	BATCH EXTRACTION	Defines the physical attributes of the application source file being processed by the Batch Extractor Program (M2X500), the databases to be used in the extraction run, and any filter criteria necessary or desired for that run
NDX	INDEX	Contains index values from the search fields and the record numbers that contain those values for your application databases.
UR	UR RECORD	Contains UR records, which either point to or contain the data that you want to access for a query
UCN	INDEX CONTROL	Contains UR record information, index status and the date and time a database's searchfields were optimized

Figure 5.12   This chart shows all query-related databases in the SDT system.

In order to execute a query, SDT utilizes the so-called "UR" file where index records containing the search field values will simply reference the above data set. The UR record does one of two things. It may point back to the source file for the contents of the entire record, or contain an abbreviated version of what was built strictly for the query.

"Upgrading" an index comes into play when a record is either changed or a new record is added to the database. A brief overview of this concept is presented in Figure 5.13. Here, the source record is made up by an index and a data portion. The index or key is built based on the database identifier field (DBID) which is also carried in the UR record for reference. Two other components of the concatenated key are made up by the employee's identifier and the department code corresponding to the value of 'VARSEGI'. The DBID is required on the source record to identify the particular database being queried. The concatenated key, on the other hand, is used to identify, for example, an employee who holds a number of temporary positions in multiple departments requiring a unique value. (The employee's I.D. alone would not be unique, since it would appear in a number of departments.) The UR record is made up of the UR database identifier along with a field acronym that refers to the previous source record. As you can see, an image of the source key is also part of the UR record, which is set up as a pointer. The index record that utilizes the NDX database also points to the RLH file in the source record showing a maximum limit.

As you recall, creating queries was discussed during the coverage of Millennium. Unless you create a "target screen" (a screen laid out exactly the way you may want to see it in its final form) your query responses will

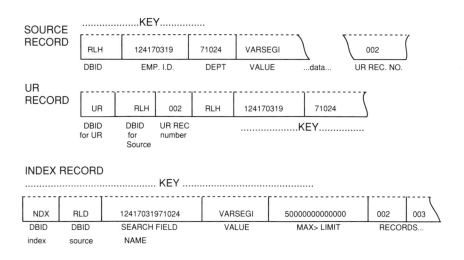

Figure 5.13 This shows components of a query which make up the index to the UR record.

always display on a system-generated answer-set screen. SDT has facilities where you can define certain data macros that allow you to store some of your more frequently used procedures for convenience.

When issuing a query, first read the CDB record (which is simply a reference table for the particular database being queried). At that point, your query will find the call sequence number and version, if any, that will identify the previously described index and UR files. During this operation, another file, the UCN (also referred to as an index control record) is read in order to locate a status indicator and to define a range. Subsequently, the query will read the index file to find the record with values identical to the search expression. Each of these records, by the way, contains the UR record number, which, as is depicted earlier in Figure 5.13 is retrieved and stored in a table.

If your source file happens to be a sequential file, the UR record will contain a copy of your source file. However, if your source file is a random access type, the UR record will have keys to reference your source database.

The final step comes into play when you need to sort the file. If you do, SDT will build all the necessary sort keys for you (based on your specification) read and rearrange the entire work set, and display it on the screen. SDT utilizes a set of routines called normalizer routines or commands to control how data passes from one place to another in your system, such as from record to screen or from record to memory and so on. The normalizer is also responsible for reformatting your record into a standard format, regardless of how data appears on your screen. Standardization, or a standardized format, is essential when you are dealing with a Millennium-based package, because of the system's way of dealing with a variety of applications.

Summary

SDT or Systems Development Tool was developed by the McCormack and Dodge Corporation based on a number of creative ideas such as the extensive utilization of databases, sophisticated screen processors, query facilities, and a full-blown fourth generation language called PDL.

Screen processing evolved from the early basic mapping support or BMS model which supported real time processing in batch mode.

A second generation screen processing concept evolved from IBM's SDF model, which allowed the user the freedom to design a panel in a purely interactive, real time environment. A more advanced concept of screen painting was triggered via a number of fourth generation languages, allowing the user some processing and prototyping capabilities. Last, but not least, a whole new screen processing technology is available today via some of the fourth generation support systems, which can access and process multiple databases and perform complicated operations, as a result. SDT essentially utilizes three basic modes or formats in defining physical file types.

The first format is designed to access a sequential file, such as an ESDS source file. The second format is used when a particular set of data is dependent on other data that must be consolidated for you to view, and the third mode is used when you need to have more than one logical database per physical file.

During the design of a particular screen, an important consideration must be emphasized, that is, whether the screen is to access one or a number of databases. When you create a screen under SDT, you must concern yourself with a fundamental design feature called screen blocks.

Screen processing in the SDT environment can be classified into pre- and postscreen processing phases. Both of these phases provide the user with substantial maintenance capabilities.

Queries allow you to find an individual or an item in a system regardless of which one of the databases such information resides on. Queries are user-oriented tools because of their relative simplicity while on-line report generators are a great deal more complex.

Search fields refer to indexes, upgrading indexes, and UR records in the SDT technology. Index records contain search field names and their associated values as well as pointers to the UR record. When you use an index, you eliminate the need for a sequential browse, that is, scanning your file record by record which is a time-consuming proposition. The execution of a query relies on the UR database where indexed records containing the search field values will simply reference the above data set.

Normalizer routines are commands to control how data is passed from one place to another in your system such as from record to screen or from record to memory.

Chapter 6

Procedure Development Language

6.1   Overview

In Chapter 5, M&D's Systems Development Software package (SDT) which is a fourth generation productivity tool, was discussed. You need to rely on SDT when you operate and design systems in a mixed environment. The term "mixed" environment indicates a practical situation where the products of different vendors along with your own proprietary software coexist. Through this Systems Development Tool, you can easily access, inquire, and update any application system in a true borderless fashion. A piece of data developed in the general ledger system, for example, can be successfully processed and "transported" to an equipment inventory or to a purchase order system, either one of which may be an old, stand-alone application.

Just what is PDL, and if SDT has so much horsepower, why would you need PDL in the first place? PDL is M&D's fourth generation language, one of the major building blocks in this extended Millennium environment. PDL stands for "Procedure Development Language," and its primary purpose is to further enhance and refine all required SDT applications using on-line, real time technology.

Think of it this way: SDT will do about 80 percent of what you need in order to develop a fourth generation system from scratch, but, if you really wish to take advantage of this environment, you want the other 20 percent, as well, which is this Procedure Development Language. For all practical purposes, SDT will enable you to design, develop, and prototype your own application. PDL will reinforce all of the above by allowing you to enhance the system's standard file maintenance processes and work with data resident on your application files.

You may think of the procedural development language as M&D's most specialized approach in producing, interfacing, and consolidating new systems. PDL is the third building block in this totally hierarchical environment. First is a powerful millennium system which is a prerequisite for the SDT module, then, a fourth generation procedure language to provide SDT an ability to handle even the most unique applications. PDL is primarily a productivity tool geared to the technician rather than to the user, that enhances the analytical and the programming capabilities of the first.

One of the most powerful aspects in the use of the Procedure Development Language is your ability to link up with conventional languages, such as ANS COBOL, or PL/I: popular and otherwise intensely utilized application languages. In a sense, PDL is a language that can provide an answer to migration technology, that is, you can start developing all your new applications under the umbrella of SDT without having to convert thousands of lines of existing code.

There is no current technology to convert a conventional language to fourth generation source code other than rewriting it from scratch. However, PDL facilitates the use of third generation programs which can be accessed, used, and manipulated as part of a full blown millennium environment. If most of your systems are developed in, for example, ANS COBOL, you will not have a way of converting those applications by using fourth generation technology. This means that a batch program that does all the editing for your gross-to-net payroll calculations cannot be "migrated" into a real time environment simply through a standard fourth generation language. (The term "standard" refers to any such language which is not fully supported by a fourth generation system, or support environment.) PDL, however, can "call" and invoke such a conventional program and enhance it by using state of the art technology. It can do this without altering a massive body of source code.

In an earlier Varsegi publication titled *Practical Business Systems, Implementation: a DP Guide*, the vast differences prevalent in third and fourth generation language technologies were discussed. The difference is really a dramatic one. Some of the conventions are highlighted to visualize the magnitude of the migration process.

If you were to compare an assembler type language with its high-level (third generation) counterpart, such as ANS COBOL, you would see that sometimes a single statement by the latter can and does translate into a number of basic, machine-oriented statements. Thus, given the conventional IBM/370 architecture, even a simple add operation requires a number of associated procedures when it is translated into assembler language. Accordingly, each field, must be packed, followed by the conversion of that data to binaries, then physically storing such data in various registers. Once the operation is completed, you will need to convert the result back to hexadecimals, then unpack each field to print or display the result.

In all this detail-oriented exercise forced by the assembler language, there is a methodology to expand a high-level statement into a machine oriented set of instructions. This logical relationship does not exist when dealing with such a high-level conventional language and its fourth generation counterpart.

When you use a fourth generation language, it is assumed that you have previously defined all editing rules and criteria in a data dictionary which makes all coding associated with editing and computational requirements redundant. Through this definition, the language can format a report or a screen layout for you automatically. Should you be dissatisfied, with the automatic set up of the system, for some reason, you would find yourself putting almost as much code into your fourth generation language to "override" these system generated "defaults" as you would in a conventional language environment. Consequently, a single statement using a fourth generation language can translate into hundreds of lines of conventional code, such as those written in PL/I or COBOL. However, unlike the translation between assembler and a high-level third generation language, this latter technology offers no common ground for a simple migratory mechanism. The power of a fourth generation language comes from the various building blocks: that is, the ability to query, the ability to utilize a centralized data dictionary, and so on. Thus, without a comprehensive support mechanism, stand-alone fourth generation languages have very little power in a sense.

PDL is a special language, one whose power comes from the total support environment, unlike stand-alone fourth generation languages, such as FOCUS. You can perform specialized tasks over and above what Millennium and SDT enable you to. You would be able to fine tune and customize procedures and to access an existing body of code in a borderless fashion.

6.2   What Is the Procedure Development Language (PDL)?

PDL has an English-like command structure with three distinct sections. The first section is a simple identification line containing the name of both the program and the author of that program. The purpose of the second section is to convey instructional and error messages. This is called the message section. The third, or procedure section, represents the main body of your program where you can define required logic and the individual tasks to be performed.

From a structural point of view, PDL derives its power from two Millennium-based files such as the CGS and the CGI databases. The CGS database performs like an internal library where all your PDL programs are kept and defined. It accommodates all PDL programs by program name and by a unique sequence number.

The CGI database, on the other hand, is like a subroutine library that contains procedures that are referenced by the different PDL programs via an INCLUDE or $INCLUDE command. Both of these databases are similar in the sense that they are made up of three components, such as a global variable member, a sequence number, and the actual line of code.

The global variable is simply your PDL identifier, that is, your program name. The sequence field defines the order in which the programs (called members) are kept on both the CGS and the CGI databases. The rest of the CGS library is allocated to the actual PDL source code.

Because PDL is a Millennium-based fourth generation language, it utilizes and has access to all those commands and databases discussed in Chapters 3 through 5.

PDL's memory can be thought of as a temporary scratch pad or work area where the fields and the values associated with those fields are stored for the program to access. One would have the notion to say, "why worry about economizing on memory? Computer environments today come with such powerful storage facilities that it is virtually impossible to saturate them."

In a way this is true. However, PDL equates the use of memory with processing efficiency, almost like the paging mechanism that shares a similar approach to IBM's concept on virtual storage. Thus, if your PDL program only needs to access a single data field on a record, then only that particular field will be brought into memory and not the rest during the execution of the program. This essentially translates into faster processing, and it gives you an altogether better response time, almost as if you were coding your program in an assembler language. This, in itself, is a lot more important than simply the memory you save as the result of processing efficiency.

The efficient use of memory relates to the way the language utilizes its terminals, responds to a request, and the way it "transports" messages back and forth between transactions. PDL's memory buffer provides each terminal initially with 6K bytes of temporary storage. After that is used up, the virtual memory system allocates memory space, as needed. Memory, like the paging mechanism, is expandable in 4K increments up to 32K. The 6K allotted to each terminal lends that terminal some local processing capabilities of its own without relying on the main-frame system. This processing or memory capability enables a terminal to function "intelligently" very much like a PC clone.

6.3   The PDL Structure

PDL, like most conventional or fourth generation languages, has its own coding structure that is made up of an identification line, a message section, and a procedure section which contains the actual PDL source code. To simplify things, you can, for all practical purposes, think of the message section as an extension of the PDL source code.

Figure 6.1 is a brief example of PDL coding. Line 100 is simply the identification line of the program displaying a PDL identifier (SAMPLE01) and the author (VENDOR) of that program. The mechanics of the rest of the messages happens to be pretty much the same type as the the first

```
100  PDL-ID. SAMPLE01                    AUTHOR. VENDOR
105  ****************************************************************
110  *    (OPTIONAL HEADER BLOCK CREATED USING COMMENTS)           *
115  *    THIS PROGRAM EDITS DATA ON THE RLA02 SCREEN              *
120  *                                                            *
105  ****************************************************************
200  MESSAGE F 0001 'PLEASE ENTER NUMERIC DATA ONLY
205         HUS RLA, SALETODTE
215  MESSAGE F 0002 'PLEASE ENTER ALPHABETIC INFORMATION ONLY
220         HUS RLA,AGENTNAME
225  MESSAGE W 0003 SALES TO DATE = @RLH, TEMPTODTE
300  TST    TEST RLA,SALTODTE NUMERIC             FM0001 FBEND
320  TST    TEST RLA,AGENTNAME ALPHA              FM0002
330  TST    REPLACE RLA, TEMPTODTE WITH STR(RLA, SALETODTE;Y092NF 0)
340  TST    CPVERB 0003
350  TST END RETURN
```

Figure 6.1 This is a brief message and procedure section for a PDL program.

message. The only exception to that is shown in line 225, where the sales-to-date information is received directly from memory via the special character "@" or @RLH.

Any message you need to define in your program is going to contain the reserved word "MESSAGE", as well as a message number along with a severity code. Severity codes are prefixes attached to a message number: F: for fatal, W: for warning, and I: for informational. These were discussed in Chapters 3, 4, and 5. This mechanism is also cloned into PDL. To be somewhat redundant, the "I" prefix attached to the message stands for the usual communication between the application program and the terminal operator which is purely informational and tends not to disrupt the processing sequences of that program.

Likewise, "W" is a warning message. Warning messages, as you recall, interrupt the processing cycle, but they interrupt only in a temporary fashion until you press enter for the second time. (Warning messages merely alert you of a potential problem, which may not necessarily be that, after all.) "F", on the other hand, is a different story. It stands for a fatal message. When you code an "F" type of message into your PDL program, you will not be able to continue the normal processing cycle unless you either correct the problem or exit the transaction by removing the maintenance subcommand. Thus, in lines 200 and 205, a fatal message was merely set up to warn the terminal operator that the field SALETODTE, which is an element on the RLA database, must be a numeric entry. If you were to enter other than numeric data in this field, line 300, which points to the corresponding message in the message section, is going to protect the field from such an entry. (Note that the acronym "HUS" preceding the RLA database represents a set of composite attribute bytes to highlight a given field on the screen in a protected mode.)

Figure 6.2 gives you a comprehensive summary of such PDL-utilized attribute combinations. Attribute characters, in general, enable the programmer to display data on the screen in various ways as required by the particular situation. When you change the original length of a field, for example (IBM refers to it as modifying a data tag), you allow the programmer to access the most recently entered information on the screen and ignore all prior data entry, which is accomplished by examining the length of each field on the screen. IBM, for one, reserves the first position or byte of any given field and allocates it internally to the various field attribute combinations.

In PDL, you also need to control the way variable fields appear on the screen such as:

• Displaying in normal intensity or highlighted,
• Displaying in a protected or in an unprotected mode, or
• Displaying on the screen at all.

```
Position     Code   Meaning      Function

One          N      Normal       Displayes the field normally
             H      Highlight    Makes the field brighter
-----------------------------------------------------------------
Two          P      Protected    Causes the cursor to skip over the
                                 field; no information can be entered in
                                 the field.
             U      Unprotected  Allows the cursor to stop at the field
-----------------------------------------------------------------
Three        S      Show         Causes the field to display on the screen
             N      No show      Prevents the field from displaying on the
                                 screen
-----------------------------------------------------------------
```

Figure 6.2 This chart demonstrates combining attributes for PDL program definition.

A normal intensity display is the one when a data field that appears on the screen does so in normal brightness. Highlighted fields are intensified to serve as warning messages, normally to pinpoint some obvious flaw. (This is more of a systems decision than anything else.)

A protected field is one that cannot be overlayed with any new information by the terminal operator. Constant information, such as the definition of function keys or field titles are normally highlighted, although security plays an important role in protecting a field. Unprotected data fields, on the other hand, represent variable type of information that can be overlayed with the most recently entered data. A third situation (besides protecting or unprotecting a field) has to do with data fields appearing in nondisplay mode. These fields are still available on the screen in a particular position, but, since their attribute bytes have been turned off, you cannot see them. (Make sure you protect such fields before they get wiped out by an unsuspecting terminal operator.) As a rule, you only want passwords to have this kind of attribute protection.

PDL also enables you to rely on a combination of attributes. For example, you may frequently run into situations where you need to highlight and, at the same time, protect a data field. To do that, you must combine a number of attribute values. In this case, you will need to protect and intensify a field. The following is a legitimate attribute combination of three such values where the first position of that attribute can be either "N" for normal intensity display or "H" for highlighting or intensifying a field.

The second position of the field may be a "P" for a protected field or a "U" for an unprotected field.

The third position may be either an "S", which causes a field to show on the screen or an "N", which prevents the same element from a display. Thus, based on the above, the following are some of the legitimate attribute combinations accommodated by PDL:

HPS   HPN
NUS   NUN
HUS   HUN
NPN

Note that you would need to have a separate code if you were to display each field differently. In order to change the attributes of more than one field in a single statement, you must list the Millennium data names separated by spaces after the attribute code.

When you code an attribute statement in your program, you can actually rely on a set of multiple statements such as:

ATTRIBUTE HUS MMA,NAME
ATTRIBUTE NPN MMA,ID
ATTRIBUTE HUS MMA,DEPT

How would you code, for example an employee name field using the above attributes. How would that be different from defining his/her employee identification field? Actually, you can also combine these statements into one for efficiency.

Millennium data names used with the attribute statement must have a screen definition on the CSV database. There is no formal separation between the message and the procedure sections. In fact, you can place a message anywhere in the program even though it is neater to place all systems messages in one place—perhaps at the top of the program. In Figure 6.1, note that in lines 300 and 320, two fields are being tested. The first one is tested for a numeric value, and the second one for a straight alpha condition. "numeric" and "alpha" are both PDL reserved words, each generating a set of required edit procedures. When you say "alpha" in your procedure section, the system expects an alphabetic entry in the "AGENTNAME" field. If the entry is a numeric one or an alphanumeric containing mixed data, PROCEDURE FM001 FBEND (over to the far right of line 300) will cause an immediate halt in the processing of that particular transaction. This is not totally different from Millennium.

PDL allows you to develop your own customized messages or to rely on those automatically generated by the environment. Customized messages must be in the sequence range of 0001 to 1000. You may also retrieve standard PDL messages. Access the TER database where all these messages are kept and refer to them through a greater than 1000 sequence code.

Say; MESSAGE I 1009 'PRESS PF2 TO CONTINUE or

MESSAGE F 1111 'ENTRY MUST BE NUMERIC. RESUBMIT

It is important to remember that when you are working with fourth generation Millennium environment does much of the work for you. If you want to do file maintenance, you may be able to get by simply by using Millennium or SDT. These systems give you access to certain subcommands (insert, replace, delete, and move) which could potentially satisfy all your processing needs.

Thus, PDL, unlike a typical fourth generation language, may never have to be used, unless you need to do something special. Only when you need to provide a high degree of product customization, or when you need to link up with a conventional environment, do you need to rely on the power of PDL. Millennium's built-in screen processing features allow you to transfer data from a screen record into memory through a set of memory switches and then execute a PDL program that uses that data. As you recall from the previous chapters, the first aspect of this processing is called prescreen processing, and the program involved therein is a prescreen PDL program. Prescreen processing, or prescreen programs have the ability to manipulate and edit information on a screen before information is actually displayed.

In order to make sure that your prescreen program functions properly, check to see that the data needed by your program are already in existence before the executing of your PDL module. During your prescreen processing you can perform a number of tasks before displaying the result on the screen. For example, you can do a great deal of editing and calculations and show the result of those calculations at the time the information is displayed. Likewise, during the postscreen cycle, you can perform edits, computations, and a host of other operations after the data is already displayed on the screen. This processing is briefly described in Figure 6.3.

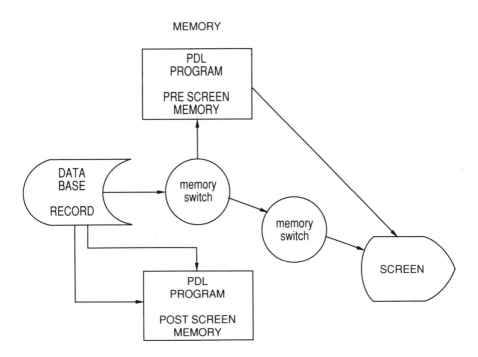

Figure 6.3   This flowchart demonstrates pre- and post-screen processing.

6.4   PDL Commands and Techniques

This discussion begins by displaying a set of tables used by PDL in its processing cycle. The first one is the PDL reserved word list (Figure 6.4). The second table gives you an overview of standard PDL statements (Figure 6.5). PDL contains seven reserved words, mainly in reference to the standard and special I/O commands which are presented to you in Figure 6.6.

In most cases, standard statements can only act on information that already exists in memory. However, once the information is stored in memory, you can manipulate it using any one of the PDL statements shown in

Reserved Word	Meaning
ALL	Can be used with the CLEAR verb and I/O verbs. * CLEAR ALL specifies that all fields should be cleared from memory * (I/O Verb)(DBID)(key value) LOAD (fdname,ALL) specifies that every occurrence of a field should be loaded from the record.
HI	Required reserved word that must be used with the LO reserved word to specify a status indicator range in a MILLSTAT statement
LO	Required reserved word that must be used with the HI reserved word to specify a status indicator range in a MILSTAT statement
IN	Required reserved word that must be used in the FINDSTRING and $FINDSTRING statements.
LOAD	Reserved word that must appear in the NEXTREC, $NEXTREC, NEXTALT, FINDREC, and PUTREC statements. For the NEXTREC,$NEXTREC, NEXTALT, and FINDREC statements, the field names specified after LOAD will be stored in memory and available to PDT for manipulation. For the PUTREC statement, the field name specified after LOAD will be written to the record on the database. (Note: The reserved word LOAD is different from the LOAD verb)
UNTIL	Optional reserved word used in the DO statement. Execution of paragraph initiated by the DO statement will continue while the condition is true
WITH	Is a reserved word required with REPLACE statements. The value after WITH will be stored in memory as the new value associated with the Millennium data name.

Figure 6.4   This chart explains PDL reserved words.

Verb	Purpose
ATTRIBUTE	Changes the display characteristics and accessibility of a field or a list of fields.
CALL	Calls a COBOL program
CLEAR	Removes fields and values from memory
CPVERB	Updates date/time, displays messages, branches to a level-2 label
CURSOR	Positions cursor over a field on the screen
DO	Executes a block of code. The code can be a paragraph within a program or another program
ENDDO	Terminates processing of a paragraph initiated by a DO statement
EOJ	Stops program execution when a condition makes further processing unlikely
FINDSTRING	Locates a substring within a string
$FINDSTRING	Locates a substring within a string; turns off wild cards, allowing you to search for question marks
INCLUDE	Copies a member stored on the CGI database into another program at compile time, changing the level-1 label of the "included" code to the level-1 label of the main program
$INCLUDE	Copies a member stored on the CGI database into another program at compile time, retaining the level-1 label from the "included" code
ITSDONE	Represents the termination switch in a DO statement, eliminating the need to code a temporary termination switch field
LOAD	Load information from a record present in a record buffer into memory, without performing I/O
LOADX	Loads portions of alphanumeric data into memory for string manipulation
MILLSTAT	Excludes specific records from I/O read by defining a range of Millennium status indicator values
REPLACE	Replaces a field in memory with a value
RESET	Resets alphanumeric fields to spaces and numeric fields to zeros in memory
RETURN	Terminates a program
SUBS	Acts upon a data expression that is coded like a symbolic expression
TEST	Compares two values or performs special tests
THISREC	Makes a record present in the screen buffer available for the LOAD verb
$REPLACE	Similar to REPLACE verb; the operand, however, must be symbolic name that represents a postfix expression
$TEST	Similar to the test verb; the operand, however, must be a symbolic name that represents a postfix expression

Figure 6.5   This chart explains standard PDL verbs

Figure 6.5. For example, if you wanted to determine that a value from the RLH,SALETODTE field was located in memory, you would issue the following standard PDL command:

TEST INHEM RLH,SALETODTE TM0001

Verb	Purpose
DELETREC	Deletes a record
ENDBROWSE	Prematurely terminates a browse; used with NEXTREC $NEXTREC and NEXTALT
FINDKEY	Verifies the existence of a record using a specific key value
NEXTALT	Obtains a record through a Millennium search field
NEXTREC	Performs a sequential read (browse) of a database in order to retrieve record data from database
$NEXTREC	Same as NEXTREC, except that it sends the key value that ends the browse to a field in memory named $$$,key.
PUTREC	Writes or rewrites a record to a database
IPUTREC	Writes a new record to a database
RPUTREC	Rewrites a record to a database

Figure 6.6   This chart shows PDL I/O statements.

Copyright © 1988 McCormack & Dodge Corporation. Used by permission.

If the RLH,SALETODTE field (where RLH points to the particular record on that database and SALETODTE to a single field associated with that database) is in memory, the program will display a message. This will be the message you have already defined in the message section of your PDL program.

Any foreign file operated on by PDL (or by SDT, for that matter) must be brought into memory before the system can "acknowledge" it and operate on it.

Input statements essentially retrieve data from your database and store the data in memory for efficiency. I/O and standard PDL statements differ in that I/O statements do not need a screen to access any data. Standard statements do need a screen. Once the data exist in memory, they can be easily manipulated with a set of standard PDL statements and then written out to a record with the use of an output statement. I/O statements allow you to browse your database for specific information, create new records, delete unwanted ones, and so on. For example, the I/O verb "FINDREC" is used to locate a record on a database and then to load the information specified by the statement into memory. Because of the extent of the total number of commands and statements used by PDL, it will not be possible to provide extensive coverage in a single chapter. However, the charts listed in Figures 6.4, 6.5, and 6.6 list all of the above statements available in the language.The charts do not provide an extensive explanation.

PDL's ability to link up with conventional programs is accomplished through one or a number of CALL statements. Briefly, CALL statements allow you to access such programs from a PDL program. This is really a time saver, since programs already written in COBOL will not have to be rewritten in PDL. To use a CALL statement, the COBOL program to be invoked must have a LINKAGE SECTION where the communication and exchange is to take place. All this is done through the Millennium memory, which is also available to PDL.

Line 601 in the PDL sample program in Figure 6.7 shows the CALL statement that accesses M2X037, which is the external COBOL module. M2X037 does not have to be converted from its current format to be utilized by this extended Millennium environment.

Code "CLEAR" in your program when there is a need for you to delete information from memory selectively. In the SDT-Millennium system, not everything is cleared automatically. Fields whose database identifier (DBID) are the same as that of the screen's are cleared automatically through this statement. (Remember, for every database, there is at least one corresponding screen.) All other fields need to be cleared of undesirable values left over from prior processing.

Three PDL statements have their origin in a conventional (third generation) language. These are the CPVERB, the DO, and the CURSOR commands. Actually, the DO statement has an ENDDO counterpart, which denotes the end of the execution of the DO function.

```
   1  PDL-ID.  $$CROPT                    AUTHOR. VENDOR.
   4  ********  EXAMPLE OF CALL STATEMENT
  36  SCR       REPLACE $$$,PARMS,,22,4 WITH 'SOPT'
  60  SCR       REPLACE MEM,PGM        WITH 'M2X037'
 100  SCR       TEST INMEM @$$$,PARMS,,1,31,$$COMQUAL,2    FBCKT
 200  SCR       REPLACE MEM,TEMPLIT    WITH @$$$,PARMS,,1,31,$$COMQUAL,2
 601  SCR CKT   CALL M2X037
9000  SCR       TEST $$$,PARMS,,10,1 EQ 'N' FM1450
9001  SCR       CLEAR *MEM
9002  SCR END   RETURN
```

Figure 6.7 This is a sample PDL program showing the three sections.

The CPVERB is an unconditional branch or an unconditional message display. It is similar to a GO TO statement in COBOL, or B (Branch) in Assembler Language (BAL). Actually, the CPVERB is a lot more flexible than a simple branch statement. You can perform a number of miscellaneous tasks such as updating the date and time fields in memory. The DO statements execute a block of code very much like a PERFORM statement does in COBOL or a Branch and Link (BAL) in an assembler environment.

Unlike assembler or COBOL, PDL executes lines of macros which means that each line is sometimes equivalent to a whole set of procedures. This is possible only because PDL is backed up by such powerful environments as those of the Millennium and the SDT systems, where everything—files, screens, procedures, and edit rules—is already defined for you in concurrently used systems.

There are two kinds of DO commands used in fourth generation language. The first one is a simple DO statement that executes a block of code with control returning to the next logical statement in the program. The second kind has to do with an "iterative DO", also referred to as a conditional DO. This is only invoked upon the truism (or falsehood) of a particular condition. Figure 6.8 includes a number of DO statements that execute the same block of code.

The simple DO statement on sequence line 400 of Figure 6.8 executes a paragraph of code associated with the level 1 label BRW. On every read activity, the program adds 1 to the counter initialized as X,CNT. The

```
  10 PDL-ID.  DOEXAMP                AUTHOR. M&d
 100           EXAMPLE OF DO STATEMENT
 150           MNL / VALIDATES AGENCY NAME FROM RLT DATA BASE
 200 MNL       REPLACE X, CNT                 WITH  0
 300 MNL       REPLACE RLT,NUMBER             WITH '???'
 400 MNL       DO BRW
 500 MNL       DO BRW WHILE     X,CNT LT 5
 600 MNL       DO BRW UNTIL     ITS DONE
 900 MNL       RETURN
2000           BROWSE RLT DATA BASE FOR AGENCY NAME
2005 BRW       REPLACE X,CNT    WITH X,CNT + 1
2010 BRW       NEXTREC RLT NUMBER LOAD NAME CODE          FBOUT
2120 BRW       REPLACE X,TABLE,@X,CNT! WITH RLT,NAME
2240 BRW OUT ITS DONE
2260 BRW       ENDDO
```

Figure 6.8   This demonstrates the use of the DO command in a PDL program. Note that some of the statements reference the Millennium system.

NEXTREC statement reads the RLT database, loading the fields NAME and CODE into memory. If no record is found, the program branches and control is returned to the main program. If a record is found, the value of RLT, NAME, is put into a table field, indicating the last record counted. The ENDDO statement on sequence line 400 ends the processing of the paragraph and returns control to the main program. The next DO statement on sequence line 500 executes the BRW paragraph only while the value of X,CNT is less than five. When the value of X,CNT reaches five, control is returned to the main program.

The last DO statement on sequence line 600 uses an "ITS DONE" statement as a termination switch. The BRW paragraph executes until the ITS DONE statement on sequence line 2240 is read. Control is then linked back to the main program.

Last, the CURSOR statement positions the cursor over a particular field when a screen is displayed. In Figure 6.9, the cursor will automatically display over the field on the screen whose CSV record name is RLA,BUD,@USR,OCC!

The system resolves the symbolic portion of the data name first. It checks the memory to find the value associated with @USR,OCC!. The system then substitutes the value it finds there for the third component of the data name. Therefore, if 1 was the value in memory, the system would place the cursor over the field whose CSV record name is RLA,BUD,1.

FINDSTRING is a typical Millennium/PDL command that allows you to compare the values of two Millennium names or literals to determine if one is contained in the other. The vendor refers to a value that is part of another or a substring. Note that you can also have (as with a number of other PDL-based commands) a "$" (dollar sign) preceding the word substring such as $FINDSTRING. Like the above command, $SUBSTRING also compares the values of two Millennium data names or literals. However, the dollar sign deactivates the wild card function so that you can

```
4000        * TEST BUDGET FIELDS FOR ZERO OR BLANK
4040  BUD     TEST RLA,BUD,@USR,OCC! EQ 0          PBOUT
4060  BUD     REPLACE USR,INVBUD WITH USR,INVBUD + 1
4080  BUD     CURSOR RLA,BUD,@USR,OCC!
4200  BUD OUT REPLACE USR,OCC WITH USR,OCC + 1
4299  BUD     ENDO
```

Figure 6.9   This represents sample use of the CURSOR statement.

search for values that contain the question mark character. Note that in Chapter 3, this particular Millennium feature that works pretty much like this is discussed.

There are essentially two types of wild card commands in PDL to perform an efficient search. The first one is referred to as the question mark (?), while the second one is an asterisk (*) type of search. The question mark indicates that any character can occupy a particular position in the key. The asterisk simply replaces an entire key component. So if you were to enter

>   _____   002,?????2_____ON RLH01_____

the system will attempt to make a character-for-character match between the key values entered in the command qualifier and a key on the record. When the system encounters a question mark in a position of the key, it selects records with any value for that position. For example, when you say ??3 the number 543 would be a match. So would be 123. Likewise the series 33456 would match the wild card numbers such as 3??5? The asterisk, on the other hand, replaces an entire low order string, not just a single character. So a string of 123* will match 123540, 1239763110, 123YBXZ and so forth.

A review of the above is shown in Figure 6.10. Note the following: The first FINDSTRING statement on sequence line 110 checks for the value "6" associated with the data name X,X. Since it does not find a 6, the false

```
    5    PDL-ID.   PDLFIND                   AUTHOR. VENDOR
    9    **********  FINDSTRING ' ?' FINDS FIRST BLANK CHAR IN LITERAL STRING
   11    **********  FINDSTRING '?'  ALWAYS FINDS A CHARACTOR IN POSITION
   13    **********  $FINDSTRING ' ?' FINDS FIRST BLANK CHAR IN LITERAL STRING
   15    **********  $FINDSTRING '?'  FINDS FIRST QUESTION MARK ? IN LITERAL STR
   20    MESSAGE I 0001 'TRUE @$$$,PARMS,,4,5
   35    MESSAGE I 0002 'FALSE
  100    MNL          REPLACE X,X    WITH '1234 ?789'
  110    MNL          FINDSTRING '6' IN X,X           TM0001 FM0002
  120    MNL          FINDSTRING '?'  IN X,X          TM0001 FM0002

  170    MNL          ?FINDSTRING '?'  IN X,X         TM0001 FM0002
  190    MNL          ?FINDSTRING ' ?' IN X,X         TM0001 FM0002
  900    MNL          RETURN

  00021- FALSE                0001I- TRUE 00001
  0001I- TRUE 00005           0001I- TRUE 00006
  0001I- TRUE 00005
```

Figure 6.10   This demonstrates the FINDSTRING command in conjunction with REPLACE.

message 0002 displays. The next FINDSTRING statement's wild card value (?) checks for any character. This type of FINDSTRING statement will always find the character in the first position of the literal string. The last FINDSTRING statement, containing a blank and wild card value (?), looks for one blank character in the string. In the FINDSTRING statements on sequence lines 130 and 150, the searched-for values are found. The starting position within the data name where the value located is stored in $$$,PARMS,,4,5. These values are displayed in the messages 0100I-TRUE 00001 and 0100I-TRUE 00005.

One of PDL's many versatilities is displayed by its use of an IN-CLUDE statement (both INCLUDE and $INCLUDE). This statement sim-

```
  50 PDL-ID. INCLUDE              AUTHOR. M&D
 100       * EXAMPLE OF INCLUDE STATEMENT — NESTED ROUTINES
 200 MESSAGE F 0001 'INVALID AGENCY
 210          HUS RLA,CODE
 220 MESSAGE W 0007 'NO AGENCY CODE ENTERED
 230 MESSAGE W 0013 'INVALID NUMBER OF AGENT
 240 MESSAGE W 0090 'NO HIT ON RLQ
 250 MESSAGE W 0100 'BAD NAME = @RLA,NAME
 260 HUS RLA,NAME
 270 MESSAGE W 0101 'GOOD NAME - @RLT,NAME
 280       * MCP - MAIN CONTROL PARAGRAPH
 290 MCP      INCLUDE EXAMP3A
1000 MCP      CLEAR *USER *RLT
2000 MCP END RETURN
```

```
MEMBER -> EXAMP3A
 400          TST - MAIN TESTING PARAGRAPH
 500 TST      TEST RLA,CODE NUMERIC            FBNX1 FM0001
 501 TST      TEST RLA,CODE BT '001' AND '020'  FBNX1 FM0001
 510 TST      INCLUDE EXAMP3B
 560 TST NX1  TEST RLA,PHONE EQ ' '            TM0007
 600 TST      TEST RLA,NUMAGENT BT 1 AND 300   FM0013
```

INCLUDE statement - first called member

```
MEMBER -> EXAMP3B
1100          NAM - VALIDATE AGENCY NAME FROM RLT DATA BASE
1120 NAM BRW REPLACE USR,BADNAMESW WITH 'N'
1140 NAM      REPLACE RLT,NUMBER WITH '???'
1160 NAM      DO BRW UNTIL ITS DONE
1180 NAM      TEST USR,BADNAMESW EQ 'Y'         FBNX1
1200 NAM      CPVERB 0100 0101
```

INCLUDE statement - second called member

Figure 6.11   This shows the entire call and called program mechanism.

ply allows you to CALL and INCLUDE an existing PDL code stored on the CGI database in another PDL program at compile time. This feature enables you to write common modules for a set of standard procedures that can be used repeatedly in multiple programs. The process is reviewed in Figure 6.11 in detail.

When you develop your source program (whether in a third or fourth generation environment), you may find it convenient to prepare "shells" that will save you a substantial amount of time in coding, while simplifying the entire process. For example, a source program written in CICS command language to add an employee to the payroll master file may also be utilized to modify data on that file via some minor programming changes. Thus, shells are generalized programs that can be customized with relatively minor effort to expedite program development time. In order to transform a set of pseudoconversational code of an add logic to a change transaction, modify a couple of statements, such as the HANDLE CONDITION (perform only when a particular record is found) and then modify the write/ rewrite statement. Thus, in addition to including an external member (program) in your PDL logic, you can customize the same program and include only the specific shell that needs to be included at the time. (This is further explained in Chapter 11.)

In the sample program shown in Figure 6.11, a nested INCLUDE statement was used. The INCLUDE statement in the main program brings the included program member, EXAMP3A, into the main program area. EXAMP3A then includes another member, EXAMP3B. When you code a LOAD command into your program, you will need to understand the relationship between the LOAD and the THISREC commands. THISREC and LOAD work together to load the information from a record currently being updated by screen processing. When a record is processed by the Millennium file maintenance it is put into a screen buffer before being rewritten on the database. This makes the record that is present in the screen buffer available for the LOAD verb. No I/O needs to be issued by THISREC or LOAD, since the current record being processed is in the buffer area.

Another typical PDL command which has no equivalency in a third generation structure is the REPLACE statement. REPLACE assigns a particular value to a Millennium data name located in memory. Thus, the command is used to initialize a data name with a value. If the data name does not exist in memory, then the statement automatically creates a data name in that storage.

Summary

When operating and designing systems in a mixed environment rely on SDT. The term "mixed" environment indicates a practical situation where the product of different vendors along with your own proprietary software coexist. Through this SDT, you can easily access, update, or issue inquiries against any application system in a true borderless fashion. Thus, a piece of data developed in the general ledger system, for example, can be success- fully processed and "transported" to an equipment inventory or to a pur- chase order system, either one of which may be an old, stand-alone applica- tion.

Procedure Development Language (PDL) is M&D's fourth generation language, one of the major building blocks in this extended Millennium en- vironment. Its primary purpose is to enhance and refine further all required SDT applications using on-line, real time technology.

One of the most powerful aspects of using the PDL is your ability to link up with conventional languages, such as ANS COBOL, or PL/I: popu- lar and otherwise intensely used application languages. In a sense, PDL is a language that can provide an answer to migration technology, that is, you can start developing all your new applications under the umbrella of SDT without having to convert thousands of lines of existing code. When you use a fourth generation language, it is assumed that you have previously defined all editing rules and criteria in a data dictionary which makes coding associated with most editing and computational requirements redun- dant. In fact, it formats reports and screen layouts for you, and, to override such automatic features, you need to generate more than the standard de- fault codes. Consequently, a single statement using a fourth generation language can translate into hundreds of lines of conventional code, such as those written in PL/I or COBOL. However, unlike the translation between assembler and a high-level third generation language, this latter technology offers no common ground for such a translation. The power of a fourth generation language comes from the various building blocks: that is, the ability to query, the ability to utilize a centralized data dictionary, and so on.

PDL has an English-like command structure with three distinct sec- tions. The first section is a simple identification line containing the name of both the program and the author of that program. The purpose of the second section is to convey messages to the user ranging from instructional to error messages. This is called the message section. The third, the procedure section, represents the main body of your program where you can define required logic and the individual tasks to be performed. From a structural point of view, PDL derives its power from two Millennium-based files, CGS and the CGI databases.

Attribute characters, in general, enable the programmer to display data on the screen in various ways as required by the particular situation. When you change the original length of a field, for example (IBM refers to it as modifying a data tag), you allow the programmer to access the most recently entered information on the screen and ignore all prior data entry simply through the manipulation of that field's length. IBM, for one, reserves the first position or byte of any given field and allocates it internally to the various field attribute combinations.

In PDL, you also need to control the way variable fields appear on the screen such as:

- Displaying in normal intensity or highlighted,
- Displaying in a protected or in an unprotected mode, or
- Displaying on the screen at all.

PDL also enables you to rely on a combination of attributes. For example, you may frequently, run into situations where you will need to highlight and, at the same time, protect a data field. To do just that, you must combine two or a number of such attribute values. Millennium data names used with the attribute statement must have a screen definition on the CSV database.

Chapter 7

Introduction to the Information Expert Environment

7.1   Overview

The MSA Information Expert (I.E.) environment is a complete fourth generation support system. It is, as briefly summarized in Chapter 2, made up of a number of building blocks, such as the expert language, a report generator module that is customized per application, a screen painter, query facilities, and an extensive software that enables you to communicate with sophisticated PC networks. The purpose of this chapter is to explore the reporting aspect of the MSA I.E. environment.

When you create a report using the Expert Language (which is MSA's nomenclature for its fourth generation language), you can do it interactively through I.E.'s on-line support facilities (OSF), or you can do it in a purely batch environment. The OSF module is a real-time dialogue manager which is supported by a number of utility programs. The primary purpose of this manager is to allow you to control the OSF Dialog Manager processing facilities. This simply means that you can create or modify a series of basic and advanced reports through OSF using I.E.'s full-screen editing capabilities. Other functions included here have to do with the on-line submission of a report series for producing information either in a printed format or for viewing it at the terminal. When you view the information, the vendor provides you with extensive Help facilities. This chapter provides an extensive coverage on the mechanics of I.E.'s step-by-step "programming" methodology. This methodology will let you create a basic flow of information, without any in-depth knowledge of the Expert Language.

The step-by-step method of creating a report is essentially a program writing technique that requires no expertise on your part other than knowing your needs, and does not require you to worry about the technology. This is because the system uses prompts that guide you through the entire programming cycle and does it on an elementary level. The Expert Language translates each one of your menu selections into a set of valid commands while it creates new procedures, a report series, queries, and whatever specifics you request. In addition to building a report, you can also create output files with I.E. these files can be used as a bridge between two or more application systems.

Once your programming definition is completed, you can prepare and submit your job through the system's job preparation and submission module on line. Remember one thing: submitting your job interactively is efficient since you do not need to worry about job control specifications, or to develop lengthy procs (job control statements placed into a library for defining a standard runstream). You do not have to follow cumbersome formalities such as a written service request and prior notifications when dealing with computer operations.

7.2   The Reporting Process

I.E. uses your own report specification, the definition from the data dictionary, and the associated data frame to create whatever information you happened to be requesting. The steps involved in producing a report include the physical preparation of a report, the running of that report, and the subsequent viewing or printing of it.

Preparing a report involves the translation of English-like commands into a complex machine-type language that remains transparent to you, but, nonetheless, is necessary for the computer. These statements are automatically expanded by I.E. into simplistic "one-on-one" procedures, such as the definition of the source data, the definition of printing requirements and how a logical or a physical data-frame is to be presented. By one-on-one procedures, I'm referring to the ability of the expert language to disseminate complex user statements into a set of single procedures.

Once you have prepared your report series, you can run it any time you wish to without having to prepare it again—unless, of course, you need to modify the original scope. Figure 7.1, reflects the above preparation process. Running a report series means initiating the automatic translation of your job by I.E. to machine language (which does not concern you at all) and generating a product that can either be printed or viewed on-line.

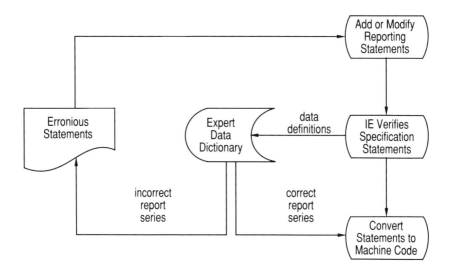

Figure 7.1   This flowchart summarizes the I.E. preparation process.

At that time the system will verify your access and extract the appropriate data (note that a complete review of security considerations will be laid out in Chapter 9). If you need sequencing for your report, I.E. will sort the contents of that data frame before printing or displaying it on the tube. Over and above what is covered in Chapter 9, the system checks your password and your logon I.D. before it allows you to proceed. If your password and your sign-on are valid, you may continue: if not, you will not be allowed to go on. To look at the overall process from an efficiency point of view, data for each report in a series are extracted from the particular data frame, but I.E. only processes the specific data you need to have in order to produce your report(s). It will not extract any other information from the data frame that is redundant.

Think about this for a moment. In a conventional environment ("conventional," refers to a third generation system), you need to consider everything that is on a record, whether you will reference it in its entirety or not. If a record contains 3000 bytes of storage, and you only need a one-position status indicator out of it, you will still have no alternative other than to define the entire file or subset. This may seem wasteful.

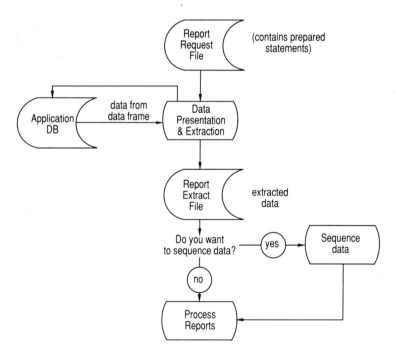

Figure 7.2   This flowchart demonstrates the process required for running a report series.

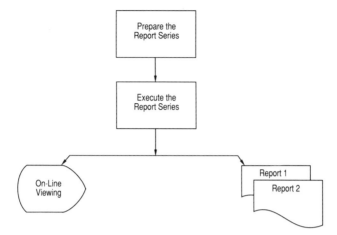

Figure 7.3   This flowchart pictures the report viewing process.

Figure 7.2 summarizes the process required to run a report series. At this point you can review that report on-line and decide if you need that information printed or else simply discard the product. This is an important feature since you do not want to produce an erroneous report, all 900 pages of it, before having a chance to correct it. This process is further depicted in Figure 7.3.

Note that, under I.E., you can selectively view a specific page in a report or you can search for a specific piece of information. For example, you may want to view the grand total of a personnel-type report which is on page 400 of the file.

7.3   How to Generate a Report through Information Expert

When you are in the process of designing and coding a report, you need to concern yourself with a number of issues very much standard in this business. Some of these are:

- Page and column headings,
- Subtotals, as well as grant totals,
- The positioning of the columns across the page,
- The various sequencing of the information,
- Specifying computations and so forth.

The I.E. reporting concept utilizes three types of resources in generating the required information. These are the particular database or databases referred to as data frames, a powerful dictionary which drives the I.E. system, and a means of communicating with the system to keep a "dialogue" going, constantly requesting and monitoring this state-of-the-art mechanism that is mostly terminal driven. In reporting, of course, I.E. is not restricted to a single data frame; rather you can combine a number of data frames successfully, depending on the requirements of a particular user.

A data dictionary, by definition, is a collection of descriptions of the data, not the actual data. A dictionary is made up of words and definitions. A data dictionary consists of items and descriptions. Figure 7.4 shows in a simplistic way how the two functions relate. The MSA Data Dictionary (referred to as the "Expert" dictionary) is made up of four components: items, groups, records, and data frames.

Items represents the lowest, most basic, form of information kept within the expert environment. An item can be a field name such as an employee's gross pay. These items, in turn, can be classified into groups that are a collection of items. For example, if a group of information is referred to as an employee address, then items within that group would be the street address, the city and state, as well as the zip code.

```
WORD:    AARDVARK

DESCRIPTION:
A large burrowing nocturnal
African mammal that has an ex-
tensile tongue, powerful claws
large ears, and heavy tail and
feeds on ants and termites.


WORD:    AARDWOLF

DESCRIPTION:
A maned striped mammal of south-
ern eastern Africa that re-
sembles the related hyenas and
feeds chiefly on carrion and in-
sects.


WORD:    ABACK

1 Archaic: BACKWARD, BACK
2 In a position to catch the
  wind upon the forward surface
  of a square sail.
```

```
ITEM:  EMPLOYEE-ID

DEFINITION:
This item is the employee's
unique identifier which is part of
the concatenated record key on the
Payroll/Personnel data frames.


WORD:   EMPLOYEE-NAME

DEFINITION:
The name of the employee as appear
on the Payroll/Personnel data
frames and is a component of the
above concatenated key. Format:
last name, comma, space, first name,
omma, space initial.


WORD:    EMPLOYEE-STREET-ADDRESS

Shows the employee's street address
and is a mandatory field to enter
when adding a new record to the
Payroll/Personnel data frames.
```

Figure 7.4   This shows the simplistic relationship between a dictionary and a data dictionary used to define data items.

Records are the third component in this hierarchy that are the logical collection of items and/or groups pertaining to an entity which has to do with a logical "view" of that data. A conventional payroll file, for example, can be made up of a number of segments, such as the employee's deduction segment, fringe benefits segment or segments, retroactive adjustments, demographic profile, and so on.

Some of these segments or records may then be referred to as data frames, which are a logical collection of records contained in the dictionary that provide the information about the data. This will tell you what is ultimately to be printed or viewed at the terminal.

The data dictionary is the place where you can define all you need to know about a piece of data, such as the name, its length, type, decimal position, print mask, column heading, code translation, and a great deal more. Remember that the data dictionary contains rules and values and not the actual data. The actual data comes from the various data frames being processed through a number of criteria listed in the dictionary. A useful term is "filter," where raw data is being filtered through a set of formalized (and totally automated) process.

Two terms need to be discussed in conjunction with the I.E. reporting structure:

1. Report request, and
2. Report series.

Report requests are essentially requests that describe a specific report or reports including a set of processing criteria, computations, and so on.

A report series, on the other hand, pertains to a number of report requests that utilize the same data frame and are submitted to the I.E. processing environment concurrently. The report series reads the data from the data frame, then extracts certain items for your request, performs the necessary computations, has the data sequenced and totaled, and generates the final product, which may be one or a dozen standard reports.

7.4   The Step-By-Step Approach

In summary, the step-by-step approach is a completely user-oriented tool that enables you to generate any number of programs through menu selection and without having to write a single line of code in the process. This is the first of two methodologies in the vendor's fourth generation language family. The second method, which involves actual coding through the text editor, will be presented to you (including a brief case study) in Chapter 8.

The step-by-step way of producing a report or a "view" encompasses a number of selfdefining steps; such as selecting or excluding a record, performing calculations, setting up a particular print format, and a great deal more.

I.E. is so extensively menu driven (and I mean it in the most positive sense) that you can actually create or modify a report and generate a program without ever having to write a single line of code. What you do have to concern yourself with is supplying the system a proper set of criteria that come from your own requirements. In reality, this method has more to do with user responsibilities than with data processing, which is what this fourth generation language is all about. Probably the easiest way to gain insight into this kind of a new technology is through a step-by-step process. Creating a report with I.E. is done in an on-line environment that enables you to view your product before submitting it.

The main menu screen presented in Figure 7.5. is the sign-on panel requiring a user I.D., a password, and other options for security reasons, some of which depends on your particular installation and shop standards. A second menu screen presented in Figure 7.6 is the primary option menu where you can select one of five major functions, such as the expert reporting facilities, source management, job preparation and submission, report

```
  M S A   INFORMATION EXPERT   ------------------ENTER SIGN ON DATA BELOW


     ENTER SYSTEM ID:  BROWNLY               REL.:   ESRR   87.01
     ENTER USER ID:    _____              DATE:   08/07/88
     ENTER PASSWORD    _____              TIME:   10:02:32


     COMMAND INPUT:    _____      (To skip the Primary Menu Option)
     USER GROUP ID:    _____      (If different from default group)
     DICTIONARY ID:    _____      (If different from System Id)




             .


     NOTE:  TO CANCEL SIGNON, PRESS THE PF3 KEY.

     COPYRIGHT (C) 1988 MANAGEMENT SCIENCE AMERICA, INC.
     All rights reserved. This is unpublished material and contains trade
     secrets and other confidential information and is subject to the
     confidentiality agreement. The unauthorized possession, use, reproduction
     distribution, display or disclosure of this material of the information
     contained herein is prohibited.
```

Figure 7.5 This is the I.E. report generator sign-on screen.

```
      M S A  INFORMATION EXPERT  ------------------PRIMARY OPTION MENU


           ENTER SELECTION BELOW:

           ER - EXPERT REPORTING
           SM - SOURCE MANAGEMENT
           JS - JOB PREPARATION & SUBMISSION
           RV - REPORT VIEWING
           SA - SYSTEM ADMINISTRATION
           EN - END OF SESSION

        SELECTION ===> ER
        LIBRARY ===> CCPUBLIC


     ACTION: _____


   PRESS:        ENTER Process      PF1 Help  PF3 End Session
```

Figure 7.6   This is the I.E. Primary Option Menu.

viewing, and systems administration. The sixth function (EN) is used to terminate the current session when you need to exit out of your current activities or simply to return to a different procedure. In order to understand the expert reporting (ER) module, it is important to discuss the I.E. source management facility first. The I.E. source management provides you with a way of entering and processing I.E. commands through a full-screen text editor. Syntax checking is done interactively to verify that your data was entered in a correct format and that you have initiated proper commands.

Using the source management facility panel, you can display a member, meaning an existing report, or create a new one, if necessary.

You can also maintain your existing set of reports to reflect new requirements. These would be changes that do not justify reprogramming. I.E. also enables you to utilize a number of standard utilities such as copying an existing member, as well as replacing, merging, adding, renaming, and deleting it. The source management facility panel is shown in Figure 7.7. I.E. utilizes three types of libraries in which to store all the required information. These libraries are as follows: a "public" library, a "semiprivate" and a "private" library. A private library can only be accessed by a user to whom the data, the specific information belongs. A public library, as the term suggests, can be accessed by anyone. A semiprivate library is partially restricted and is normally within the jurisdiction of the system

```
  M S A   INFORMATION EXPERT ------------------ SOURCE MANAGEMENT FACILITY


         ENTER SELECTION BELOW:

         LS - DISPLAY MEMBER LIST
         CR - CREATE A NEW MEMBER
         CH - CHANGE A NEW MEMBER
         UT - COPY/DELETE/RENAME/MERGE MEMBERS
         RE - RETURN TO PRIMARY OPTION MENU


       SELECTION     ===>  ____
       MEMBER NAME   ===>  _____
       LIBRARY NAME  ===>  DEMOGR

      ACTION:  _____


    PRESS:   ENTER Process   PF1 Help  PF3 Return to Primary Option Menu
```

Figure 7.7   This is the I.E. source management facility menu.

administrator, a function synonymous with that of a database administrator in a more formal environment. In selecting the expert reporting module to generate a report, I was also required to define the library which will contain the data for such a report. This library I named CCPUBLIC. This was referenced through the CCPUBLIC library. Thus, the next frame, which is shown in Figure 7.8 requires you to supply I.E. with the following basic information about your report: You will need to give your report series a name. This will be a common term used by any number of reports that will be logically tied to this series.

The next selection topic has to do with choosing the proper data frame or frames you need for your report. Because of the fragmented nature of information, it is frequently necessary to extract a logical view from two or more physical data frames. A logical view represents a consolidated database, an extract, in fact, of any number of physical databases that point to a particular user's view in the system.

Next, give your report a name and define its width to I.E. which, by the way, cannot exceed 160 print positions. (I doubt seriously if you will ever need that much width.) Note that once you exceed an 80-position standard IBM card image entry, (which is the width of the screen), you will have to scroll either to your left or to your right to view a typical report layout on line. What follows after giving your report a name and defining its physical characteristics is a definition of your selection and extraction criteria.

```
  M S A  EXPERT REPORTING   ----- BUILD / CHANGE REPORTS

  This function will take you through a step by step process to build a
  report or series of reports (Report Series). Listed below are the steps:

      1 - Give the Report Series a Name
      2 - Select a Dataframe
      3 - Give your Report a Name
      4 - Define Selection/Exclusion Criteria
      5 - Define how Report is to be Sequenced
      6 - Define any Calculations Required
      7 - Define Page Headings
      8 - Select Data to be Displayed
      9 - Define how Data is to be Totalled
     10 - Repeat Steps 3 - 9 for the Next Report


  Your Reports will be stored in Library CCPUBLIC


  PRESS:   ENTER Begin     PF1 Help    PF3 Return to Primary Option Menu
```

Figure 7.8 This is a documentary panel describing 10 steps for creating a report in an on-line environment.

In this step, you need to select (or exclude) records from the data frame so that only the data you specify show up on the report. The way you select, or exclude a record will make a great deal of difference in your processing efficiency.

Since every report is generated in a specific order, your next move is to define a particular sequence (starting with the major sort criteria). You may also refer to this statement as an ORDER statement that specifies the physical order for your report if it is different from the original sequence of the primary input data frame. Once the order is established, the next step is to specify to I.E. the type of calculations to be performed using the four basic arithmetic operations such as adding (+), subtracting (-), multiplying (*), and dividing (/). When performing these arithmatic operations, you can store the result in an "interim" storage area, just like in COBOL or in PL/I. These items do not have to be defined in the data dictionary, and, once they are no longer required, I.E. will simply delete them for you at the end of the process.

Page heading is next. Actually, there are two internally kept items, the page number, and the system date, both of which can be invoked automatically in the step-by-step process.

When you do the actual programming you are to code both the page counter and the system date ('DATE' #SYSDATE, and 'PAGE' #PAGE-

NUMBER) into your program. Note that the page counter monitors your lines and pages for the purpose of generating correct page numbers. Actually, the page mechanism is responsible for generating an overflow condition, producing page totals, or resetting a set of internal counters after a page break. The system date, on the other, hand displays the current date for you on the top of each report.

Next, define your data requirements for printing. Earlier, you selected one or a number of data frames for entering your selection and exclusion criteria. You did that mainly to minimize the redundant data cluttering your report. In this frame, you essentially need to repeat the same process, but for a different purpose: for example, to define what is to be printed—regardless of what was read into the system before. Last, but not least, you want to specify the totals or subtotals utilized by your report. If there are any, you will need to highlight them.

This may sound a bit confusing. Figure 7.8 provides you with an overview of what needs to be prompted in this path, the rest is totally transparent. When you press enter, you will invoke a panel (Figure 7.9) requiring some decision-making on your part.

Do you wish to change or modify an existing report series? If the answer is "YES", you can select from among a set of available report series names by entering the character "S" (standing for selection) next to the particular series. If no selection is specified to I.E., it will assume that a new report series is to be created in which case you will be prompted for a new name.

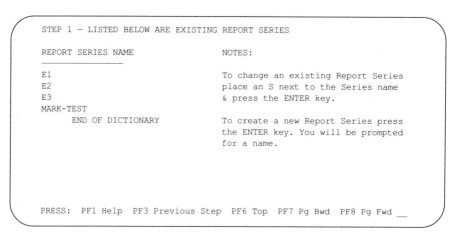

Figure 7.9   This is the report series selection menu.

```
STEP 1 -- ENTER A NAME FOR YOUR REPORT SERIES: DEMO 1_____


PRESS: ENTER CONTINUE  PF1 Help   PF3 Previous Step
```

Figure 7.10   This is the entry panel for identifying a report series.

Copyright © 1988 Management Science America, Inc. Used by permission.

Notice the standard command key assignments on the bottom of each panel that also enable you to invoke Help when you are stuck. You can also return to the previous step by pressing function key 3. Function keys 7 and 8, on the other hand, are allocated to scrolling (up and down this time), in order to view the information presented on multiple pages.

The "Enter A Name For Your Selection Series" (Figure 7.10) was prompted to create a brand new series rather than utilize an existing one, and I.E. needs to be aware of such an event.

When you are creating a report series, the name should be at least one position long, but should not exceed 30 characters in length. You can utilize hyphens, but not embedded blanks, and the first character of the name should be an alphabetic character. (Special characters are unprocessable at this point.)

Once you have selected a name for your report series, which is DEMO1 in this case, press enter to continue the selection process. This will trigger a "Select Dataframe for Your Reports" panel presented in Figure 7.11. Why do you need this particular panel? You need it because you have to tell I.E. about your input requirements for a specific database or databases that must be selected in this process. These, by the way, are the data frames currently indicated on the CCPUBLIC library accessible to all I.E. users.

If you are not sure whether you are dealing with the proper data frame, you may have to expand further on your definition. This is done by placing an "L" (rather than an "S") next to the name of the data frame and pressing enter. In the above example, the IECUSBAS data frame was selected, which carries a basic customer master layout and, thus, continued processing through the enter key which triggered the report naming panel. Figure 7.12 is a familiar panel already invoked once during the definition of a report series. But this time, instead of defining a series, it is used to create a report member to be included in the DEMO1 series.

Each screen invoked in the path provides you with a single task: not two, or three, almost as if you were conversing with I.E. The system will

```
STEP 2 -- SELECT A DATAFRAME FOR YOUR REPORTS


   DATAFRAME        DESCRIPTION OF DATAFRAME
   ---------        ------------------------------------      Place S or L beside
   ---------        ------------------------------------      desired Dataframe &
                    * INDICATES THAT THIS DATAFRAME IS        press the ENTER key
                      NOT RECOMMENDED FOR USE WITH
                      EXPERT REPORTING
   ---------        ------------------------------------      S - Use Dataframe
                                                              L - List Contents
   IEABBREV         ABBREVIATION REGISTER
   IECUSBAS         BASIC CUSTOMET MASTER DATAFRAME
   IECUSBIL         BILLING MASTER FILE                       Press the PF3 key
   IECUSINS         UTILITY INSTALLATION FRAME                to cancel this
   IEDICENT         I.E. DICT ENTITY DETAIL DEF             * function & return
   IEDICENU         I.E. DICT ENTITY USAGE DEF              * to the previous step
   IEDOCDEC         I.E. DICTIONARY DOC DESC                *
   IEDOCDV          DATAFRAME DOCUMENTATION                 *
   IEDOCIT          ITEM AND GROUP DOCUMENTATION            *
   IEHIST           CUSTOMER HISTORY FRAME                  *
   IEIMSDOC         IMS DATAFRAME DOCUMENTATION             *


   PRESS:    ENTER Process PF1 Help  PF6  Top  PF7 Page Bwd  PF8 Page Fwd --
```

Figure 7.11   This demonstrates selecting the basic customer master data frame from a number of dictionary-driven databases.

not let you skip a mandatory panel (those without the automatic default values), and, if you make a mistake, you can easily recover from it just by pressing Function Key 3 which takes you back to the previous frame to start over. On the Report Name panel has been selected and named the report DMREPT1 and enter has been pressed to move onto the next frame. This brings you to the "Set the Width of Your Report" panel that operates

```
STEP 1 — ENTER A NAME FOR YOUR REPORT SERIES: DEMO1_____


   PRESS:   ENTER Contiue    PF1 Help    PF3 Previous Step
```

Figure 7.12   This is the entry panel for identifying a report series.

```
STEP 3B — SET THE WIDTH OF YOUR REPORT : 132

NOTE: The width must be greater than zero and less than 160


PRESS:  ENTER Contiune   PF1 Help   PF3 Previous Step
```

Figure 7.13   This is the entry panel for defining the width of the report.

on a 132 print position default value. I.E. requires that you define a minimum of one print position in your reports, but not exceeding 160 positions. This panel is shown in Figure 7.13. It has been possible, thus far to spec out the requirements just by responding to an on-line questionnaire saying "yes" or "no", allowing the I.E. environment to assemble and generate code out of it. This is a new dimension in programming technology where the physical aspect of coding is no longer viable, or viable only with complex update type programs. The next frame was invoked to expand on the contents of the data frame (Figure 7.14). Those items needed to produce a report were

```
STEP 4A — PLACE AN S BESIDE THE ITEM TO BE USED TO SELECT RECORDS

      IE-CUST-ACCT-CLASSIFICATION        IE-CUST-SUB-ACCOUNT
      IE-RECORD-TYPE                     IE-CUST-UTILITY-CODE
      IE-CUST-MONTH-CODE                 IE-CUST-ACCT-DELETE-CODE
      IE-CUST-ACCT-DELETE-DATE         S IE-CUST-NAME
    S IE-CUST-PHONE-NUMBER             S IE-CUST-ADDRESS-LINE-1
    S IE-CUST-ADDRESS-LINE-2             IE-CUST-ADDRESS-LINE-3
      IE-CUST-COUNTRY-CODE               IE-CUST-POSTAL-CODE
      IE-CUST-UTIL-DATE-INSTALLED        IE-CUST-ACTIVE-INACTIVE-CODE
      IE-CUST-ACTIVE-INACTIVE-DATE       IE-CUST CURR-BEG-METER-READ
      IE-CUST-CURR-END-METER-READ        IE-CUST CURRENT-METER-READ-DATE
      IE-CUST-CURR-BILLING-DATE          IE-CUST-CURR-DUE-DATE
      IE-CUST-DATE-BILLED              S IE-CUST-AMOUNT-BILLED
      IE-CUST-AMOUNT-USED                IE-CUST-PAYMENT-DATE
    S IE-CUST-PAYMENT-AMOUNT             IE-CUST-BALANCE-OWED



    PRESS:   ENTER Return  PF1 Help  PF6 Top  PF7 Page Bwd  PF8 Page Fwd
```

Figure 7.14   This demonstrates selecting data fields from a particular data frame for reporting purposes.

flagged, and the rest were simply omitted from the task. After reviewing the "item selection screen," an "S" was again placed next to the specific fields and enter was pressed afterward. If you have requested too many items on your report, I.E. won't let you get away with it. The system will calculate its spacing requirements, and, if you exceeded it, do one of two things:

1. You may restructure your request by specifying fewer items, or
2. You may increase the original width of your view, which may not be a practical solution. After all, How many shops use printers that print in excess of 132 positions?

For every item selected on this list, you will receive a corresponding panel starting with the IE-CUST-NAME as shown in Figure 7.15. Note that the lines associated with the FROM VALUE (and that of the THRU VALUE) vary in length depending on the actual width of the field. You can visualize this by just comparing Figure 7.15 and Figure 7.16.

If you were to select six items from the items directory panel (Figure 7.14), you would be getting six corresponding selection panels (one for every field), displayed in a continuous flow. These panels can be thought of as a bunch of "IF" statements where certain values are associated with a particular item. Single values are placed in the FROM value column. Ranges,

```
STEP 4A — DEFINE SELECTION CRITERIA FOR REPORT DMREPT1

ENTER SELECTION VALUES BELOW FOR IE-CUST-NAME

FROM VALUE                              THRU VALUE
A_____        C_____
 _____         _____
 _____         _____
 _____         _____
 _____         _____
 _____         _____
 _____         _____
 _____         _____
 _____         _____
 _____         _____
 _____         _____



PRESS:    ENTER Continue  PF1 Help  PF3 Previous Step  PF5 Select Data
```

Figure 7.15 This demonstrates creating a set of selection criteria for report DMREPT1.

```
STEP 4A — DEFINE SELECTION CRITERIA FOR REPORT DMREPT1

ENTER SELECTION VALUES BELOW FOR IE-CUST-PHONE-NUMBER

FROM VALUE                         THRU VALUE

_____                        _____
_____                        _____
_____                        _____
_____                        _____
_____                        _____
_____                        _____
_____                        _____
_____                        _____
_____                        _____
_____                        _____
_____                        _____
_____                        _____


PRESS:   ENTER Continue  PF1 Help  PF3 Previous Step  PF5 Select Data
```

Figure 7.16 There are no selection criteria with regards to the customer phone field.

on the other hand are entered into both the FROM and the THRU VALUE columns. In Figure 7.15, I.E. is requested to consider only those customers whose names are between "A" (FROM) and "C" (THRU VALUE). Thus, data pertaining to American Automobile Systems would be selected, while York Paper Supply Company would be excluded. If a value, or a set of values, is erroneously stated, and it is to be erased, simply move the cursor to the beginning of the value and press the EOF key. If this is done for all values for an item, the selection criteria for that item are completely removed.

The next step in this highly structured hierarchical path is the definition of your exclusion criteria presented in Figure 7.17.

Here, the field name IE-CUST-ACTIVE-INACTIVE-CODE was selected. (Selection, again, was done by placing an "S" next to the item.) This means that the goal is to control record exclusion based on a particular value (or values) contained in that field. What that value should be will be described on the next sequential panel (Figure 7.18). Selection of the IE-CUST-ACTIVE-INACTIVE-CODE was triggered by an exclusion criterion. When a customer is inactive ('I'), it is necessary to exclude him or her from the reporting series to save space and valuable processing time. It also

```
STEP 4B — PLACE AN S BESIDE THE ITEM TO BE USED TO EXCLUDE RECORDS

     IE-CUST-ACCT-CLASSIFICATION        IE-CUST-SUB-ACCOUNT
     IE-RECORD-TYPE                     IE-CUST-UTILITY-CODE
     IE-CUST-MONTH-CODE                 IE-CUST-ACCT-DELETE-CODE
     IE-CUST-ACCT-DELETE-DATE           IE-CUST-NAME
     IE-CUST-PHONE-NUMBER               IE-CUST-ADDRESS-LINE-1
     IE-CUST-ADDRESS-LINE-2             IE-CUST-ADDRESS-LINE-3
     IE-CUST-COUNTRY-CODE               IE-CUST-POSTAL-CODE
     IE-CUST-UTIL-DATE-INSTALLED      S IE-CUST-ACTIVE-INACTIVE-CODE
     IE-CUST-ACTIVE-INACTIVE-DATE       IE-CUST CURR-BEG-METER-READ
     IE-CUST-CURR-END-METER-READ        IE-CUST CURRENT-METER-READ-DATE
     IE-CUST-CURR-BILLING-DATE          IE-CUST-CURR-DUE-DATE
     IE-CUST-DATE-BILLED                IE-CUST-AMOUNT-BILLED
     IE-CUST-AMOUNT-USED                IE-CUST-PAYMENT-DATE
     IE-CUST-PAYMENT-AMOUNT             IE-CUST-BALANCE-OWED



  PRESS:   ENTER Return  PF1 Help  PF6 Top  PF7 Page Bwd  PF8 Page Fwd
```

Figure 7.17   This demonstrates excluding records based on an item value from a report.

```
STEP 4B — DEFINE EXCLUSION CRITERIA FOR REPORT DMREPT1

ENTER EXCLUSION VALUES BELOW FOR IE-CUST-ACTIVE-INACTIVE-CODE

FROM VALUE THRU VALUE
i              _
_              _
_              _
_              _
_              _
_              _
_              _
_              _
_              _
_              _
_              _
_              _
_              _
_              _
_              _

  PRESS:   ENTER Continue  PF1 Help  PF3 Previous Step  PF5 Select Data___
```

Figure 7.18   This is a panel to select exclusion values.

```
STEP 5 — LISTED BELOW IS THE ORDER FOR REPORT DMREPT1

1 #REPORTID               Renumber to change the order of the list
2 IE-CUST-NAME
3 IE-CUST-PAYMENT-DATE     To remove an item from the list, blank out the
                           number next to the item

                           To select additional data, press the PF5 key

                           Press the ENTER key to process changes or
                           continue to the next step.



PRESS:    ENTER Process    PF1 Help  PF3 Previous Step
```

Figure 7.19 This is an example of establishing order for a report.

is not desirable to clutter up the report with irrelevant information. With the exclusion criteria defined, the next step is to determine a specific order in which a report is to be presented. When you specify a particular sequence for a report, you can also create control breaks for it. Actually the two go hand in hand. You cannot set up control breaks without specifying a particular sort sequence to I.E., which is only logical. The "order definition" panel also enables you to add other items to the screen, renumber them, or completely remove them, if necessary. (Figure 7.19)

When this report, is printed it will come out with the report identifier as the major sort field, followed by the name of the business and the date of the customer payment.

You must sort on the report identifier, since you may have a number of reports in the series. You will want to make sure that all of those reports are kept straight and not intermixed. Once the order is established in this fashion, you will need to define to I.E. the type of calculation to be performed and the items involved in those calculations (Figure 7.20). Items you choose are assigned letters toward the bottom of the calculation screen (which is depicted in Figure 7.21). Note the following:

- Any free letter can be assigned a numeric value,
- OP1 specifies what will be to the left of the sign,
- OP2 specifies what will be to the right of the sign, and
- (+, -, *, /) indicates the arithmetic sign you can use.

```
STEP  6   -- PLACE  AN  S  BESIDE  THE  ITEMS  TO  BE  USED  IN  CALCULATION


        IE-CUST-ACCT-DELETE-DATE           IE-CUST-UTIL-DATE-INSTALLED
        IE-CUST-ACTIVE-INACTIVE-DATE       IE-CUST-CURR-BEG-METER-READ
        IE-CUST-CURR-END-METER-READ        IE-CUST-CURR-METER-READ-DATE
        IE-CUST-CURR-BILLING-DATE          IE-CUST-CURR-DUE-DATE
        IE-CUST-DATE-BILLED             S  IE-CUST-AMOUNT-BILLED
        IE-CUST-AMOUNT-USED                IE-CUST-PAYMENT-DATE
     S  IE-CUST-PAYMENT-AMOUNT             IE-CUST-BALANCE-OWED




     PRESS:      ENTER Return PF1 Help  PF6 Top  PF7 Page Bwd  PF8 Page Fwd___
```

Figure 7.20   Items are selected to be used in calculation.

```
STEP  6  —  DEFINE  CALCULATIONS  FOR  REPORT  DMREPT1

Build the calculation using letters assigned to the items below

OP1      (+,-,*,/)     OP2        RESULT    OPTIONAL  RESULT  NAME
A_           -         B_    =    R1    ( CURR-CUST-BALANCE_____ )
__                     __    =    R2    ( _____ )
__                     __    =    R3    ( _____ )
__                     __    =    R4    ( _____ )
__                     __    =    R5    ( _____ )
__                     __    =    R6    ( _____ )

Numeric values may be assigned to any free letter.
 A: IE-CUST-BALANCE-OWED_____     B: IE-CUST-PAYMENT-AMOUNT_____
 C: _____      D: _____
 E: _____      F: _____
 G: _____      H: _____
 I: _____      J: _____
 K: _____      L: _____

PRESS:  ENTER  Process  PF1 Help  PF3 Previous Step  PF5 Select Data  ___
```

Figure 7.21   Define your calculation requirements to I.E.

In Figure 7.21, EI-CURR-CUST-BALANCE was subtracted from the IE-CUST-BALANCE-OWED and the result, CURR-CUST-BALANCE became a "working storage" type data field. Working storage items are of temporary nature and as such, you do not have to define them in the dictionary. However, once you have completed your report cycle, the above information gets flushed from the system. This is fine, but field attributes and information pertaining to column headings are only referenced in the dictionary. How will the new information appear when viewed or printed?

When you use the full blown Expert Language (rather than the step-by-step approach), you can define both of those attributes directly in the body of the program. In this particular situation, the system will assume a default header which would be "CURR CUST BALANCE" (without the hyphens) and a length accommodating the resulting computations.

Notice, that you were only allowed to choose from what the dictionary recognizes as numeric fields. Other items were simply excluded from display.

The panel shown in Figure 7.21 is made up of two sections. The first one is where the actual computation is defined. This, in turn points to the data fields used in the calculation. The page-header builder is invoked in the next sequential step (Figure 7.22). Several things should be noted at this point. DMREPT1 is automatically displayed on the first line of the panel for a quick reference. You may designate a particular date for your report if you want to override the current system date. I.E. allows you to use two lines to define your header. In the current customer balance report, Figure 7.22, only a single line was utilized.

Note that the new working storage item (CURR-CUST-BALANCE) is also part of the selection displayed. In fact that particular item was selected to appear on DMREPT1. This panel is shown in Figure 7.23. A "subset" of

```
STEP 7 - BUILD PAGE HEADINGS FOR REPORT DMPERT1


DATE FOR THE REPORT:  __ / __ / __      (Default is Today's Date)

FIRST  HEADING LINE: CURRENT CUSTOMER BALANCES REPORT_____
SECOND HEADING LINE: _____


  PRESS:    ENTER Process   PF1 Help  PF3 Previous Step
```

Figure 7.22 Define your report heading to I.E.

```
STEP 8  - PLACE AN S BESIDE THE ITEM TO BE PRINTED ON THIS REPORT

 S #REPORTID                         S  CURR-CUST-BALANCE
   IE-CUST-ACCT-CLASSIFICATION          IE-CUST-SUB-ACCOUNT
   IE-RECORD-TYPE                       IE-CUST-UTILITY-CODE
   IE-CUST-MONTH-CODE                   IE-CUST-ACCT-DELETE-CODE
   IE-CUST-ACCT-DELETE-DATE          S  IE-CUST-NAME
   IE-CUST-PHONE-NUMBER             S  IE-CUST-ADDRESS-LINE-1
   IE-CUST-ADDRESS-LINE-2               IE-CUST-ADDRESS-LINE-3
   IE-CUST-COUNTRY-CODE                 IE-CUST-POSTAL-CODE
   IE-CUST-UTIL-DATE-INSTALLED          IE-CUST-ACTIVE-INACTIVE-CODE
   IE-CUST-ACTIVE-INACTIVE-DATE         IE-CUST CURR-BEG-METER-READ
   IE-CUST-CURR-END-METER-READ          IE-CUST CURRENT-METER-READ-DATE
   IE-CUST-CURR-BILLING-DATE            IE-CUST-CURR-DUE-DATE
   IE-CUST-DATE-BILLED                  IE-CUST-AMOUNT-BILLED
   IE-CUST-AMOUNT-USED                  IE-CUST-PAYMENT-DATE
 S IE-CUST-PAYMENT-AMOUNT               IE-CUST-BALANCE-OWED




 PRESS:   ENTER Return  PF1 Help  PF6 Top  PF7 Page Bwd  PF8 Page Fwd
```

Figure 7.23   Define what must be printed on the report to I.E .

```
STEP 8  -  POSITION ITEMS TO BE PRINTED ON REPORT DMREPT1

Items listed below will be printed from left to right

   1  #REPORTID                   Renumber to change the order of the list
   2  IE-CUST-NAME
   3  IE-CUST-ADDRESS-LINE-1       To remove an item, blank out the number
   4  IE-CUST-PAYMENT-AMOUNT       next to the name of the item
   5  CURR-CUST-BALANCE
                                   To select additional data, press PF5 key

                                   Press the ENTER key to process changes
                                   or to continue to the next step



 PRESS:   ENTER Process  PF1 Help  PF3 Previous Step  PF5 Select Data
```

Figure 7.24   This panel shows the position of each item to be printed (displayed) by I.E.

the above screen needs to be looked at and presented in Figure 7.24. This screen (position items to be printed on report DMREPT1), lets you define the required order in which to print your report. This is accomplished by numbering each one of the items on the screen, if they are different from the original sequence. Based on this numbering scheme, the system will calculate the proper spacing between the columns and generate title headings for each data items in conjunction with the data dictionary. Since totals were required in the listing, Figure 7.25 which would have otherwise been used was skipped. Once the Expert Program is generated and submitted, I can look at its contents on the tube via Selection 5 and decide on the next task through Figure 7.26.

Now, the report can be saved for later use, and the current session can simply be exited, if so desired. There is also the opportunity to modify or delete any member in the current series. As indicated before, the report can be viewed on-line and aborted if it is erroneous, before printing a couple of boxes of paper in vain, a costly and frustrating experience.

If you have a number of reports to code in the series, I.E. enables you to do just that without going back to step one of the overall process.

Figure 7.27 is a machine-generated code of the above activities. While going through the menu selection process, the system promptly recorded every single decision and assembled a source program out of it. The end product of this machine developed code is shown in Figure 7.28 which is the "current customer balances report."

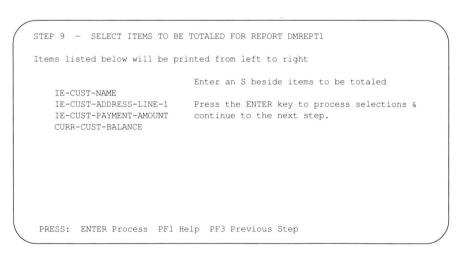

```
STEP 9  —  SELECT ITEMS TO BE TOTALED FOR REPORT DMREPT1

Items listed below will be printed from left to right

                              Enter an S beside items to be totaled
        IE-CUST-NAME
        IE-CUST-ADDRESS-LINE-1     Press the ENTER key to process selections &
        IE-CUST-PAYMENT-AMOUNT     continue to the next step.
        CURR-CUST-BALANCE




   PRESS:  ENTER Process  PF1 Help  PF3 Previous Step
```

Figure 7.25   This is the panel that defines to I.E. each subtotal break.

```
     STEP 10 — REPORT DMREPT1 COMPLETED FOR SERIES DEMO1

          ENTER SELECTION BELOW

          1 - Save this Series & Exit
          2 - Save this series & Return
          3 - Review/Change this Series
          4 - Build another Report
          5 - View the IE Commands
          6 - Prepare this Series
          7 - Prepare, Run and Print Reports
          8 - Prepare, Run and View Reports
          9 - Cancel this Function and Exit

          ===> 5


       PRESS:   ENTER Process   PF1 Help   PF3 Previous Step
```

Figure 7.26   This panel shows various courses of action.

```
     STEP 10 — REPORT COMMANDS FOR REPORT SERIES DEMO1
     ----+----1----+----2----+----3----+----4----+----5----+----6----+-----7----
     ****** ****************** TOP OF DATA ********************************
     000100 INPUT       IECUSBAS
     000200
     000300 REPORT      DMREPT1
     000400
     000500 SELECT                              ;
     000600   IE-CUST-NAME                      ;
     000700   ( 'A'                             ;
     000800     'C' )
     000900
     001000  EXCLUDE                            ;
     001100     IE-CUST-ACTIVE-INACTIVE-CODE    ;
     001200     'I'
     001300
     001400  CURR-CUST-BALANCE       (15P02)  =    ;
     001500        IE-CUST-BALANCE-OWED  -  IE-CUST-PAYMENT-AMOUNT
     001600
     001700  DEFINE    PAGEHEADINGS             ;
     001800     'DATE: #SYSDATE'                ;
     001900     'CURRENT CUSTOMER BALANCES REPORT'  ;
     002000     'PAGE #PAGE'
     002100
     002200  LIST                              ;
     002300     #REPORTID                      ;
     002400     CURR-CUSTOMER-BALANCE          ;
     002500     IE-CUST-NAME                   ;
     002600     IE-CUST-ADDRESS-LINE-1         ;
     002700     IE-CUST-PAYMENT-AMOUNT         ;
     002800     IE-CUST-BALANCE-OWED
     ****** ****************** BOTTOM OF DATA  ********************************
```

Figure 7.27   This demonstrates I.E.-generated code in Expert Language based on prior menu screen selections.

```
                         -------------------------------VIEW A REPORT
                                  REPT1          00001          001
                                                          021   099
----+----1----+----2----+----3----+----4----+----5----+----6----+----7----+----
                CURRENT CUSTOMER BALANCES REPORT

                         ADDRESS               CUSTOMER       CUSTOMER
     CUSTOMER NAME       LINE 1                PAYMENT        BALANCE


     ALLEN AND SIMS INC  702 W SPRUCE VALLEY   1254.67         879.02
     APPLIED SERVICES    222 CHANDLER           345.09         976.98
     BROWNLY INTERNATIONAL 12 W GUINEA PLAZA       .00         578.00
     DANIELSON LIMITED   4445 W 32ND STREET    2230.99            .00
     EGGHEAD BREAKFAST   1236 CHERRY LANE       113.09         678.07
     GEORGETOWN STATION  223 WESTMINSTER        237.00         567.00
     HODGES, E&O         44523 N MOZART         200.00         759.04
     TRAMMEL STEEL       44 LAWNDALE AVE       3456.00        8097.01
                         ***   END OF REPORT DMREPT1 ***
     ************************  END OF REPORT LISTING  **************************
```

Figure 7.28 This printout is a direct result of the command statement shown in Figure 7.27.

The step-by-step way of producing a view or a report series is probably the quickest way to get results. However, you may not always be able to accommodate some of the more complex issues within this framework. Rather you need to utilize a different format which will be addressed in Chapter 8.

Summary

The MSA Information Expert (I.E.) environment is a complete fourth generation support system. It is made up of a number of building blocks, such as the Expert Language, a report generator, module customized per application, a screen painter, query facilities, and an extensive software that enables you to communicate with sophisticated PC networks.

When you create a report using the Expert Language, you can do it online via I.E.'s On-line Support Facilities (OSF), or you can do it in a batch environment. The OSF module is a real time dialogue manager supported by a number of utility programs.

The purpose of this chapter is to present to you a step-by-step reporting facility to enable you to create basic I.E. reports without an in-depth knowledge of the Expert Language. (Please note that the term "Expert Language" is a vendor term, denoting one of the many building blocks that are part of a fourth generation support environment.)

MSA's Source Management Facility enables you to manage, control and manipulate your data, and you need to rely on this facility extensively to accomplish results. In addition to building a report, you can create output files that can be used as a bridge between two or more application systems.

I.E. uses your own report specification, the definition from the data dictionary, and the associated data frame to create whatever information you have requested. The steps involved in producing a report include the physical preparation of the report(s), the running of that report, and the subsequent viewing of it.

Preparing a report involves the translation of English-like commands into a complex language, which remains transparent to you, but, nonetheless, is necessary for the computer. These statements describe the requested reports in detail, such as the source of the data, which report should be printed, which should be viewed on-line, and if there are processing requirements mutual to a number of reports and report series.

To look at the overall process from an efficiency point of view, data for each report in a series is extracted from the particular data frame. But I.E. only processes data required to produce your report(s). It will not extract undefined information in order to produce that report. The I.E. reporting concept utilizes three types of resources in generating the required information. These are the particular database or databases referred to as data frames, a powerful dictionary that drives the I.E. system, and a means of communicating with the system to keep a "dialogue" going while monitoring the process, which is terminal driven.

The MSA Expert Dictionary is made up of four components: items, groups, records, and data frames. Items represents the lowest, most basic form of information kept within the Expert environment.

Report requests are basically requests that describe a specific report or reports including a set of processing criteria, computations, and so on.

A report series, on the other hand, pertains to a number of report requests that utilize the same data frame and, as such, are submitted concurrently regardless of the number of requests in the series.

To look simplistically at the working of the report series it reads the data from the data frame, then selects it for the report or reports you have requested, performs the required calculations, has the data sequenced, and generates the final product, as the result.

Chapter 8

MSA's Fourth Generation Expert Language: How It Works

8.1   Overview

In Chapter 7, you learned how to generate a report or a series of reports and view it on-line without really having to understand I.E. and its technical requirements. This process, which is referred to as a step-by-step approach to fourth generation programming techniques, is undoubtedly both efficient and productive, and it shows a great deal of tutorial sensitivity on the part of the vendor. However, more complex programming projects need to be addressed outside the framework of this step-by-step approach, and to do that you must learn some of the conventions and capabilities inherent in the Expert Language.

The Expert Language is merely a building block in the big picture that can permeate through both MSA-driven, as well as non-MSA (or non-I.E.) environments. This chapter will concentrate on the mechanics and the conventions of the Expert Language.

8.2   Using the I.E. Text Editor

If you have any prior ISPF experience, you will find I.E.'s text editor facilities quite easy to learn because of the similarities involved. (ISPF is an IBM software for text editing and library management.) There is, of course, a very practical reason for choosing the ISPF model as the focal point for the MSA text editor. ISPF enjoys a great deal of popularity and is probably one of the most widespread productivity packages currently on the market.

Before focusing on I.E. coding conventions it is best to give a cursory overview of the use of this text editor. Figure 8.1 shows the structure of the text editor, which can be triggered internally by the sign-on screen.

Invoke the primary option panel which was presented earlier in Chapter 7, and which is triggered internally by the sign-on screen. To simplify things, this screen will be displayed one more time. In Figure 8.2, there are six functions associated with the primary option menu including what amounts to an end of session task which will take you back to the main menu. However, rather than choosing ER (stands for the Expert Reporting module), which is the route I taken during the step-by-step process, Function SM or Source Management was selected and a library (CCPUBLIC) specified for retrieval. This selection invoked the Source Management Facility panel (shown in Figure 8.3), where the three basic requirements relevant to the system are described.

The first requirement was to create a new member, denoted by the term

```
EDIT REPORT SERIES: IE-CUSTOMER-BALANCES-LIST          COLUMNS 001  072
COMMAND INPUT ===>                                     SCROLL ===> HALF
   ----+----1----+----2----+----3----+----4----+----5----+----6----+----7----

000900   ***************** TOP OD DATA *****************************
001000
001100   INPUT   IECUSBAS
001200
001300   SELECT IE-CUST-ACTIVE-INACTIVE-CODE   ;
001400   AND
001500   IE-CUST-UTILITY-CODE = 'W'
001600   REPORT   SELCUST
001700   ORDER BY IE-CUST-NAME
001750   IE-CUST-SUBACCOUNT                    ;
001790
001800   DEFINE PAGEHEADINGS 'DATE:' #SYSDATE  ;
001900   'CUSTOMER REPORT'                     ;
002000   'PAGE' #PAGE-NUMBER
002100   LIST                                  ;
002200   IE-CUST-NAME                          ;
002300   IE-RECORD-TYPE                        ;
002400   IE-CUST-SUBACCOUNT                    ;
002500   IE-CUST-UTILITY-CODE                  ;
002600   IE-CUST-ACTIVE-INACTIVE-CODE


ACTION _____   1 Help  3 End  5 Find  6 Change  7 Pg Bwd  8 Pg Fwd
```

Figure 8.1 THis is the text editor structure for managing the Expert Language.

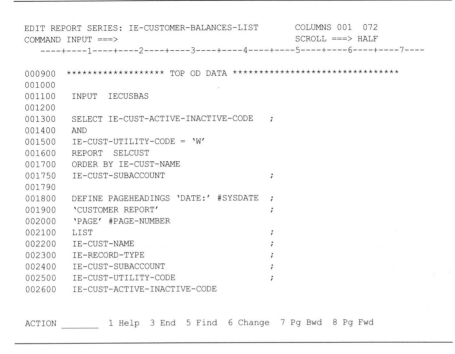

```
 M S A   INFORMATION EXPERT  --------------------PRIMARY OPTION MENU


         ENTER SELECTION BELOW:

         ER - EXPERT REPORTING
         SM - SOURCE MANAGEMENT
         JS - JOB PREPARATION & SUBMISSION
         RV - REPORT VIEWING
         SA - SYSTEM ADMINISTRATION
         EN - END OF SESSION

       SELECTION ===> SM
         LIBRARY ===> CCPUBLIC


    ACTION: _____


  PRESS:      ENTER Process       PF1 Help  PF3 End Session
```

Figure 8.2   This is the I.E. primary option menu.

```
  M  S  A   INFORMATION EXPERT ------------------ SOURCE MANAGEMENT FACILITY


        ENTER SELECTION BELOW:

        LS - DISPLAY MEMBER LIST
        CR - CREATE A NEW MEMBER
        CH - CHANGE A NEW MEMBER
        UT - COPY/DELETE/RENAME/MERGE MEMBERS
        RE - RETURN TO PRIMARY OPTION MENU


          SELECTION     ===>  ____
          MEMBER NAME   ===>  _____
          LIBRARY NAME  ===>  DEMOGR

       ACTION:  _____


    PRESS:   ENTER Process   PF1 Help  PF3 Return to Primary Option Menu
```

Figure 8.3   This is the I.E. source management facility menu.

CR, since the intention is to write a new program rather than to modify an existing set of code. The second requirement pertains to naming the new member (DEPRT1). The third requirement was already referenced in the previous step, the designation of the library that is automatically displayed on this panel.

With this in mind, the next logical step involving the display of the "DEFINE TYPE OF SOURCE MEMBER" screen was invoked. Since a new member needs to be created in this step (note that the term member is now synonymous with an application program), function 1 was selected and enter pressed. Now the text editor screen can be used.

Figure 8.4 shows the layout of the MSA text editor. The Command Input **1** in the upper-right-hand corner of the screen is available for entering a specific instruction for a number of things (such as SAVing your program or simply CANCELing the edit screen).

Column (**2**) simply displays those members that are shown on the edit screen. If there are messages to display, the system will display them instead of displaying the column number. SCROLL (**3**) is invoked when you require forward or backward spacing on the screen. "PAGE" allows you to go forward or backward a full screen at a time. If you need to reduce it, you may specify "HALF". This function moves screen images a

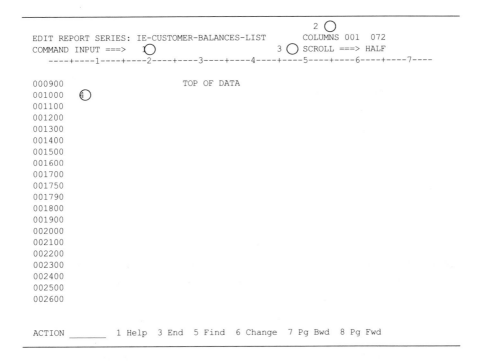

```
                                             2 ◯
EDIT REPORT SERIES: IE-CUSTOMER-BALANCES-LIST    COLUMNS 001   072
COMMAND INPUT ===>     ◯                  3 ◯ SCROLL ===> HALF
   ----+----1----+----2----+----3----+----4----+----5----+----6----+----7----

000900                        TOP OF DATA
001000    ④
001100
001200
001300
001400
001500
001600
001700
001750
001790
001800
001900
002000
002100
002200
002300
002400
002500
002600


ACTION _____   1 Help  3 End  5 Find  6 Change  7 Pg Bwd  8 Pg Fwd
```

Figure 8.4   This is the text editor layout.

half a page (roughly twelve lines at a time), depending on the current position of the cursor.

The direction (whether you go forward or backward) is done with function keys. For example, PF8, or function key 8 enables you to proceed downward toward the end of your data, while PF7 takes you back to the top.

Line numbers (**4**) are automatically generated by the I.E. system corresponding to each line of the source code. The MSA text editor utilizes two types of commands. These are line commands and command input commands.

When you are in the process of editing a member, you may want to copy, delete, insert, move, or repeat one or a number of lines. In order to perform a specific function, you need to enter line commands over the line number of the edit screen and then press ENTER. Actually, you can enter several line commands at once, as long as there is no conflict among them.

The MSA text editor let's you use single-character line commands to change a specific instruction. The editor also lets you use double-character line commands by specifying the first and the last lines of a block of lines you want changed. For example, to copy a single line of text, enter a 'C' over the line number such as:

BEFORE: 000100 AFTER: C00100, then press enter.

To copy a block of text, enter 'CC' to mark the beginning and the end of the text, as I did in Figure 8.5.

Figure 8.5 is made up of six frames to illustrate some of the features of simple and block commands.

In Frame 1, there is a record layout which needs to be rearranged through the I.E. Text Editor. As you can see, each field name (such as street address and city) is associated with a locational value. Street address encompasses positions 48 through 83 on the record. The objective is to move both the vendor number and the name fields ahead of street address to maintain an ascending sequence for the above record description.

So in Frame 2, I have marked lines 00007 and 00008 by placing the characters 'MM' in the first two positions of the line number. 'MM' designates "block moves" that is, moves involving more than a single line. Thus the MM in column 0007 is to designate the beginning area of what needs to be moved, while 0008 represents the ending of it.

In Frame 3 the character 'B' has been entered in line 00003 which is a destination description for the move. 'B' means before, that is move lines 7 and 8 before line 3.

Frame 4 shows the result of the move after enter has been hit, thus the move with regards to fields vendor number and vendor name was successfully completed and now the record is in an ascending order.

In Frame 4, I inserted an extra field between lines 7 and 8 which are the zip code and the last paydate fields. By placing an 'I' in the first position of line 7, and pressing the enter key, the I.E. text editor gave me an extra line on which to enter the new field, which is the county code. Frame 6 shows the new field entered. In addition to the above line commands, there is a set of command input commands shown in Figure 8.6. The MSA text editor relies on 10 basic input commands as follows:

FIND	CANCEL
LOCATE	SUBMIT
MAX	CHANGE
SAVE	CHECK
RENUMBER	RESET

```
 EDIT - VENDFLE  ------------------------------------ COLUMNS 001 072
 COMMAND ===>                                           SCROLL ===> HALF
 ****** ******************** TOP OF DATA  ******************************
 000001 RECORD LAYOUT FOR VENDOR ANALYSIS FILE:
 000002
 000003      STREET ADDRESS:        48 - 83
 000004      CITY          :        85 -102
 000005      ZIP CODE      :       104 -108
 000006      LAST PAYDATE  :       111 -116
 000007      VENDOR NUMBER :  COL:   1 - 10
 000008      VENDOR NAME   :        12 - 46
 ****** ****************** BOTTOM OF LIST ******************************
```

Figure 8.5—Part I. Frame 1   This is the layout of the vendor analysis file.

```
 EDIT - VENDFLE  ------------------------------------ COLUMNS 001 072
 COMMAND ===>                                           SCROLL ===> HALF
 ****** ******************** TOP OF DATA  ******************************
 000001 RECORD LAYOUT FOR VENDOR ANALYSIS FILE:
 000002
 000003      STREET ADDRESS:        48 - 83
 000004      CITY          :        85 -102
 000005      ZIP CODE      :       104 -108
 000006      LAST PAYDATE  :       111 -116
 CC0007      VENDOR NUMBER :  COL:   1 - 10
 CC0008      VENDOR NAME   :        12 - 46
 ****** ****************** BOTTOM OF LIST ******************************
```

Figure 8.5—Part I. Frame 2   This is the layout of the vendor analysis file. Note the block markers in lines CC0007 and CC0008.

```
 EDIT - VENDFLE  ------------------- COLUMNS 001 072
 COMMAND ===>                                           SCROLL ===> HALF
 ****** ******************** TOP OF DATA  ******************************
 000001 RECORD LAYOUT FOR VENDOR ANALYSIS FILE:
 000002
 B00003      STREET ADDRESS:        48 - 83
 000004      CITY          :        85 -102
 000005      ZIP CODE      :       104 -108
 000006      LAST PAYDATE  :       111 -116
 CC          VENDOR NUMBER :  COL:   1 - 10
 CC          VENDOR NAME   :        12 - 46
 ****** ****************** BOTTOM OF LIST ******************************
```

Figure 8.5—Part I. Frame 3   This is the layout of the vendor analysis file. In addition to the CC markers, a B is placed in the first position of line B00003.

```
 EDIT — VENDFLE  ------------------------------------- COLUMNS 001 072
 COMMAND ===>                                          SCROLL ===> HALF
 ****** ******************** TOP OF DATA  ******************************
 000001 RECORD LAYOUT FOR VENDOR ANALYSIS FILE:
 000002
 000003      VENDOR NUMBER :  COL:   1 - 10
 000004      VENDOR NAME   :        12 - 46
 000005      STREET ADDRESS:        48 - 83
 000006      CITY          :        85 -102
 000007      ZIP CODE      :       104 -108
 000008      LAST PAYDATE  :       111 -116
 ****** ******************* BOTTOM OF LIST ****************************
```

Figure 8.5—Part II. Frame 4   This is the layout of the vendor analysis file.
Vendor number and Name items are moved from lines 9 and 10.

```
 EDIT — VENDFLE  ------------------------------------- COLUMNS 001 072
 COMMAND ===>                                          SCROLL ===> HALF
 ****** ******************** TOP OF DATA  ******************************
 000001 RECORD LAYOUT FOR VENDOR ANALYSIS FILE:
 000002
 000003      VENDOR NUMBER :  COL:   1 - 10
 000004      VENDOR NAME   :        12 - 46
 000005      STREET ADDRESS:        48 - 83
 000006      CITY          :        85 -102
 I00007      ZIP CODE      :       104 -108
 D00008      LAST PAYDATE  :       111 -116
 ****** ******************* BOTTOM OF LIST ****************************
```

Figure 8.5—Part II. Frame 5   This is the layout of the vendor analysis file.
Vendor number and Name items are eliminated from the bottom. An "I"
insert is placed in line 000007 to allow for a county code. A "D" placed in
line 000008 will eliminate the LAST PAYDATE field.

```
 EDIT — VENDFLE  ------------------------------------- COLUMNS 001 072
 COMMAND ===>                                          SCROLL ===> HALF
 ****** ******************** TOP OF DATA  ******************************
 000001 RECORD LAYOUT FOR VENDOR ANALYSIS FILE:
 000002
 000003      VENDOR NUMBER :  COL:   1 - 10
 000004      VENDOR NAME   :        12 - 46
 000005      STREET ADDRESS:        48 - 83
 000006      CITY          :        85 -102
 000007      ZIP CODE      :       104 -108
 ,,,,,,      COUNTY-CODE   :       109 -110

 ****** ******************* BOTTOM OF LIST ****************************
```

Figure 8.5—Part II. Frame 6   This is the layout of the vendor analysis file.
Vendor number and name items are eliminated from the bottom. An "I"
insert placed in line 000007 to allow for a county code. Note that the field
LAST PAYDATE is now deleted.

Command	Entry	Description
FIND	F	scans a member for one or all occurrences of a character string.
LOCATE	L	Locates a specific line number.
MAX	M	Scrolls the maximum number of lines to the top or the bottom of the member. Used with the PF7 and PF8 function keys to page forward and backward.
SAVE	S	Saves and stores member for future use. Once you save a member, you can continue editing it.
RENUMBER	R	Renumbers line-numbers in incrememts of 100.
CANCEL	CAN	Cancels an edit session without saving member.
SUBMIT	SUB	Submits a report series, print series, or subroutine for preparation, or submits a run statement member for execution.
CHANGE	C	Replaces one or all occurrences of one character string with another.
CHECK	CHECK	Checks the syntax of the reporting statements entered for a report series, run statement, or subroutine. Similar to prepare function.
RESET	RES	Removes editing messages from the edit screen and clears out line commands that were entered incorrectly.

Figure 8.6   This chart lists command input commands.

The functions of these commands vary, but they give you tremendous flexibility with regards to file handling and utilizing a comprehensive set of utilities, very much like the IBM ISPF productivity tool.

Look at the blank text editor layout presented in Figure 8.7 which was invoked with a number of menu selections. Using the customer data frame (Figure 7.23 in Chapter 7), I entered a list program (Figure 8.8). This program needs to exclude records with an activity status code of 'I'. (This was the same criterion during the step-by-step approach.) Thus, status 'I' records will be omitted altogether by the Expert Language.

First, the heading requirements (CUSTOMER PROFILE) was specified to I.E. along with a couple of automatic features, such as the current (system) date and a page numbering scheme. Then, the print requirements were established in the report section of the program which consists of displaying the customer name, the account number, the utility code and so forth.

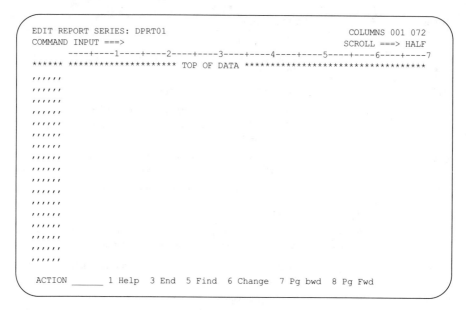

```
EDIT REPORT SERIES: DPRT01                              COLUMNS 001 072
COMMAND INPUT ===>                                      SCROLL ===> HALF
        ----+----1----+----2----+----3----+----4----+----5----+----6----+----7
****** ******************** TOP OF DATA ********************************
'''''''
'''''''
'''''''
'''''''
'''''''
'''''''
'''''''
'''''''
'''''''
'''''''
'''''''
'''''''
'''''''
'''''''
'''''''

 ACTION _____  1 Help  3 End  5 Find  6 Change  7 Pg bwd  8 Pg Fwd
```

Figure 8.7   This is the blank text editor invoked for specifying an Expert program.

To verify that the coding is accurate, the "CHECK" command was entered next to the command input arrow (===>), shown in Figure 8.8 and enter was pressed. Subsequently, I.E. ran a quick check interactively to determine if there was any error in the coding which is reflected in line 000401. The actual error was made in the line above it, in 000400 (line 000401 is a machine-generated line), while displaying an error message.

What is wrong? Figure 8.8 now says that an "UNIDENTIFIED PARAMETER (IEL-1261)" was submitted, which does not conform to I.E. conventions. The mistake made was simply that the word "HEADING" was used which is not a reserved word, nor is it to be found in any tables or in the dictionary. The system scanned the statement, and found the next instruction, this time a legitimate one such as PAGEHEADING, and generated the error message as the result. In the next frame (Figure 8.9) this situation was resolved, and, when resubmitting the program for the second time, the CHECK command did not turn up any additional flaw in the code. A "clean" run of this source program is now shown in Figure 8.10 which is the report on queue. Actually, Figure 8.10 is viewed through a CRT in an on-line fashion. Once you have viewed the report (and are satisfied with the way it looks), you can submit it for printing on-line, it is executed in a conventional batch environment.

```
EDIT REPORT SERIES: DPRT01                         COLUMNS 001 072
COMMAND INPUT ===> CHECK                            SCROLL ===> HALF
      ----+----1----+----2----+----3----+----4----+----5----+----6----+----7
****** ******************** TOP OF DATA ********************************
000100 INPUT   IECUSBAS
000110
000200 EXCLUDE IE-CUS-ACTIVE-INACTIVE-CODE 'I'
000210
000300 REPORT  DEMO1
000310
''''''
000400 DEFINE HEADING PAGEHEADINGS 'DATE:' #SYSDATE            ;
000401      IEL-1261 UNDEFINED PARAMETER. FOUND PAGEHEADINGS.
000500 'CUSTOMER PROFILE'                                      ;
000600 'PAGE' #PAGE-NUMBER
000610
000700 LIST IE-CUST-NAME                                       ;
000800 IE-CUST-ACCT-CLASSIFICATION                             ;
000900 IE-CUST-SUB-ACCOUNT                                     ;
001000 IE-CUST-UTILITY-CODE
****** ********************* BOTTOM OF DATA ****************************

 ACTION _____ 1 Help  3 End  5 Find  6 Change  7 Pg bwd  8 Pg Fwd
```

Figure 8.8 This is an error condition shown as the result of the CHECK command.

```
EDIT REPORT SERIES: DPRT01                         COLUMNS 001 072
COMMAND INPUT ===> CHECK                            SCROLL ===> HALF
      ----+----1----+----2----+----3----+----4----+----5----+----6----+----7
****** ******************** TOP OF DATA ********************************
000100 INPUT   IECUSBAS
000110
000200 EXCLUDE IE-CUS-ACTIVE-INACTIVE-CODE 'I'
000210
000300 REPORT  DEMO1
000310
000400 DEFINE PAGEHEADINGS 'DATE:' #SYSDATE            ;
000500 'CUSTOMER PROFILE'                                      ;
000600 'PAGE' #PAGE-NUMBER
000610
000700 LIST IE-CUST-NAME                                       ;
000800 IE-CUST-ACCT-CLASSIFICATION                             ;
000900 IE-CUST-SUB-ACCOUNT                                     ;
001000 IE-CUST-UTILITY-CODE
****** ********************* BOTTOM OF DATA ****************************

 ACTION _____ 1 Help  3 End  5 Find  6 Change  7 Pg bwd  8 Pg Fwd
```

Figure 8.9 This is the corrected version of the program shown in Figure 8.8.

```
M S A  INFORMATION EXPERT ----------------------------- VIEW A REPORT
SERIES: DEMO1                   REPORT: DEM01    PAGE 00001  LINE 001
COMMAND INPUT ===>                              COLUMNS 001 079
----+----1----+----2----+----3----+----4----+----5----+----6----+----7----+-
DATE: 08/22/88                   CUSTOMER PROFILE


                                ACCT          SUB          UTIL
    CUSTOMER NAME               CLASS       ACCOUNT        CODE
    ----------------------------  -----      -------       ----
    HAMMOND FINANCIAL SERVICES    B          01-002         E
    HAMMOND FINANCIAL SERVICES                              G
    HAMMOND FINANCIAL SERVICES                              W
    ALLEN AND SIMS INC                       01-004         E
    ALLEN AND SIMS INC                                      G
    GRIFFIN ADVERTISING COMPANY              04-084         G
    GRIFFIN ADVERTISING COMPANY                             W
    APPLIED SERVICES                         06-043         E
    MOSS AUTOMATIC SYSTEM                    10-013         E
    MOSS AUTOMATIC SYSTEM                                   G
    WELCH CONSULTANTS                        12-110         E
    WELCH CONSULTANTS                                       G
    WELCH CONSULTANTS                                       W


 ACTION: _____   PF3 End  PF6 Top  PF7 Pg Bwd  PF8 Pg Fwd  PF9  Last Pg
```

Figure 8.10   This is what is seen when viewing the on-line report of the list program.

8.3   The Expert Language: How It Works

Unlike using a conventional (third generation) language, where some of the complexities require time and a great deal of skill, I.E. enables you to be efficient with only a few commands and the willingness to "experiment."

These conventions are covered using the following organizational criteria:

- Specifying variable items and values,
- Sequencing and formatting commands,
- Calculating and performing conditional logic,
- Accessing data type statements,
- Defining items in working storage, and
- Utilizing stop/exit/ and next record commands.

The list is far from a complete one. However, it covers a substantial portion of the Expert "vocabulary" you initially require.

I.E. relies extensively on groups or clusters of data arranged in data frames, which is the logical view of a database. In order to access, format, and report on the various data frames, you need to tell I.E. what specific data frame(s) you will be selecting or excluding from the process.

Once you have decided on a particular source of information, all you need to do is to point to the right data frame using an INPUT command, as follows:

INPUT data frame-name, or

INPUT PERSONL

The Expert Language is made up of three sections: the INPUT section (which most programs have, but nonetheless is not required), a COMMON section, and a REPORT section, the last section being the only mandatory portion of the language.

Note that the INPUT statement must be the first command in your series, and, of course, the data frame in reference, must be a valid one already in existence on the data dictionary. Each report request needs to be identified by a name, so that you can describe, print, or display them individually. To conform with I.E. conventions, the report name must be made up of a minimum of one (alpha) character (the first position must be alpha, and the rest may be alphanumeric), but not exceeding eight characters in total length. For example, REPORT PAY001B is a legitimate name. So is the expression REPORT DEDUCT.

Statements used in the language can be coded in a free format starting in column 1 all the way to column 72. You can continue on the next line using semicolons (;). If you need to create a comment line, you may do so simply by placing an asterisk (*) in column 1 of each statement.

Internally, these statements reside and are stored in the source management facility using the text editor to create the necessary commands which will drive the report series. In order to print with the Expert Language, you essentially need to tell I.E. the exact data to be retrieved, item-by-item, data frame by data frame.

8.3.1 Specifying Variable Items and Values

Having defined your INPUT section to I.E., you may or may not have a common section to code.

SELECT and EXCLUDE statements belong to the common section, sometimes for reasons of programming efficiency. They can also be part of the REPORT section of this fourth generation language.

What are SELECT and EXCLUDE statements?

You can select or exclude certain records from displaying or printing based on whatever processing criteria are given. If the value of an item is equal to any one of the external values, the entire record containing that value is either kept or rejected. Both the SELECT and the EXCLUDE commands have the same standard format which is as follows:

SELECT item-name value ... or

EXCLUDE item-name value.

The following are examples for your review:

- SELECT IE-EMPLOYEE-DEPARTMENT '123'.

  This means to select only those departments whose value is equal to '123'.

- EXCLUDE IE-EMPLOYEE-DEPARTMENT (120 129).

  Here, you are telling I.E. through the EXCLUDE command to simply ignore (or exclude) an entire range of employee departments starting with department 120 and including department 129.

- SELECT IE-EMPLOYEE-STATUS-CODE 'A' 'I'.

  This statement will look at the actual value of the EMPLOYEE-STATUS-CODE and make the selection only when the compare value is equal to 'A' or 'I'. "OR" is the logical default value that is automatically assumed in this case.

- EXCLUDE IE-EMPLOYEE-STATUS-CODE 'I' OR IE-EMPLOYEE-DEPARTMENT '123'.

  This statement will exclude all records whose status code is equal to an 'I' with an employee department code of 123.

Although you can select or exclude records in your REPORT section, it is probably not the recommended way of doing it.

When you generate a report, the execution of such a record, in fact, passes through a number of phases such as a data extraction phase, a sort phase, a print phase, and so forth. All of this is done in a predetermined order. Assume now that you have 100,000 records to select from and that the definition for the select criteria is defined in the REPORT section, as opposed to the COMMON section. Selection specifically during the print phase means that you probably have to sort all those records, a substantial portion of which could have been eliminated had you performed your selection earlier in the COMMON Section.

8.3.2   Sequencing and Formatting Commands

You can essentially describe the body of your report with the LIST statement, which will print the item listed, left to right, across the report page in a columnar format. (To be more specific, I.E. prints from left to right and from top to bottom.) Column headings are automatically generated for each item. Note that only one LIST statement is allowed in a report request. For example:

LIST IE-EMPLOYEE-NAME ;

IE-EMPLOYEE-ID ;

IE-EMPLOYEE-DEPARTMENT ;

IE-EMPLOYEE-CLASS

Figure 8.11 shows what an actual I.E. program would look like in a given setting, and Figure 8.12 displays the result of that code based on the data residing on the customer information data frame. Notice that the title heading was initially defined in the data dictionary, otherwise I.E. would have relied on the item names for heading, replacing the separating hyphens with blanks. Thus, instead of DEPT, the title heading —— would have been IE EMPLOYEE DEPARTMENT. ————————————————————

```
    M S A  INFORMATION EXPERT ------------------------ VIEW A REPORT
    SERIES:  DEMO5                  REPORT: REPT01   PAGE 00001  LINE 001
    COMMAND INPUT ===>                                COLUMNS 001  079
    ----+----1----+----2----+----3----+----4----+----5----+----6----+----7-


    DATE: 07/12/88                           SYSTEMS MAINTENANCE LISTING
    TIME: 12:07:08                               INFORMATION EXPERT


    ------------------------------------------------------------------

    0001   000100  INPUT PERSNL
    0002   000200
    0003   000300  REPORT PAY-ONE
    0004   000400
    0005   000500  LIST    IE-EMPLOYEE-NAME           ;
    0006   000600          IE-EMPLOYEE-ID             ;
    0007   000700          IE-EMPLOYEE-DEPARTMENT     ;
    0008   000800          IE-EMPLOYEE-CLASS

      * DEMO5  HAS BEEN PREPARED AND ADDED TO THE REPORT REQUEST FILE
                      * END OF REPORT LISTING

    ACTION:  _____PF3 End  PF6 Top  PF7 Pg Bwd  PF8 Pg Fwd  PF9  Last Pg
```

Figure 8.11   This shows the LIST command using the Expert Language.

```
EMPLOYEE NAME            ID#    DEPT     CLASS
-------------           ------  ----     -----

KEELING, ROSE L         127645  123      OD748
KRAMER, JOHN Q          238711  123      OD748
LANGSTON, ALEX          970082  147      ACCTA
POWELL, JOSEPH R        129017  147      ACCTB
SCHAFFORT, MARIE A      300199  147      ACCTC
TOMCZAK, CROLL R        301397  892      PRODE
VALENTINO, PAUL         501132  111      LCE01
WALLACE, LARRY D        450111  111      LCE02
WALTON, DAN O           213087  112      XINGW
```

Figure 8.12 This is a list generated via I.E. LIST statement from Figure 8.11.

Complementary to the list command, the Expert Language also relies on its PRINT counterpart, which gives you complete control over the design and format of a report. This is useful if you are in the process of designing a report, for preformatted statements such as a W2 layout or a quarterly report.

You can also tell I.E. how to sequence the data in your report, if the sequence you need is different from the initial sequence of the data frame. To do that, you can identify the sequence of each report request using the ORDER command. The ORDER command works in conjunction with the REPORT statement. Only the SELECT and the EXCLUDE commands can be between the REPORT and the word "ORDER" which also sets up sequence breaks at levels that you indicate. Unless you state it specifically, the order of your report is going to default to an ascending sequence. If this is not satisfactory, you need to specify DESCENDING or DESC. For example:

ORDER BY IE-EMPLOYEE-ID   ;
IE-EMPLOYEE-DEPARTMENT DESC

In this particular situation, information is going to be arranged by employee number, which will be the major field, and by the department code, as the secondary sort field.

Title headings need to be set up in the beginning of your definition through the DEFINE PAGEHEADINGS statement. (Note that the term PAGEHEADINGS is one word.) Page headings are made up of constants (such as the title header itself), as well as special values such as #SYSDATE and #PAGE-NUMBERS. #SYSDATE will grab the current date used by the computer. Normally, it is presented in standard MMDDYY format, where MM designates the month, DD the day, and YY the year. To that

MSA adds a two-digit century indicator (CC). The PAGE mechanism is a feature that gets updated every time an overflow condition is created. (Remember, in ANS COBOL, it is up to you to update the page counter and to count lines to force an overflow condition.)

Additional lines can also be accommodated using the NEXT LINE option.

8.3.3 How to Calculate and Perform Conditional Logic

The ability to compute and perform conditional logic is very much part of this fourth generation product.

In a conventional environment, even the calculation of a simple PAGE mechanism can be a major hassle. You add to a line counter, then keep comparing it until a value is reached to perform an overflow. Then, clear the counter and start all over again after resetting all the internal values. To compute a control level break, you must continuously monitor the key value or values in a record against an internal counter set up in the program logic. You keep accumulating the data until a key value in the record changes resulting in a control level print out.

Using the Expert Language, however, you will find all of the above functions to be automatic. In fact, you need to develop an elaborate scheme should you decide to override those capabilities. In order to perform a set of calculations, you want to use the ASSIGN statement. The result of your calculations could be stored in a work field, which is a temporary item that exists only in the current report series. For example: AMOUNT-DUE = IE-UNIT-SOLD * IE-RATE, is a legitimate statement where I have created a temporary item (AMOUNT-DUE), by multiplying two dictionary terms such as IE-UNIT-SOLD times IE-RATE. (I assumed in my example that both IE-UNIT-SOLD and IE-RATE were dictionary terms.) Note that any combination of items, names, numeric values and other previously calculated work field names can be used in the computation. Totals, such as sub- and grand totals are computed automatically using the TOTAL option in conjunction with the LIST statement.

When you use the term BY, it will cause your subtotals to be printed at specified levels. Subtotal levels must be items from the ORDER statement (or the initial sequence of the data frame), if no ORDER statement was specified. If you need to get a grand total, in addition to the subtotals, the variable #REPORTID must be used as part of the BY clause.

Standard format for the above command is as follows:

LIST item-name...

(TOTAL item-name) (BY total-level) (NEWPAGE)).

The keyword NEWPAGE enables you to initiate printing on a new page (depending on the exact location of this command). To complement the ability of the language to perform computations, I.E. also provides you with the ability to perform extensive conditional logic as follows:

You can perform basic conditional logic, which executes a set of criteria based on the truism of a condition. In addition, I.E. operates on a sequence break logic executing a set of statements based on changes in the sequence of the item. First-and-last, time logic on the other hand is invoked when a procedure needs to be triggered for the first or for the last time during the processing of a report series.

One of the rules applicable when you use conditional logic is to issue an "END" command after the last conditional statement. (Actually, you may use a number of "END" statements, if you utilize consecutive "IF" statements in a string.)

Why do you need to rely on conditional logic?

Normally you can use an "IF" statement when a certain action needs to be triggered, depending on the true (or false) outcome of your comparison. This is what the basic premise of conditional logic is all about.

I.E. relies on six types of value comparison commands as follows:

EQ: for an "equal" condition

NE: for a "not equal" to condition

GT: for a "greater than" condition

GE: for a "greater than" or equal to condition

LT: for a "less than" condition

LE: for a "less than or equal to" condition.

In Figure 8.13, a compound "IF" statement was issued to list data off the IECUSBIL data frame based on some predefined criteria. First of all it is necessary to report on two types of customers; one with the utility code 'E' and another with a utility code 'G'. Also, for current analysis, only customer balances showing zero amounts are of interest. Note that the "AND" command allows you to combine at least two or a number of conditions, so that in the given situation, both the utility criteria as well as the customer balances are satisfied.

Finally, an "END" command is placed to denote the last "IF" statement once the condition is completed.

A printout shown in Figure 8.14 is a brief overview of what the above "IF" statement generated while reading the ISCUSBIL database. In addition to using single compound "IF" statements, as above, I.E. also enables you to use a number of them connected through the "AND" and "OR" operands.

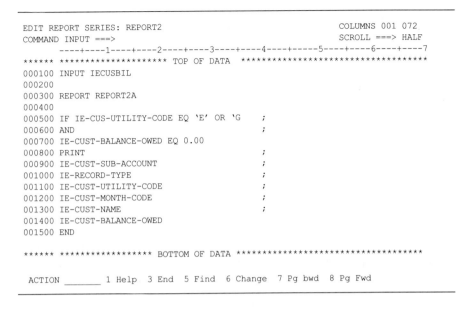

```
EDIT REPORT SERIES: REPORT2                           COLUMNS 001 072
COMMAND INPUT ===>                                    SCROLL ===> HALF
     ----+----1----+----2----+----3----+----4----+-----5----+----6----+----7
****** ******************** TOP OF DATA  ********************************
000100 INPUT IECUSBIL
000200
000300 REPORT REPORT2A
000400
000500 IF IE-CUS-UTILITY-CODE EQ 'E' OR 'G     ;
000600 AND                                     ;
000700 IE-CUST-BALANCE-OWED EQ 0.00
000800 PRINT                                   ;
000900 IE-CUST-SUB-ACCOUNT                     ;
001000 IE-RECORD-TYPE                          ;
001100 IE-CUST-UTILITY-CODE                    ;
001200 IE-CUST-MONTH-CODE                      ;
001300 IE-CUST-NAME                            ;
001400 IE-CUST-BALANCE-OWED
001500 END

****** ****************** BOTTOM OF DATA ********************************

ACTION _____  1 Help  3 End  5 Find  6 Change  7 Pg bwd  8 Pg Fwd
```

Figure 8.13 This is an example of the I.E. conditional statement.

Copyright © 1988 Management Science America, Inc. Used by permission.

```
M S A  INFORMATION EXPERT ------------------------- VIEW A REPORT
SERIES: DEMO3                  REPORT: REPORT1  PAGE 00001  LINE 001
COMMAND INPUR ===>                              COLUMNS 041  119
----+----1----+----2----+----3----+----4----+----5----+----6----+----7----+

   SUB      REC    UTIL   MON   CUSTOMER NAME                   BALANCE
   ACCOUNT  TYPE   CODE   CD                                    OWED
   -------  ----   ----   ---   -----------------------------   -------

   01-002    2      E     10    HAMMOND FINANCIAL SERVICES       0.00
   01-002    2      E     10    HAMMOND FINANCIAL SERVICES       0.00
   01-002    2      E     10    HAMMOND FINANCIAL SERVICES       0.00
   01-004    2      G     10    ALLEN AND SIMS INC               0.00
   01-004    2      G     10    ALLEN AND SIMS INC               0.00
   04-004    2      G     10    GRIFFIN ADVERTISING COMPANY      0.00
   04-004    2      G     10    GRIFFIN ADVERTISING COMPANY      0.00
   06-043    2      E     10    WALKER PRESS INC                 0.00
   07-098    2      G     10    MOSS AUTOMATIC SYSTEMS           0.00
   07-098    2      G     10    MOSS AUTOMATIC SYSTEMS           0.00
   07-098    2      G     10    MOSS AUTOMATIC SYSTEMS           0.00
   07-098    2      G     10    MOSS AUTOMATIC SYSTEMS           0.00
   10-887    2      E     10    WELCH CONSULTANTS                0.00

ACTION: _____  PF3 End  PF6 Top  PF7 Pg bwd  PF8 Pg Fwd  PF9 Last Pg
```

Figure 8.14 This is a subsequent list generated from the prior code.

Copyright © 1988 Management Science America, Inc. Used by permission.

8.3.4 Data Access Type Statements

Frequently you need to refer to more than one data frame at a time. After all, in a database environment, you always concern yourself with the logical, rather than with the physical, database. The relationship here, however, is like having a master data frame against which updates are applied and matched. (Actually, you can issue a MATCH command to extract information from a number of data frames.) To produce a match, each data frame must be in the same sequence that is further specified by the ORGANIZED BY clause.

How does the MATCH command work? When you use MATCH in place of an INPUT command, I.E. reads the first record of each data frame referenced by the above MATCH statement. After the system retrieves the required data from the appropriate data frames, it compares the sequence items defined in the ORGANIZED BY clause for the same values. If the values match, each record becomes available for printing. Otherwise the record with the lowest key will be printed first.

You can think about the RELATE command perhaps as a logical extension of the above MATCH. But, in addition to processing two or more data frames concurrently, by using such a command, you can also retrieve data from a "secondary" data frame while processing the first uninterrupted.

While processing a primary data frame via the INPUT command, you can also retrieve information from a second data frame depending on the values of the primary (invoking) data frame. Before you can issue a RELATE command, make sure that a KEY IS clause is also defined in the data dictionary. This clause, in fact, can contain any combination of item names and literals necessary to identify the individual record.

Note that you can refer to a data frame using a RELATE statement only if the record definitions of the given data frame contains a KEY IS clause and that the values for those items (and literals) will be supplied by you.

8.3.5 Items in Working Storage

When you need to define items in working storage to I.E., you must fully describe them in terms of attributes, disposition, and other characteristics. The reason for that is that they do not exist in the data dictionary for reference.

"WORK" is a reserved word that precedes the item described in the program, and the following information must be supplied before you can refer to it: the item name, its length and type, and in the case of a numeric field you also need to supply its decimal positions as well as other requirements. (This, by the way also includes format definitions for all date items.)

With regards to printing, you need to define further column and title headings, and specific print formats and occurrences if you attach sub-scripting values to a particular item.

To add a work statement to a series, you must describe the characteristics of each item using the following syntax:

WORK WK-EMPLOYEE-ID (9A)

WK-EMPLOYEE-ID = IE-EMPLOYEE-ID

In this particular instance, an item in working storage has been defined. The rationale is that there is a need to store the contents of the IE-EMPLOYEE-ID field, which is a data dictionary driven item, and as such, part of one of the data frames. The format, WK-EMPLOYEE-ID (9A), points to the working storage name of the item and its LTD. LTD simply refers to an item's length, type, and decimal position, which, under the circumstances, would be a nine-character-long field, described as alphanumeric. A seven-position numeric field with three decimal positions (1234.556), would look like: 7N3.

The syntax: WORK GROSS-PAY (7P2 'GROSS-PAY';'$$$,$$$.99') simply means to print out the field "GROSS-PAY, which is a seven-position-long work field followed by two decimal positions in a $$$,$$$.99 format using standard floating dollar signs. When you issue a WORK command to describe a column heading, you must enclose those headings in apostrophes. Commas are used to indicate when to break between heading lines. Thus, if you were to enter 'EMPLOYEE,RETROACTIVE,PAY', it would show up on the report as follows:

EMPLOYEE RETROACTIVE PAY ——————

8.3.6   Stop/Exit/and Next Record Commands

When you use the NEXT RECORD command in your program, it bypasses all subsequent processing with regards to your current record. For example:

IF RECORD-INDICATOR EQ 'A' OR 'B' NEXT RECORD END

means that if your current record type is either "A", or "B", you want to ignore it and concentrate on the next record in the buffer. Note the END command is there to terminate a set of logic.

The EXIT command has a somewhat similar function used by I.E. It, in fact, bypasses the remaining statements within a specified group of statements when you determine that the remaining statements do not need to be executed. There are five versions of the above available in the system. These are as follows:

- EXIT REPORT
- EXIT COMMON
- EXIT PROC
- EXIT SUBROUTINE

EXIT is used to terminate a loop, reset it, and begin processing from the next record or transaction on. Figure 8.15 describes the use of the EXIT command. In the example, there was a need to accumulate an employee's last five salary increases since January 1, 1982. Note that the EXIT command appears just before the END command, each time it finds a review date before January 1 1982 rather than incrementing the item TOTAL-SALARY-INCREASES again. Each of the five occurrences of the item review date will be checked, but only when the date criterion is satisfied (greater than January 1, 1982) will the counter be updated. As soon as the value of the item review number is greater than five, processing for the current record will continue, so that the TOTAL-SALARY-INCREASE will print for the employee. Afterward, the record of the next employee will be initiated.

An EXIT REPORT command causes I.E. to skip statements contained in the entire report section, while EXIT COMMON will omit statements that are part of the COMMON section. The EXIT PROC command simply

```
INPUT EMPMST

REPRT EMP001

WORK REVIEW-NUMBER (S)
WORK TOTAL-SALARY-INCREASES   (11P2)

FOR REVIEW-NUMBER = 1 TO 5 DO
IF REVIEW-DATE/REVIEW-NUMBER GE 820101
TOTAL-SALARY-INCREASES = TOTAL-SALARY-INCREASES  + ;
SALARY-INCREASE/REVIEW-NUMBER
ELSE
  EXIT
  END

PRINT AT 5 EMPLOYEE-NUMBER               ;
AT 20 REVIEW-DATE/REVIEW-NUMBER          ;
AT 30 SALARY-INCREASE/REVIEW-NUMBER      ;
AT 30 TOTAL-SALARY INCREASES             ;
NEXT LINE ADVANCE 1
```

Figure 8.15   This is an example of using working storage Items with I.E.

bypasses those statements that remain in the procedure. The EXIT SUB-ROUTINE command, on the other hand, is a call routine to invoke another program in the application. Finally, the STOP command terminates the current processing before its normal or scheduled termination, utilized mainly to avoid a fatal error or a core dump.

DATE 08/12/88   BILLING ANALYSIS BY UTILITY AND CUSTOMER CLASSIFICATION   PAGE 1

ACCOUNT NUMBER	PHONE NUMBER	CUSTOMER NAME	AMOUNT BILLED	UTIL CODE	DUE DATE	METER READING	METER READING	AMOUNT USED	UTILITY RATE
801-002	954 7323	BROWNLY INTERNATIONAL	122.50	E	11/11/88	049681	051089	1,408	$ .087
801-004	878-0081	AUTOMATIC SYSTEMS INC.	261.00		11/05/88	002000	005000	3,000	$ .087
806-004	767-9432	APPLIED GARBAGE	568.57		11/09/88	002745	007187	4,442	$ .128
808-877	755-0098	TRIANGLE AUTO	46.98		11/29/88	769118	769658	540	$ .087
907-009	833 4357	WILSON STORAGE FACILITIES	259.86		11/19/88	386409	389396	2,987	$ .087
909-002	988 7611	CAROL, SCHOOL OF BEAUTY	12.26		11/01/88	832706	832847	141	$ .087

TOTAL FOR UTILITY $99,999,999.99

TOTAL FOR CUSTOMER CLASSIFICATION $999,999,999.999

Figure 8.16   This is a report to be generated for the case study.

8.4 Case Study

Assume, that you want to generate a report that will combine the utility usage of certain firms in a given geographical area. You want this information for billing purposes of and for calculating consumption. Figure 8.16 shows what needs to be produced as the end product, which is a billing

```
M S A   INFORMATION EXPERT   ----------- LIST CONTENTS OF DATAFRAME IECUSBIL

    FIND DATA NAME:
                                              FLD   NBR   DEC   DT
    ITEM / GROUP NAME           LVL  DISPL  TYPE  SIZE  DIG   POS   CD   OCCS
    ------------------------    ---  -----  ----  ----  ---   ---   --   ----

    IE-CUST-ELECTRIC-USAGE-INFO  01   11    A     5                        3
    IE-CUST-ELECTRIC-RATE-CODE   02   11    A     1
    IE-CUST-GAS-USAGE-INFO       01   11    A     5                        3
    IE-CUST-GAS-RATE-CODE        02   11    A     1
    IE-CUST-ACCT-CLASSIFICATION  02    0    A     1
    IE-CUST-UTILITY-CODE         01    8    A     1
    IE-CUST-WATER-USAGE-INFO     01   11    A     5                        3
    IE-CUST-WATER-RATE-CODE      02   11    A     1
    IE-CUST-NAME                 01   48    A    30
    IE-CUST-PHONE-NUMBER         01   58    A    22
    IE-CUST-ACTIVE-INACTIVE-CODE 01   17    A     1
    IE-CUST-CURR-BEG-METER-READ  01   24    N     6     6     0
    IE-CUST-CURR-END-METER-READ  01   30    O     6     6     0
    IE-CUST-CURR-DUE-DATE        01   48    A     6     6     6    2
    IE-CUST-SUB-ACCOUNT          02    1    A     6
    IE-CUST-AMOUNT-BILLED        01   17    N     7     7     2
    IE-CUST-AMOUNT-USED          01   24    N     6     6     0
    ------------------------
              ------------------------
                        ------------------------
                                  ------------------------

    M S A INFORMATION EXPERT   ----------- LIST CONTENTS OF DATAFRAME IERATE
    FIND DATA NAME:
                                              FLD   NBR   DEC   DT
    ITEM / GROUP NAME           LVL  DISPL  TYPE  SIZE  DIG   POS   CD   OCCS
    ------------------------    ---  -----  ----  ----  ---   ---   --   ----

    IE-RATE-RECORD               00    0    A    80
    IE-RATE-UTILITY-CODE         01    0    A     1
    IE-RATE-CUST-CLASSIFICATION  01    1    A     1
    IE-RATE-CODE                 01    2    A     1
    IE-RATE-AMOUNT               01    3    N     3     3     3
    FILLER                       01    6    A    74
    ------------------------
              ------------------------
                        ------------------------
```

Figure 8.17 This is a detail from two data frames to be referenced in the case study.

analysis by utility and customer classification. (Incidentally, you can make this the title of your report.) This is only a partial list that goes on for pages. Note that there is only a single utility code (E) shown in the beginning of the report, meaning rate calculations pertaining to electricity. In reality, tabulate the other utility types as well such as the "G" type ("G" stands for gas) and the "W" type, meaning water. At the end of the report, grand total is needed that will show all three utilities lumped into two counters; one, which is a final total for all customers (TOTAL FOR UTILITY) and another total reflecting dollar amounts by customer classification. The AMOUNT BILLED can be attained as follows: Subtract the BEGINNING METER READING from the ENDING METER READING and multiply the result by the applicable rate. Figure 8.17 shows the individual items you need to perform the necessary calculations.

The majority of the items come from the IECUSBIL data frame. However, you also need to relate to the IERATE data frame from which you access the current billing rates and classification. At this point, you want to check the actual utility usage against a rate table.

In calculating utilities, you can arrive at a rate depending on the amount of electricity or water used. In this program, three rates are used. If your usage is less than the first entry on the table you pay so much; if your usage is greater than the first entry, but less than the second, you pay a different rate. Finally, when your usage exceeds the second entry on that table, you pay an altogether different rate.

Select only the active customers (IE-CUST-ACTIVE-INACTIVE-CODE = 'A'). Make sure the usage is a numeric field. The report should be sequenced by the customer account classification item, which is the major order, then by the utility code, and by the customer subaccount.

A sample solution is presented in Figures 8.18 and 8.19. Note that three working storage fields were selected for temporarily storing the IE-RATE-CODE, the IE-ACCOUNT-NUMBER, and the IE-CUST-SUB-ACCOUNT.

Note the coding conventions used for subscripting (/1, /2, etc). Figure 8.17 shows the second data frame used in this problem. The LIST command handles both variable data, as well as the constant title header information in the report section of the program. You can actually create "shells" via the Expert Language so that you can use and reuse parts of a particular source program with some minor changes.

```
INPUT   IECUSBIL

SELECT IE-CUST-ACTIVE-INACTIVE-CODE 'A'        ;
AND                                            ;
IE-CUST-AMOUNT-USED (000001 999999)

REPORT UTILBILL

ORDER BY IE-CUST-ACCT-CLASSIFICATION           ;
         IE-CUST-UTILITY-CODE                  ;
         IE-CUST-SUB-ACCOUNT

WORK RATE-CODE        (1A)
WORK ACCOUNT-NUMBER (7A)
WORK AMOUNT-USED      (6N)

ACCOUNT-NUMBER = IE-CUST-ACCT-CLASSIFICATION . IE-CUST-SUB-ACCOUNT
AMOUNT-USED    = IE-CUST-CURR-END-METER-READ - ;
IE-CUST-CURR-BEG-METER-READ

WHEN IE-CUST-UTILITY-CODE                      ;
IS 'E'
    IF AMOUNT-USED LE IE-CUST-ELECTRIC-USAGE/1
    RATE-CODE = IE-CUST-ELECTRIC-RATE-CODE/1
END
    IF AMOUNT-USED GT IE-CUST-ELECTRIC-USAGE/1  ;
    AND                                         ;
    AMOUNT-USED LE IE-CUST-ELECTRIC-USAGE/2
    RATE-CODE = IE-CUST-ELECTRIC-RATE-CODE/2
END
    IF AMOUNT-USED GT IE-CUST ELECTRIC-USAGE/2
    RATE-CODE = IE-CUST-ELECTRIC-RATE-CODE/3
END
IS 'G'
    IF AMOUNT-USED LE IE-CUST-GAS-USAGE/1  ;
    RATE-CODE = IE-CUST-GAS-RATE-CODE/1
END
    IF AMOUNT-USED GT IE-CUST-GAS-USAGE/1       ;
    AND                                         ;
    AMOUNT-USED LE IE-CUST-GAS-USAGE/2
    RATE-CODE = IE-CUST-GAS-RATE-CODE/2
END
    IF AMOUNT-USED GT IE-CUST-GAS-USAGE/2
    RATE-CODE = IE-GAS-RATE-CODE/3
```

Figure 8.18 This is a partial listing of the case study program and is continued in Figure 8.19.

```
    IS 'W'
        IF AMOUNT-USED LE IE-CUST-WATER-USAGE/1
        RATE-CODE = IE-CUST-WATER-RATE-CODE/1
    END
        IF AMOUNT-USED GT IE-CUST-WATER-USAGE/1  ;
        AND                                      ;
        AMOUNT-USED LE IE-CUST-WATER-USAGE/2
        RATE-CODE = IE-CUST-WATER-RATE-CODE/2
    END
        IF AMOUNT-USED GT IE-CUST-WATER-USAGE2
        RATE-CODE = IE-CUST-WATER-RATE-CODE/3
    END

END
        RELATE IERATE                                ;
        WHERE IE-CUST-ACCT-CLASSIFICATION =          ;
        IE-RATE-CUST-CLASSIFICATION                  ;
        AND                                          ;
        IE-CUST-UTILITY-CODE = IE-RATE-UTILITY-CODE  ;
        AND                                          ;
        RATE-CODE = IE-RATE-CODE

DEFINE PAGEHEADINGS 'DATE' #SYSDATE                  ;
        'BILLING ANALYSIS BY UTILITY AND CUSTOMER CLASSIFICATION ';
        'PAGE' #PAGE-NUMBER
  LIST      ACCOUNT-NUMBER                       ;
            HEADING IS 'ACCOUNT,NUMBER'          ;
            IE-CUST-PHONE-NUMBER                 ;
            IE-CUST-NAME                         ;
            IE-CUST-AMOUNT-BILLED                ;
            HEADING IS '   AMOUNT,   BILLED'     ;
            IE-CUST-UTILITY-CODE                 ;
            HEADING IS 'UTIL.,CODE'              ;
            IE-CUST-CURR-DUE-DATE                ;
            IE-CUST-CURR-BEG-METER-READ          ;
            IE-CUST-CURR-END-METER-READ          ;
            IE-CUST-AMOUNT-USED                  ;
            IE-RATE-AMOUNT                       ;
            ADVANCE 2                            ;
            TOTAL IE-CUST-AMOUNT-BILLED BY IE-CUST-UTILITY-CODE  ;
                    HEADING IS 'TOTAL FOR UTILITY'                  ;
                    IE-CUST-ACCT-CLASSIFICATION                     ;
                    HEADINGIS 'TOTAL FOR CUSTOMER CLASSIFICATION'
```

Figure 8.19 This is the case study program continued from Figure 8.18.

Summary

This chapter concentrates on the mechanics and conventions of the Expert Language. More complex programming projects need to be addressed outside the framework of the step-by-step approach, and, to do that, you must learn some of the conventions and capabilities inherent in the Expert Language.

If you have any prior ISPF experience, you will find I.E.'s text editor facilities quite easy to learn as a result of the similarities between the MSA and IBM software.

The MSA text editor, which is made up of line commands and command input commands, enables you to utilize single-character-line commands to change a specific instruction, as well as double-character-line commands specifying the first and the last lines of a block of lines you want changed.

To copy a block of text, enter CC to mark the beginning and the end of the text.

Unlike using a conventional (third generation) language, where some of the complexities require time and a great deal of skill, I.E. enables you to be efficient with only a few commands and the willingness to "experiment."

Chapter 9

The Expert Data Dictionary and Security Functions

9.1   Overview

The data dictionary is one of the building blocks of a fourth generation environment. In fact, one may consider such a dictionary to be the sole driver of this state-of-the-art apparatus, where everything you need to know or access is centrally defined. This chapter will give you a very specific insight into the technical aspect of MSA's Expert Dictionary, reflecting a high level of sophistication by the vendor company.

A data dictionary, is a central repository of rules and definitions describing how data is used. A dictionary does not contain actual data, as a file does, only a mechanism to evaluate and enhance the contents of such data being inputed.

During the late sixties and early seventies, database systems relied extensively on data dictionaries, such as the IMS DB/DC hierarchical model or the IDMS/DC technology. (DC stands for data communication, which is a teleprocessing monitor.) Non-database systems on the other hand, utilized a one-dimensional file structure without the ability to expand or implode their component segments and, of course, lacking the ability to respond well to highly volatile situations. In a typical fourth generation business environment, all data requirements are filtered through an active data dictionary that defines a set of attributes for the incoming data in terms of length, type, disposition, storage, contents, associated edit rules, and a number of additional format requirements.

If you were to change the length of the zip code from five to nine positions, for example, and perhaps the disposition of the field from alphanumeric to numeric one, you only need to do it in a central place and without having to overhaul every single file connected with that particular piece of data.

When you write code using a fourth generation language, you need to reference the very same item name both in your program and in the data dictionary. Thus, you need to define the requirements in the dictionary prior to referencing them in your code.

In a fourth generation business environment, the dictionary is where certain logical rules and procedures, which would otherwise require extensive programming, are defined. This concept of utilizing a dictionary rather than an application program will enable you to define a rule only once, not repeatedly in every program referring to that rule.

This does several things for you. First of all, it simplifies the sometimes complex and repetitious task of program development. Second, this methodology gives the user a greater degree of responsibility and involvement in standardizing a set of procedures.

The Expert Dictionary, like any state-of-the-art dictionary has its own maintenance mechanism that enables you to maintain this infrastructure, that is, the ability to add change, delete, replace, inquire, browse, and report on any number of data items contained in the dictionary.

The maintenance of the Expert Dictionary is normally accomplished through a set of vendor utilities or through the fourth generation Expert Language. Overall, it is made up of four types of data entity definitions: items, groups, records, and data frames. Items are the smallest unit in the structure, which represents a single data field. They are the lowest level at which you can access and describe data to I.E. The employee's social security number, starting date, or marital status can be viewed as a single item classifiable into a logical unit, such as a group. An item in the data dictionary is made up of a number of attributes:

- an item name and its associated length;
- its type, determining whether the item is an alphanumeric or a numeric field or simply a subscript;
- decimal positions, if that piece of information happens to be a numeric entity;
- date storage format (mainly for internally generated date fields);
- default column headings;
- default print format; and
- value description.

The item name is a mandatory attribute for reasons of reference. Once placed on the dictionary, it needs to conform to certain edit rules. It must be made up of at least one, but not exceeding thirty characters, and the first position must be an alpha character. Storage format describes specific data to the dictionary, that is just how the data appear to the computer, whether it is numeric or packed, or whether it has a sign, and so forth. A more comprehensive "type" list is as follows:

Type "A" represents an alphanumeric field;

Type "N" is a signed zoned numeric item;

Type "O" (alpha "O") refers to an unsigned numeric (zoned) item;

Type "P" is a signed packed numeric field;

Type "Q", an unsigned packed numeric; and

Type "S", which is a subscript.

The length and the decimal position of an item is also important: the first tells the dictionary just how many characters are stored in the item, the latter shows its decimal positions.

In order to print or display the contents of the dictionary, print formats and conventions in general need to be understood. Print formats describe how an item is to be printed and "masked" in case it is different from the original definition. Actually, print formats are optional; if none is given for an item, I.E. defaults to a set of rules. Among these are zero suppression for numbers as well as negative or positive flags such as "-", "CR", "DR", parentheses, floating dollar signs, and so on. Figure 9.1, illustrates certain item values and the resulting printouts.

The second level of information in this dictionary structure is the group. The group is a collection of items that can be viewed as a single unit. This flexibility enables you to refer to more than one item at a time in reference to a group. For example, an address is normally made up of a number of items such as a street address, city and state, zip code (and a country)—some five components, overall, that can be subclassified into the group: "EMPLOYEE-ADDRESS".

The third level of information in this hierarchical structure is the record, which is the further expansion of the above group concept. Look, for example, at an employee database and arrange it into segments such as a "deduction segment," a "demographic segment," a "retroactive pay segment," and so on. (Please note that the term "segment" is this author's terminology meaning a logical category of information.) Thus, a demographic segment, in this particular instance, contains several logical categories or groups such as the employee's educational background, formal work experience, skills inventory, position control, and so on, all of which could be thought of as a physical record.

ITEM VALUE	TOTAL LENGTH	PRINT FORMAT	PRINTED RESULT
0001234567	10N2	$99,999,999.00	$00,012,345.67
0001234567	10N2	$ZZ,ZZZ,ZZZ.99	$ 12,345.67
1234567	7N2	$$$,$$$.99	$12,345.67
-1234567	7N2	$ZZ,ZZZ.99CR	$12,345.67CR
-1234567	7N2	($ZZ,ZZZ.99)	($12,345.67)
1234567	7N2	$ZZ,ZZZ.99+	$12,345.67+
0001234567	10N2	$** ,***,***.99	$****12,345.67

Figure 9.1   These are print formats through various masks used by I.E.

This leads to the definition of a single data frame, which is a collection of application-related data that need to be accessed for a specific reporting purpose. A data frame is a logical entity of a database; it is made up of at least one (or more) physical databases required by your application system. For example, you may view the customer vendor database, which is part of your accounts payable system, but, in order to produce the necessary detail, you will also need to utilize parts of the general ledger year-to-date file. What you must do in this particular instance is combine the two physical databases into a logical data frame. Combining the two, does not simply mean merging them. Rather, it refers to a situation where you extract only the necessary items from each physical file and move them into their logical counterpart.

To create a data frame, you need to define the following delimiters to I.E.:

- A name: In order to reference a data frame you need to give it a name.

- You also need to define the type, which refers to a particular access method processable by the I.E. environment. This can be a sequential batch dataset, VSAM, a logical type, or a report view. Sequential datasets are the simplest kind. VSAM data sets offer a number of options, but from a practical point of view only the KSDS (Key Sequenced Dataset) method is viable. Logical types refer to the relationship between the logical data frame and its associated physical databases. A Report view is I.E.'s ability to allow viewing of a report on-line before a printout is requested to make sure that such a report is in its final format.

- A logical interface module (LIM) name is an optional entry. To expand on this a bit, LIM gives the I.E. reporting module the flexibility to satisfy more demanding I/O processing requirements to take on relatively complex tasks.

- File assignment name is an optional feature, which describes the name of the particular file to the I.E. system. (To clarify these topics, a file assignment name is simply the DDNAME that follows the IBM JCL nomenclature for an OS or DOS environment.)

- Dataset name is the definition of the file known as the DSN (or simply DSNAME) that further describes the file.

- Maximum record length refers to the number of positions in the record, which cannot exceed 4096 bytes per record.

- Record format can be fixed blocked, fixed, variable blocked and variable.

- Block size and key length are also required delimiters.

Block size (BLKSI) specifies the length of a block of records (in bytes) that makes up the data frame. Note that the block size cannot exceed 32K. Key length (KEYLN) refers to the length of the physical key in each record (whether simple or concatenated) that works in conjunction with the location of such a key (KEYLOC) to indicate just where in that record the key is located. Most of these delimiters will be discussed further in subsequent sections.

9.2 Data Dictionary and the Expert Language

Once you have defined all the required terms to the Expert Dictionary, it is important to have some sort of a methodology to either print or display all that information for future reference. After all, what good is all that wealth of information if you have no access to it. For one thing, you can use a number of vendor utilities to find out about the contents of your dictionary, which involves a series of dictionary reports. This is a valuable tool since you need to know the specific application window to perform a job effectively. This, incidentally, is the purpose of a machine generated-documentation—to keep your vital information current and in a readily usable format. Figure 9.2 shows the detail associated with a data frame. EICUSBAS is the short name for a basic customer data frame using a total of eight characters to identify the contents of that data frame. In order to develop code using such a data frame, you need to look at the individual item components.

Figure 9.2 is a comprehensive summary of the I.E. documentation report, which gives you a fairly good explanation as to why and how a particular data frame has been created, its uses, and its relation to other data frames in the I.E. environment.

The technical information definition relates to whether the data frame is structured or nonstructured. A structured data frame is a way that I.E. identifies a particular record to this fourth generation environment. The term "RELATE" should be a familiar one. As you recall from the case study in Chapter 8, you have used the RELATE statement to combine two or more of physical databases to arrive at a single (logical) data frame for your reporting needs. "ORGANIZED BY" specifies the sequence of the information. Fields displayed here represent the actual sequence of the data. For example:

ORGANIZED BY IE-EMPLOYEE-ID

IE-EMPLOYEE-DEPARTMENT-NUMBER

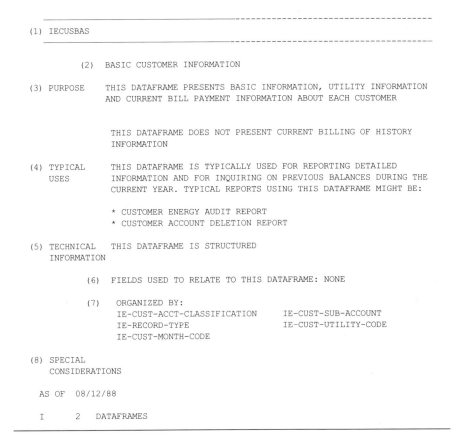

```
(1) IECUSBAS    -----------------------------------------
                -----------------------------------------

        (2)  BASIC CUSTOMER INFORMATION

(3) PURPOSE     THIS DATAFRAME PRESENTS BASIC INFORMATION, UTILITY INFORMATION
                AND CURRENT BILL PAYMENT INFORMATION ABOUT EACH CUSTOMER


                THIS DATAFRAME DOES NOT PRESENT CURRENT BILLING OF HISTORY
                INFORMATION

(4) TYPICAL     THIS DATAFRAME IS TYPICALLY USED FOR REPORTING DETAILED
    USES        INFORMATION AND FOR INQUIRING ON PREVIOUS BALANCES DURING THE
                CURRENT YEAR. TYPICAL REPORTS USING THIS DATAFRAME MIGHT BE:

                * CUSTOMER ENERGY AUDIT REPORT
                * CUSTOMER ACCOUNT DELETION REPORT

(5) TECHNICAL   THIS DATAFRAME IS STRUCTURED
    INFORMATION

        (6)  FIELDS USED TO RELATE TO THIS DATAFRAME: NONE

        (7)  ORGANIZED BY:
             IE-CUST-ACCT-CLASSIFICATION    IE-CUST-SUB-ACCOUNT
             IE-RECORD-TYPE                 IE-CUST-UTILITY-CODE
             IE-CUST-MONTH-CODE

(8) SPECIAL
    CONSIDERATIONS

   AS OF   08/12/88

   I    2   DATAFRAMES
```

Figure 9.2   This is an overview of a data frame through the I.E. documentation report.

IE-EMPLOYEE-STATUS-CODE means that the report series will be ordered by the employee's identifier, which is the major sort component, followed by the department (also known as an intermediate sort field), and last by the status code, which is the minor sort component.

Special consideration pertains to a number of special topics relative to both the user and the specific data frame in question. A more refined way to dictionary reporting is achieved on the item level which is listed alphabetically the same way as the data frame. Figure 9.3 is an overview of that listing. Note that the item indicator tells I.E. whether the system is dealing with a single item or a group of items. Accordingly, an "I" tells you that you are dealing with an item, and a "G" simply refers to a group of such items.

```
(1)   EI-CUS-SUB-ACCOUNT                          (2)  (I)


(3)   COL HEADING:   SUB
                     ACCOUNT

(4)   LENGTH:    6 (5) TYPE:  ALPHANUMERIC  (6) DECIMAL:  0   (7) DATE: N/A

(8)   FORMAT:

(9)   DESCRIPTION:  THE NUMBER WHICH UNIQUELY IDENTIFIES THE ACCOUNT. THIS
                    NUMBER IS COMBINED WITH THE ACCOUNT CLASSIFICATION
                    TO FORM THE CUSTOMER ACCOUNT NUMBER
```

Figure 9.3 The summarizing an item in the dictionary report series is demonstrated.

Copyright © 1988 Management Science America, Inc. Used by permission.

Column heading essentially describes the constant or the title header that appears over the corresponding item. In this particular situation the column header will bear the title "SUB,ACCOUNT". If this is left out, the title "IE CUST SUB ACCOUNT" will appear, which is an automatic default. I.E. allows you to define and print a maximum of four header or title lines. Each line may not exceed thirty characters in length. The header will be centered over each column of the data. When you use commas, they will simply indicate that you need a break in the title heading.

```
 M S A  INFORMATION EXPERT———— DATAFRAME DIRECTORY LIST

  DATAFRAME        DESCRIPTION OF DATAFRAME            NOTES:
  ————            ——————————————
                               To list the contents
                                                     of a dataframe,
  IEABBREV        ABBREVIATION REGISTER              enter an S next to
  IECUSBAS        BASIC CUSTOMER MASTER DATAFRAME    the name, press the
  IECUSBIL        BILLING MASTER FILE                ENTER key
  IECUSINS        UTILITY INSTALLATION FRAME
  IEDICENT        I.E. DICT ENTITY DETAIL DEF
  IEDICENU        I.E. DICT ENTITY USAGE DEF
  IEDOCDEC        I.E. DICTIONARY DOC DESC
  IEDOCDV         DATAFRAME DOCUMENTATION
  IEDOCIT         ITEM AND GROUP DOCUMENTATION
  IEHIST          CUSTOMER HISTORY FRAME
  IEIMSDOC        IMS DATAFRAME DOCUMENTATION

  PRESS:   ENTER Process  PF1 Help  PF6  Top  PF7 Page Bwd  PF8 Page Fwd —
```

Figure 9.4 This demonstrates displaying the data frame contents of the dictionary.

```
M S A  INFORMATION EXPERT  ――― LIST CONTENTS OF DATAFRAME IECUSBAS

FIND DATA NAME:

                                          FLD   NBR  DEC  DT
ITEM / GROUP NAME             LVL  DISPL  TYPE  SIZE  DIG  POS  CD  OCCS
────────────────         ─  ─     ─   ─ ─ ─  ─


IE-CUST-ACCT-BASIC-INFO-REC   00    0     A     80
IE-CUST-ACCOUNT-NUMBER        01    0     A      7
IE-CUST-ACCOUNT-CLASSIFICATION 02   0     A      1
IE-CUST-SUB-ACCOUNT           02    1     A      8
IE-RECORD-TYPE               01    7     A      1
IE-CUST-UTILITY-CODE         01    8     A      1
IE-CUST-MONTH-CODE           01    9     A      2
IE-CUST-ACCT-DELETE-CODE     01   11     A      1
IE-CUST-ACCT-DELETE-DATE     01   12     O      6   6    0    2
IE-CUST-NAME                 01   18     A     30
IE-CUST-PHONE-NUMBER         01   48     A     10
FILLER                       01   58     A     22

IE-CUST-ADDRESS-RECORD        00    0     A     80
IE-CUST-ACCOUNT-NUMBER        01    0     A      7


ACTION _____  1 HELP  3 End  4 File Attr  6 Top  7 Pg Bwd  8  Pg Fwd
```

Figure 9.5 This is the contents of the IECUSBAS data frame.

Print facilities are part of the I.E. utilities since you always need to know the contents of a particular data frame for your programming reference. However, the system also enables you to display the required information on-line, as was indicated in the step-by-step overview of the language. An expansion of this is shown in Figure 9.4. The actual contents of the above data frame are further magnified in Figure 9.5.

Figure 9.4 gives you a list of all data frame definitions available in reference to a particular library. You may choose from the list by placing an S next to the data frame and by pressing enter. This will initiate a detailed list of all those items that make up the data frame. In the previous chapter, a similar on-line item/group definition panel was presented for the customer billing and customer rate databases, which were a prerequisite for developing source code.

9.3   How to Maintain the Expert Dictionary

Think of the Expert Dictionary as an on-line file that needs to be maintained periodically, just like any other file, against a great number of transactions. This means that the Data Dictionary is an unusually volatile "master" file, since any minor change you make on the application would immediately be reflected here.

You can maintain the Expert Dictionary either batch or on-line. In batch mode, you need to specify an UPDATE DICTIONARY command, which will alert the system that all subsequent entries will relate to a set of dictionary maintenance related activities. The on-line dictionary procedures are a great deal more user friendly. Once you invoke the On-line Support Facilities (OSF), you can simply bypass the UPDATE DICTIONARY route and have most of the required utility statements automatically generated by the system. Although the Expert Dictionary can be maintained on-line on several levels, this discussion will focus on the technical aspect of maintaining a particular data frame (as opposed to an item), or other smaller data components.

By definition, a data frame is a logical collection of data needed for specific business reporting. Since most of the reporting in the I.E. environment depends on a number of physical files or databases, a data frame is merely a logical view, or a composite of these physical databases. There are three commands associated with the maintenance of a data frame, these are the ADD DATAFRAME, the DELETE DATAFRAME, and the REPLACE DATAFRAME commands.

If you look at the syntax of an ADD command (Figure 9.6), you will see that the individual statements therein are standard OS/MVS or else DOS (VSE) job control type statements. In order to add a new data frame to the dictionary, say "ADD DATAFRAME", followed by the specific name of that data frame. The term "type," which is a required piece of information, refers to one of four types of data frames. The first type is sequentially organized. A second type may be defined as a VSAM dataset, accommodating all three access methods. A third type pertains to one that is processable by MSA's logical interface module. A fourth type is commonly referred to as a "report view" containing extracted records used in a print series.

The "MODNM" delimiter is a logical interface module (which is a program written in ANS COBOL) that retrieves a given application or a particular database. Note that this is only required when your data frame is specified as "logical," otherwise you can simply omit this delimiter. To clarify what is mandatory and what is not, look at Figure 9.7 which will

```
ADD DATAFRAME dataframe-name

TYPE (dataframe-type)

[MODNM (logical-interface-module-name)]

[DDNAME (ddname)]

[DSN (data-set-name)]

[LRECL (maximum-record-length)]

[RECFM (record-format)]

[BLKSI (blocksize)]

[KEYLN (length-of-key)]

[KEYLOC (key-location)]

[ORGANIZED BY component1.....]

CONTAINS [AT component2 [LEVEL]] record-name...
```

Figure 9.6 These are the syntax requirements for the ADD DATAFRAME command.

	TYPE			
PARAMETER	LOGICAL	REPORT VIEW	SEQ	VSAM
MODNM	R	N	N	N
DDNAME			O	O
DSN			O	O
LRECL			R	O
RECFM			R	R
BLKSI			O	O
KEYLN			O	O
KEYLOC			O	O
ORGANIZED BY	O		O	O
CONTAINS	R		R	R

```
R= REQUIRED
O= OPTIONAL
BLANK = NOT USED OR NOT APPLICABLE
```

Figure 9.7 This shows parameters in the add syntax and their respective function.

explain some of the basic requirements in the ADD syntax. Make a note of the symbols used to identify the various types: "R" meaning mandatory and "O" meaning optional. Also note that certain delimiters are not used or applicable in a given situation designated by the lack of an entry.

Suppose you need to add a nonstructured data frame to the Expert Dictionary that is a sequential file. Records on this file are 200 positions long, blocked 10, and contain fixed blocking. Also, the key referring to the employee's identification number (which happens to be his or her social security number) is a nine-position-long field starting in column 1. There is only a single record type on this file which is the PAYROLL-PAY-SEGMENT. Figure 9.8 is a brief overview of the above requirements. The RECL (definition for the record length), the RECFM (denoting a specific record format, such as fixed or fixed block or a variable record type), and the BLKSIZE (block size) are standard JCL delimiters.

In Figure 9.8, the file is organized by the EMPLOYEE-NUMBER, which is the major sort sequence, then, by the PAY-CENTER, and finally by the DEPARTMENT-CODE. The CONTAIN clause tells I.E. that the incoming file contains a single record type (PAYROLL-PAY-SEGMENT) that pertains to some gross-to-net calculations.

The mechanics of the REPLACE DATAFRAME are identical to the ADD command in terms of syntax. The purpose of this command, is to replace the definition of a data frame that already exists in the dictionary. Note that, in both instances, the CONTAINS AT clause refers to a structured data frame.

A NONSTRUCTURED data frame can contain one or more records defined to the dictionary. When triggering such a data frame, I.E. presents one record at a time for processing and printing. If you have more than a single record type in a data frame, the system will make no attempt to distinguish one record type from another.

A STRUCTURED data frame, on the other hand, contains a natural structure or hierarchy, defined to I.E. Structured data frames usually contain at least two different record types. The set of records is determined by the ORGANIZED BY and the CONTAINS AT LEVEL clauses of the data frame definition. If these two clauses are present, the data frame is said to be a structured one. The set of records refers to one of each records defined in the CONTAINS AT LEVEL clause. Thus, as an addendum to Figure 9.8, the structured concept, which is the purpose of Figure 9.9, is also illustrated.

In order to delete a data frame, you only need to specify to I.E. the name of the data frame to be deleted. Thus, the Syntax is short and sweet:

DELETE DATAFRAME PAYFILE

```
ADD DATAFRAME  PAYFILE        ;
TYPE (SEQ)                    ;
DDNAME (PAYREC)               ;
LRECL (200)                   ;
RECFM (FB)                    ;
BLKSIZE (2000)                ;
KEYLEN (9)                    ;
KEYLOC (1)                    ;
ORGANIZED BY EMPLOYEE-ID      ;
             PAY-CENTER       ;
             DEPARTMENT       ;
CONTAINS PAYROLL-PAY-SEGMENT
```

Figure 9.8   These are commands to add a new nonstructured data frame.

```
ADD DATAFRAME  PAYFILE        ;
TYPE (SEQ)                    ;
DDNAME (PAYREC)               ;
LRECL (200)                   ;
RECFM (FB)                    ;
BLKSIZE (2000)                ;
KEYLEN (9)                    ;
KEYLOC (1)                    ;
ORGANIZED BY EMPLOYEE-ID      ;
             PAY-CENTER       ;
             DEPARTMENT       ;
CONTAINS                      ;
   AT EMPLOYEE-ID             ;
      LEVEL EMPLOYEE-RECORD   ;
   AT PAY-CENTER              ;
      LEVEL CHECK-REGISTER    ;
   AT DEPARTMENT              ;
      LEVEL DEPT SUMMARY
```

Figure 9.9   These are commands to add a new structured data frame .

9.4   I.E. Security Models

I.E. is a comprehensive network of security modules allowing you to secure the following:

- data frames defined on the Expert Dictionary,
- functions of I.E. OSF and corresponding batch functions, and
- access to public libraries.

The primary purpose of this section is to explore the first aspect of I.E. security only, which deals with that of a data frame. In order to establish security for data frames, there are certain basic components that make the preceding possible. These are the access list and the security group. An access list is merely a set of rules defined by your company authorizing some specific users or user groups to have access to certain data frames. Who has access to what information, of course is an administrative issue that is normally handled by a security administrator once the rules are agreed upon by the responsible parties. Each time a user attempts to access a data frame that has been secured to an access list, I.E. determines the user's access by evaluating the access list.

To visualize this process of evaluation, you need to understand the use of access list statements and key words that function practically like reserved words do in a program. One of the key-words used in this system is "ALLOW" which defines a list of users or user groups and the access type allowed for each. ALLOW works in conjunction with IF and ELSE conditional logic. An access list, as a rule, can and does contain many conditional statements, each specifying a combination of users and accesses as well as user groups and accesses for a given condition.

"DEFAULT" is another keyword that defines an access type for all users not specifically mentioned in the access list. Actually, both ALLOW and DEFAULT statements can be expressed in terms of certain access values, such as allowing (or simply denying) a user to view a specific set of data on the terminal. When you use the IF and ELSE logic, I.E. enables you to rely on a set of Boolean statements such as:

EQ when conditions are equal,

NE when conditions are not equal,

GT a greater than condition,

LT a less than condition,

GE meaning a compound situation such as greater than or equal to, and

LE meaning less than or equal to.

Along with these logical operands, the vendor also provides you with a set of "Globals." Globals are values that are maintained by the system using predefined formats, such as the one shown in Figure 9.10.

Another component of securing a data frame has to do with the security groups, which represent a collection of data frames that have a common security need. A security group is simply a pointer from the data frames to an access list. Using security groups, you can change the security of a number of data frames without changing each data frame individually. You establish security for a data frame when you point it (reference it) to an

Name	Length & type	Values, notes formats, etc.
#DAY-OF-WEEK	12AN	Values: 'Sunday' — 'Saturday'
#GROUPID	8AN	Description: specifies the ID of the user group with which the operator is associated during this session job
#TERMINAL.ID	8AN	Description: specifies the terminal the operator is using
#THIS-MONTH	2N	Format: MM
#THIS-DATE	2N	Format: DD
#THIS-YEAR	4N	Format: YYYY
#TIME	5AN	Format: HH:MM
#TODAYS-DATE	7N	Format: YYYYDDD
#USERID	8AN	Description: specifies the user ID of the operator

Figure 9.10   This is the global value table used by I.E.

access list. Another aspect of defining security is that, instead of pointing a data frame directly to an access list, you can point it to a security group.

To illustrate this point note the following paths:

DF ————————> AL
DF ————————> SG
DF————————> SG ————————> AL

where DF stands for a data frame (or frames), AL for an access list and SG for a security group.

Typically, groups of data frames are based on the level of security needed (for example, high, medium, low) and the category of the data (for example, specific parts of an application or business entity—salary, invoice, journal entry, etc.). An overview of this concept is presented in Figure 9.11. I referred to the term "SECURing" before. You need to use the SECURE statement, that is to point a data frame to an access list or to a security group.

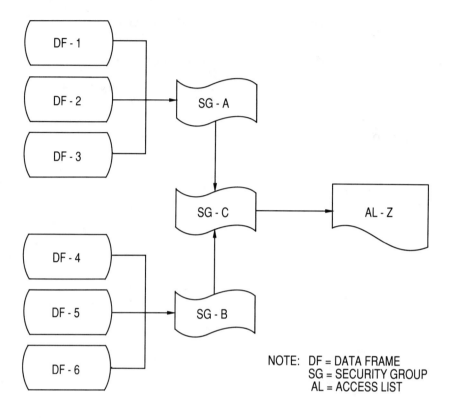

Figure 9.11   This diagram summerizes the concepts behind security groups.

Another component in this environment identifies a particular user or user group for security considerations. Actually, a user can be included in a number of (user) groups, not just one. However, the user can only be associated with one user group during a given on-line session or batch job. To simplify things, the user will have to specify the user group with which he or she wants to be associated during a given session. This is important, since the security system only recognizes the user group with which the user is associated during the current job/session. This concept has numerous advantages. If several individual users share a security need, you can define a user group to contain these users. Once you have defined such a group, you can refer to the group, rather than to the individual users when you create the access list. (In other words, you can refer to the entire group rather than to the individual users.) Thus, if security rules for a user group change, then only one maintenance change is required, versus maintenance for each individual user.

Users can be grouped in terms of types of functions they perform in their jobs, their responsibility levels, etc. Users might also be grouped in terms of the type of data they access; such as personnel, budget marketing, or business entity, like salary, invoice, journal entry, etc.

Assume you want to set up two data frames (PERSNL and PAYRL) to be viewed by John, Fred, and Mark. Combine the two data frames into one security group (RESOURC1) and the three individuals—John, Fred, and Mark into a user group (USRJFM). Statements describing the implementation of these requirements are shown in Figure 9.12. In the above example, the term "USRJFM" was used to describe such a group that is made up by John, Fred, and Mark.

A brief overview of the preceding material is presented in Figure 9.13. Suppose that you now want to combine data frames PERSNL and PAYRL into a security group such as RESOURC1. Afterward, you want to specify the individual users, a situation highlighted in Figure 9.14. Assume John, Fred and Mark can see the data associated with the particular data frames, while a fourth person, Rick, can only see it during the first of the month.

First you must consolidate both PERSNL and PAYRL data frames into a security group RESOURC1, then, combine the three users with the unrestricted view (John, Fred, and Mark) into a user group (USRJFM). Using a conditional criteria (as illustrated in Figure 9.15) add Rick's security arrangements to it.

```
UTILITY
ADD USER-GROUP USRJFM            ;
INCLUDE IN USRJFM                ;
      JOHN                       ;
      FRED                       ;
      MARK                       ;
UPDATE DICTIONARY
ADD ACCESS-LIST SECPAY1 FOR DATAFRAME    ;
DEFAULT (NONE)                           ;
ALLOW USRJFM (VIEW)
ADD SEC-GROUP RESOURC1 FOR DATAFRAME
SECURE PERSNL USING RESOURC1
SECURE PAYRL USING RESOURC1
SECURE RESOURC1 USING SECPAY1
```

Figure 9.12 This is the initial security set-up for the first case.

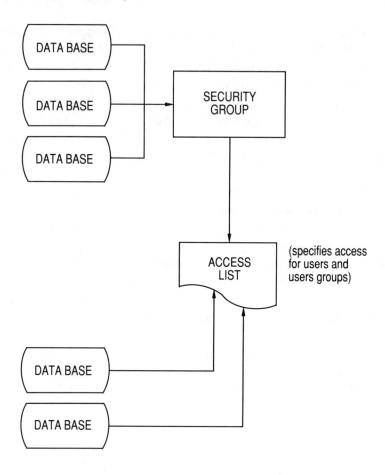

Figure 9.13   This flowchart represents the basic concept of data security (arrow represents SECURE statements).

Suppose Fred leaves the department no longer requiring access to the PERSNL and PAYRL data frames. You simply say

UTILITY

REMOVE FROM USRJFM FRED

Assume now, that Fred's transfer triggers new security measures that are to become effective immediately. Accordingly, Rick is now the only person to have access to the PERSNL data frame. Another data frame POSCNT has the same security criteria as PAYRL. Rick can see the data on the first and the fifteenth of each month, but has no access to the file the rest of the time. Figure 9.16 shows the required statements for the implementation of this particular policy.

```
 UPDATE DICTIONARY
 ADD ACCESS-LIST SECPAY1 FOR DATAFRAME     ;
 DEFAULT (NONE)                            ;
 ALLOW JOHN (VIEW)                         ;
 ALLOW FRED (VIEW)                         ;
 ALLOW MARK (VIEW)
 ALLOW USRJFM (VIEW)
 ADD SEC-GROUP RESOURC1 FOR DATAFRAME
 SECURE PERSNL USING RESOURC1
 SECURE PAYRL USING RESOURC1
 SECURE RESOURC1 USING SECPAY1
```

Figure 9.14   This is the second security case review.

```
 UTILITY
 ADD USER-GROUP USRJFM           ;
 INCLUDE IN USRJFM               ;
       JOHN                      ;
       FRED                      ;
       MARK                      ;
 UPDATE DICTIONARY
 ADD ACCESS-LIST SECPAY1 FOR DATAFRAME     ;
 DEFAULT (NONE)                            ;
 ALLOW USRJFM (VIEW)                       ;
 IF #THIS-DATE EQ 01                       ;
 ALLOW RICK (VIEW)
 ADD SEC-GROUP RESOURC1 FOR DATAFRAME
 SECURE PERSNL USING RESOURC1
 SECURE PAYRL USING RESOURC1
 SECURE RESOURC1 USING SECPAY1
```

Figure 9.15   This is the third security implementation.

```
 UPDATE DICTIONARY
 ADD ACCESS-LIST SECPAY2 FOR DATAFRAME     ;
 DEFAULT (NONE)                            ;
 IF #THIS-DATE EQ 01                       ;
 OR #THIS-DATE EQ 15                       ;
 ALLOW RICK (VIEW)
 SECURE PERSNL USING SECPAY2
 SECURE POSCNTL USING USRJFM
```

Figure 9.16   These are maintenance security specifications.

Before establishing data frame security, you will have to evaluate your security needs. Security needs in general fall into two main categories—those having to do with users, and those having to do with data. Your best bet is to evaluate each of these areas independently of the other and then combine the results of the evaluation through a matching process—a combined data and user evaluation.

The steps involved in such a data evaluation are as follows:

- List your data frames. You can list the data frames in your Expert Data Dictionary using standard Expert Language reports.

- Determine which applications are used for the same application or business entity—such as invoice, vendor, or salary information.

- Determine which data frames have like security requirements.

- Determine any overlap between the groups of data frames with like security requirements and the groups of data frames used by the same business entity. Ask yourself the following questions:

–Can anyone see the information in this data frame? Collect all data frames that you answer "yes" into one group. Since there are no restrictions on who can see the data in the field(s) supported by the data frame, the DEFAULT access is VIEW in the access list associated with the group of data frames.

–Can almost anyone see the information in the file supported by the data frame? Collect all data frames whose data are available to anyone into one group. For other data frames, ask yourself, "Under what circumstances can someone see the data in the data frame?" By answering the above (and similar) questions, you will be able to develop a set of standard criteria instrumental to provide (or deny) a particular user group access to data. If the answer to the above question is conditional based on time-related variables, date-related variables or user- or terminal-related variables, access to the data frame can be controlled using stand-alone ALLOW statements and/or the IF ELSE statement with DEFAULT and/or ALLOW statements for each conditional statement.

If the answer to the above question involves data-related variables (such as a pay frequency or an account number, for example), you cannot conditionally secure the data frame. If you decide that certain users can see the data conditionally, or unconditionally, you can place data frames with like security access requirements together or you can create an access list just for that data frame.

Summary

The Expert Dictionary is the sole driver of this state-of-the-art apparatus where everything you need to know or access is centrally defined.

A data dictionary, by definition, is a central repository of rules and definitions pertaining to the data, but not the actual data. In the earlier days, only formal database systems relied on data dictionaries, such as the IMS DB/DC or IDMS DC technology. (DC stands for data communication, which is a teleprocessing monitor.) Conventional systems, on the other hand, utilized a one-dimensional file structure, without the ability to expand or implode their component segments.

In a typical fourth generation business environment, all data requirements are filtered through an active data dictionary that defines a set of attributes for the incoming data in terms of length, type, disposition, storage, contents and a number of associated edit rules. In a fourth generation business environment, the dictionary is a place where certain rules (and logic) are defined, so that all that criteria need not be incorporated into each application program referencing the same procedure.

The Expert Dictionary is made up of items groups, records and data frames. Items are the smallest unit in the structure representing a single data field. They are the lowest level at which you can access and describe data to I.E. Print formats tell I.E. how an item is to be printed and "masked" in case it's different from the original definition. The second level of information in this dictionary structure is the group, which is a collection of items that can be viewed as a single unit. This flexibility enables you to refer to more than one item at a time via a group. The third level of information is the record, which is the expansion of the above group concept.

I.E. has a comprehensive network of security modules allowing you to secure:

- data frames defined on the Expert Dictionary,
- functions of I.E. OSF and corresponding batch functions, and
- access to public libraries.

Chapter 10

Installing a Fourth Generation System—the Technician's View

10.1   Overview

This chapter focuses on the technician's responsibilities during the implementation process. Vendor packages do not follow the peculiarities of a system cycle. They essentially entail the requirements study phase and some modest programming activities either to customize or to enhance certain features inherent in the package. Systems testing takes on a totally different aspect, and it is normally marked by the following activities:

1. The testing of a demo module provided by the vendor mainly for tutorial reasons.

2. The testing of a limited portion of the system identical to the vendor's demo module, but utilizing the user's own database. This, in fact, requires the reinitialization of all demo files to create a "near" production environment.

3. Last, the saving of all interim files other than those that are transaction related.

In an accounts receivable system, for example, the user normally enters permanent customer related information on the customer master. Assuming that these are valid customers, you need to develop a routine to save that information when switching to a live, production environment. Transactions, on the other hand, need not be saved, since they are normally copies of past activities modified in some fashion. When you acquire a vendor package, you normally receive it on a tape containing both on-line and batch source code along with a set of load modules representing the object version of your programs. Also included on this tape, you will have all of the required Job Control Statements (JCL's), vendor utilities, control tables and an "unabridged" database for the demo system.

Fourth generation business systems deliver more than conventional utilities. They deliver an entire support environment in which to operate, modules such as the I.E. subsystem, the Millennium software, DCI, SDT, PDL, or the Financial Controller package and so forth. (Note that most, if not all of these items have been already discussed in prior chapters.)

Two major activities need to be highlighted here, both within the grasp of the technician involved in the implementation process. These are:

1. The selection of specific options from a more generalized set of vendor criteria; a process referred to as APPLICATION SYSTEMS GENERATION (or simply Sys.Genning), and

2. the customization of some of the control statements that will be used to set up daily or other timely activities.

10.2   The Application Systems Generation Process

IBM defines the systems generation process as one that "builds systems libraries that reflect your operating system's requirements. The systems generation or sysgen process selects modules from the IBM distribution libraries (DLIBs), optionally combines them with installation provided routines from one or more specified partitioned datasets, and places the modules and routines in the appropriate systems libraries." (OS/MVS XA Systems Generation Reference Guide.)

The Systems Generation process essentially runs a series of jobs in two stages. In the first stage, it assembles a set of macro instructions you provide and expands them into a job stream that consists of JCLs and utility type statements. Before the second stage is described, an explanation of the meaning of macros or macro instructions is needed.

The term DATASET, for example, is a macro statement because it can be used to define not just one, but a number of activities or instructions, such as to allocate space and catalog a particular file. It can also be used to invoke, among other things, user-written routines, parameters, or procedures that will then become part of the above file or dataset. The term IODEVICE, another macro statement, describes the characteristics of an input/output device, such as a printer, a telecommunications control unit, a terminal, or a variety of other devices.

The second state of the Systems Generation process continues utilizing the job stream created in stage I to assemble, link, edit, and copy modules from the DLIBs to the new systems datasets. The output from stage II is the new updated operating system's libraries including a documentation listing. An overview of this process is presented in Figure 10.0. The process of Systems Generation may not entirely be a doable process by the application side alone, without a substantial effort by the systems support side as well.

When you acquire a vendor package the Systems Generation process is normally channeled through the vendor's own set of programs, which are a combination of logical procedures, as well as standard IBM utilities. This will greatly simplify the sysgen-ning process to a set of choices presented to the analyst for his review and decision. Among these you will pick criteria applicable in your specific environment. Each criterion is presented in the form of questionnaire-like statements, similar in concept to macro

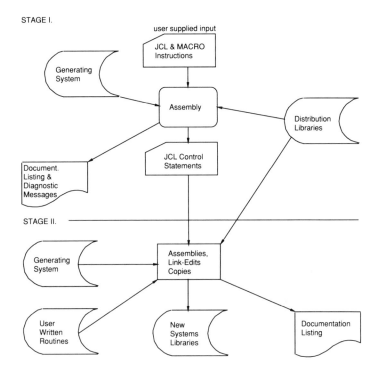

Figure 10.0 This shows the two stages of the systems generation process.

type instructions. The purpose of these macro base instructions is to generate a number of machine readable commands, thereby allowing the system to substitute each parameter and substitute it in an automatic fashion.

Step 11 of Figure 10.1 requires you to define a standard device for a direct access unit. Thus, if a generic vendor option is not applicable in your operating environment—such as using VSAM.DISK.UNIT(3380) spindles instead of 3350's—you may easily override the valid option by substituting it for the generic device type.

The term VSAM.DISK.UNIT(3380) is a dataset macro that I described to you in the beginning of this section. Actually you may also use an expression, such as "SYSDA", or "TEMP" to further qualify a dataset so it would be meaningful to you in differentiating temporary from permanent datasets or those especially allocated for a particular (dedicated) assignment.

The vendor makes it easy for you to activate the new device (VSAM.DISK.UNIT(3380)) by allowing you to remove the asterisk (*), so that the command that was previously "commented out" would be promptly activated. In this fashion, the above statement will scan the vendor's generic sets of JCL's, replacing all original (3350) device types with those of

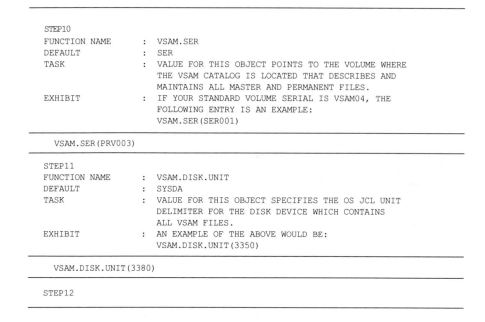

```
STEP10
FUNCTION NAME      :  VSAM.SER
DEFAULT            :  SER
TASK               :  VALUE FOR THIS OBJECT POINTS TO THE VOLUME WHERE
                      THE VSAM CATALOG IS LOCATED THAT DESCRIBES AND
                      MAINTAINS ALL MASTER AND PERMANENT FILES.
EXHIBIT            :  IF YOUR STANDARD VOLUME SERIAL IS VSAM04, THE
                      FOLLOWING ENTRY IS AN EXAMPLE:
                      VSAM.SER(SER001)
```

```
   VSAM.SER(PRV003)
```

```
STEP11
FUNCTION NAME      :  VSAM.DISK.UNIT
DEFAULT            :  SYSDA
TASK               :  VALUE FOR THIS OBJECT SPECIFIES THE OS JCL UNIT
                      DELIMITER FOR THE DISK DEVICE WHICH CONTAINS
                      ALL VSAM FILES.
EXHIBIT            :  AN EXAMPLE OF THE ABOVE WOULD BE:
                      VSAM.DISK.UNIT(3350)
```

```
   VSAM.DISK.UNIT(3380)
```

```
STEP12
```

Figure 10.1   This is the application system genning process.

3380's and resetting the location of that disk to point to the pack that contains volume PRV003. As previously mentioned, a simple statement can change and generate hundreds of corresponding statements and provide an automatic methodology to customize part of a generic software. Likewise, all VSAM04 variables will be replaced in step 10.1 with a specific unit, such as PXR003.

In reality, the application sysgenning process sometimes entails hundreds of steps ranging from file definitions to VSAM catalogs, to source program filters, to backup tape assignments, and so on. Consider some related questions on this topic:

- What release of CICS does your shop utilize: 1.6 or 1.7?

  Reply: 1.7

- Name the load library to be used in the system.

  Reply: NIRXT.AMCONS.ACCREC.CICSLIB

- Name your sort library Reply: SYS1.SORTLIB
- Name the "vol ser" number of the backup tape to be used to retain the Data Dictionary Reply: BACKUP.TAPE.VPLSER.DDICT(112342)
- Define the VOL SER (volume serial), on which your permanent disk files will be located: Reply: PERM.DISK.SER(PRIV009)

- Name your sort library to be used and referenced in this application.

  Reply: SORTLIB.NAME(SYS1.SORTLIB)

- Define your COBOL step library:

  Reply: COBOL.STEPLIB(SYS1.VSCLIB)

- Define your COBOL library:

  Reply: COBOL.LIBRARY(SYS1.COBLIB)

- Define your COBOL compiler:

  Reply: COBOL.COMPILER(IKFCBL00)

- Define you basic assembler macro library

  Reply: ASM.MACRO.LIB(SYS1..MACLIB)

- Define the prefix to be used in the accounts receivable application process

  Reply: PROC.PREFIX(AR)

In section 10.7 you will see how all these definitions will be generated after you have successfully loaded your application runstreams.

10.3   Definition of Generation Data Group Files

Since the system requires the definition of a series of files, this is probably the best time for you to set up all Generation data groups. A generation data group (GDG) is chronologically and functionally related datasets. GDG's, in fact, simplify the batch processing aspect of the system, since they essentially enable you to retain different versions of the same file without altering the dataset name.

Assume your company runs a semimonthly payroll. This means that you need to update the check register file twice a month, utilizing the latest information. Without relying on GDG's, you would need to keep track of each dataset separately, rather than to have the system do it for you, which could be a messy, if not a totally unmanageable task when placed into a production environment. Using the GDG concept, the most current version of the file is always zero: it will drop down to a -1, at the time another version of the same file is created, then to a -2 and a -3 until the "depth" definition of the file is finally exhausted. Thus, if you want to refer to a certain check register that was generated during the last processing cycle, you can simply say "-1". Likewise, -2 refers to the check register that was

```
//VARSEG  JOB  (1233,AVR),NOTIFY=VARSEGI,CLASS=A,
//     MSGLEVEL=(1,1),MSGCLASS=X,REGION=4096K
//* BUILD GENERATION DATA GROUPS
//DEFGDG  EXEC PGM=IDCAMS
//SYSPRINT DD SYSOUT=(*)
//SYSIN  DD  *,DCB=BLKSIZE=80
  DEFINE GENERATIONDATAGROUP
  (NAME(PAYROLL.SEMIMO.PROC1)
  LIMIT(6)
  SCRATCH)
  DEFINE GENERATIONDATAGROUP
  (NAME(PAYTOLL.MONTHLY.PROC1)
  LIMIT(6)
  SCRATCH)
  DEFINE GENERATIONDATAGROUP
  (NAME(PAYTOLL.BIWEEK.PROC1)
  LIMIT(6)
  SCRATCH)
```

Figure 10.2 This is a screen for creating generation data groups for the new system.

created a month ago, while -6 contains transactions that were created some 90 days prior to that, provided that the depth of the generations is extensive enough for such a retention.

Just how many file generations you should keep depends on the circumstances. Back-up frequencies are important issues, especially if there is a need to refer to historical generations. GDG's can be expensive, since they tend to tie up machine resources, depending on the overall volume of each file and the device type, such as a 3380 direct access device as opposed to a couple of reels of tapes.

Generation numbers, of course, are automatically monitored (and assigned) by the system and updated every time a new dataset is about to be created. (IBM limits each GDG to a maximum of 255 entries.) With regards to the previously mentioned check register, it is altogether possible that you need to rerun a particular job before producing a final version. What this amounts to is that during such a reiterative process, you may be creating a number of extra generations, some of which will need to be uncataloged to maintain normal generation patterns. Figure 10.2 gives you an example of building such GDG indices for three files. These are the PAYROLL.SEMIMO.PROC1, PAYROLL.MONTHLY.PROC1, and PAYROLL.BIWEEKLY.PROC1 files. Note that an IBM utility called IDCAMS is used to define to the system the above GDG files.

The term LIMIT refers to the number of generations that should be monitored by the operating system, so that when the new (+1) generation is created, the oldest generation catalogued would be dropped from the GDG "library." Technically speaking, the file in this discussion does not actually get deleted. It simply gets uncataloged and dropped from the GDG index,

```
//VARSEG  JOB  (1233,AVR),NOTIFY=VARSEGI,CLASS=A,
//     MSGLEVEL=(1,1),MSGCLASS=X,REGION=4096K
//* DEFINE VSAM CLUSTERS
//DEFVSAM EXEC PGM=IDCAMS
//SYSPRINT DD SYSOUT=(*)
//SYSIN  DD  *,DCB=BLKSIZE=80
  DEFINE CLUSTER (NAME(AR.TRANSACT) -
  FILE(ARVSAM) -
  VOL(VOLS02) -
  CYL(55, 2) -
  RECORDSIZE(550 550) -
  KEYS(9 0) -
  UNIQUE) -

  DEFINE CLUSTER (NAME(AR.INVOIC) -
  FILE(INVSAM) -
  VOL(VOLS03) -
  CYL(10, 1) -
  RECORDSIZE(150 150) -
  KEYS(9 5) -
  UNIQUE) -
```

Figure 10.3   These are the VSAM clusters for the new system.

which, unless the file is overlayed with new information, still contains the original data.

10.4   Cluster Definition for VSAM

Another step in the implementation process is to build the required direct access files, a process referred to as creating VSAM clusters. The term "clusters" simply means data sets, a nomenclature, designed to differentiate what IBM calls a virtual storage access method technology from the sequential access type. Just like creating GDGs, you need to rely on the same type of general utility (IDCAMS) to develop clusters for Virtual Storage Access Method (VSAM) datasets.

Actually, VSAM files can be used for both on-line and batch systems, although most vendors utilize VSAM KSDS technology in conjunction with interactive, realtime applications. Figure 10.3 shows a number of utility statements used in building (and defining) VSAM clusters. When you define a VSAM cluster, you need to do it through the DEFINE CLUSTER command. All VSAM datasets must be catalogued in both user and master catalogs.

In order to define a VSAM dataset, you need to supply the following information to the operating system:

- a FILE or CLUSTER name.
- VOLUME, abbreviated as "VOL", which will specify the particular volume occupied by the VSAM cluster.
- For a FILE definition, you can reference a dataset which is normally the DD name using standard OS/MVS JCL's. (DLBL under a Disk Operating System definition.)
- CYL, which is short for cylinder, is another required parameter that tells the computer the amount of space required for the file.
- RECORDSIZE specifies the maximum and the average length for the above VSAM cluster, if the record has a variable length. If the record is of fixed length, then both the maximum and the average length of the record need to be identical.
- KEYS tell VSAM that the length and the relative position of that record is a KSDS file. Remember that the relative position of the key is always byte zero.
- IMBED (or NOIMBED) tells VSAM whether the sequence set, or the lowest level of index, contains two or a number of levels of indices to expedite the search of a record by index. "IMBED" will simply enhance your performance when using a KSDS file.
- The term "UNIQUE" means that you have allocated space for this VSAM file at the time you have defined the cluster. The opposite of this is having files that are suballocated (SUBALLOCATION) sharing VSAM space with other files in the system.
- REPLICATE indicates whether each index record is to be written on a track just as often as it will fit, to enhance overall performance. I suggest that you define "REPLICATE" for all KSDS files.
- REUSE/NONREUSE means whether a file is reusable to VSAM or not. Reusable files are normally used as work files or "scratch pad" files, so that permanent files should be made NONREUSABLE.

10.5   The CICS Table Entry Process: FCT, PCT and PPT Entries

The majority of mainframe environments today utilize the CICS telecommunications monitor in providing on-line, realtime processing technology for their installation. Historically, the use of CICS has gained so dramatically over the last decade or so that the majority of vendor companies that previously relied on their own teleprocessing monitors have eventually abandoned them in favor of CICS.

CICS is a table-driven system. This means that all of your on-line processing requirements need to be defined to the system through a set of tables. Among these tables are a File Control Table (FCT), a Processing Program Table (PPT) and a Program Control Table (PCT). The tables are the topic of Figures 10.4 through 10.6.

Note that these tables are already coded by the vendor, and by selecting certain options during the genning, or systems generation process, you can easily supply the system with the missing information required by the FCT, such as the DSNAME. The other tables, the PPT and the PCT, are automatically generated for you by the vendor, since all that information (for example the programming language, transaction identifier, the name of each on-line program or mapset) is vendor defined.

The following is a brief overview of the FCT, PPT and PCT tables:

```
DFHFCT  TYPE=DATASET,                                       X
DATASET=AR715A,                                             X
DSNAME=FIN.ARSY88.CUST.715,                                 X
DISP=SHR,                                                   X
ACCMETH=VSAM,                                               X
SERVREQ=(READ,ADD,UPDATE,DELETE,BROWSE,),                   X
LSPOOL=NONE,                                                X
STRNO=2,                                                    X
BUFNO=3,                                                    X
BUFNI=2,                                                    X
RECFORM=(FIXED,BLOCKED),                                    X
FILSTAT=(ENABLED,CLOSED)
DFHFCT  TYPE=DATASET,                                       X
DATASET=AR716A,                                             X
DSNAME=FIN.ARSY88.OPEN.716,                                 X
DISP=SHR,                                                   X
ACCMETH=VSAM,                                               X
SERVREQ=(READ,ADD,UPDATE,DELETE,BROWSE,),                   X
LSPOOL=NONE,                                                X
STRNO=2,                                                    X
BUFNO=3,                                                    X
BUFNI=2,                                                    X
RECFORM=(FIXED,BLOCKED),                                    X
FILSTAT=(ENABLED,CLOSED)
DFHFCT  TYPE=DATASET,                                       X
DATASET=AR717A,                                             X
DSNAME=FIN.ARSY88.CLOSED.717                                X
DISP=SHR,                                                   X
ACCMETH=VSAM,                                               X
SERVREQ=(READ,ADD,UPDATE,DELETE,BROWSE,),                   X
LSPOOL=NONE,                                                X
STRNO=2,                                                    X
BUFNO=3,                                                    X
BUFNI=2,                                                    X
 RECFORM=(FIXED,BLOCKED),                                   X
FILSTAT=(ENABLED,CLOSED)
```

Figure 10.4   This table shows coding for the File Control Table (FCT).

The FCT, (Figure 10.4) tells CICS which files will be used in an on-line environment. (Clusters, for some of these files were created in Section 10.4). So, as you can see, during the systems generation process, you can essentially segregate the batch from the on-line portions beginning with the file definition.

Glancing at the first set of entries shown in Figure 10.4, the data definition name will be AR715A. (This you can also associate with a DD Name using standard JCL conventions.) A second reference to the FCT requires a DSNAME, or Dataset Name (FIN.ARSY88.CUST.715), which, by the way, is the file description for the customer master (using a third-level qualifier). Likewise, the other two file definitions shown in the above example pertain to an "OPEN" and a "CLOSED" dataset. DISP=SHR, is a standard IBM term for the sharing of a file by a number of concurrent users.

The reason this is so important is that in a typical on-line system you may have dozens, if not hundreds, of users simultaneously accessing a particular database. ACCMETH or Access Method accommodates the structural makeup of a file. For example,

SERVREQ=(READ,ADD,UPDATE,DELETE,BROWSE,),

means that you can read the customer master and are allowed to perform a number of tasks. Among these, you can add a record to the file using a file

```
DFHPPT    TYPE=ENTRY,PROGRAM=PROG715A,PGMLANG=COBOL
DFHPPT    TYPE=ENTRY,PROGRAM=PROG716A,PGMLANG=ASSEMBLER
DFHPPT    TYPE=ENTRY,PROGRAM=PROG717A,PGMLANG=COBOL
DFHPPT    TYPE=ENTRY,PROGRAM=PROG718A,PGMLANG=COBOL
DFHPPT    TYPE=ENTRY,PROGRAM=PROG719A,PGMLANG=COBOL
DFHPPT    TYPE=ENTRY,PROGRAM=PROG720A,PGMLANG=COBOL
DFHPPT    TYPE=ENTRY,PROGRAM=PROG721A,PGMLANG=COBOL
DFHPPT    TYPE=ENTRY,PROGRAM=PROG722A,PGMLANG=COBOL
DFHPPT    TYPE=ENTRY,PROGRAM=PROG723A,PGMLANG=COBOL
DFHPPT    TYPE=ENTRY,PROGRAM=PROG724A,PGMLANG=COBOL
DFHPPT    TYPE=ENTRY,PROGRAM=PROG725A,PGMLANG=COBOL
DFHPPT    TYPE=ENTRY,PROGRAM=PROG726A,PGMLANG=COBOL
DFHPPT    TYPE=ENTRY,PROGRAM=PROG730A,PGMLANG=COBOL
DFHPPT    TYPE=ENTRY,PROGRAM=PROG735A,PGMLANG=ASSEMBLER
DFHPPT    TYPE=ENTRY,PROGRAM=PROG740A,PGMLANG=COBOL
DFHPPT    TYPE=ENTRY,PROGRAM=PROG777A,PGMLANG=COBOL
DFHPPT    TYPE=ENTRY,PROGRAM=PROG787A,PGMLANG=COBOL
DFHPPT    TYPE=ENTRY,PROGRAM=PROG788A,PGMLANG=COBOL
DFHPPT    TYPE=ENTRY,PROGRAM=PROG792A,PGMLANG=COBOL
DFHPPT    TYPE=ENTRY,PROGRAM=PROG795A,PGMLANG=COBOL
DFHPPT    TYPE=ENTRY,PROGRAM=PROG797A,PGMLANG=COBOL
DFHPPT    TYPE=ENTRY,PROGRAM=PROG870A,PGMLANG=COBOL
DFHPPT    TYPE=ENTRY,PROGRAM=PROG880A,PGMLANG=COBOL
DFHPPT    TYPE=ENTRY,PROGRAM=PROG890A,PGMLANG=COBOL
```

Figure 10.5 This chart shows coding for the Processing Program Table (PPT).

```
DFHPCT    TYPE=ENTRY,TRANSID=AR75,PROGRAM=PROG715A
DFHPCT    TYPE=ENTRY,TRANSID=AR76,PROGRAM=PROG716A
DFHPCT    TYPE=ENTRY,TRANSID=AR77,PROGRAM=PROG717A
DFHPCT    TYPE=ENTRY,TRANSID=AR78,PROGRAM=PROG718A
DFHPCT    TYPE=ENTRY,TRANSID=AR79,PROGRAM=PROG719A
DFHPCT    TYPE=ENTRY,TRANSID=AR80,PROGRAM=PROG720A
DFHPCT    TYPE=ENTRY,TRANSID=AR81,PROGRAM=PROG721A
DFHPCT    TYPE=ENTRY,TRANSID=AR82,PROGRAM=PROG722A
DFHPCT    TYPE=ENTRY,TRANSID=AR83,PROGRAM=PROG723A
DFHPCT    TYPE=ENTRY,TRANSID=AR84,PROGRAM=PROG724A
DFHPCT    TYPE=ENTRY,TRANSID=AR85,PROGRAM=PROG725A
DFHPCT    TYPE=ENTRY,TRANSID=AR86,PROGRAM=PROG726A
DFHPCT    TYPE=ENTRY,TRANSID=AR87,PROGRAM=PROG730A
DFHPCT    TYPE=ENTRY,TRANSID=AR88,PROGRAM=PROG735A
DFHPCT    TYPE=ENTRY,TRANSID=AR89,PROGRAM=PROG740A
DFHPCT    TYPE=ENTRY,TRANSID=AR90,PROGRAM=PROG777A
DFHPCT    TYPE=ENTRY,TRANSID=AR91,PROGRAM=PROG787A
DFHPCT    TYPE=ENTRY,TRANSID=AR92,PROGRAM=PROG788A
DFHPCT    TYPE=ENTRY,TRANSID=AR93,PROGRAM=PROG792A
DFHPCT    TYPE=ENTRY,TRANSID=AR94,PROGRAM=PROG795A
DFHPCT    TYPE=ENTRY,TRANSID=AR95,PROGRAM=PROG797A
DFHPCT    TYPE=ENTRY,TRANSID=AR96,PROGRAM=PROG870A
DFHPCT    TYPE=ENTRY,TRANSID=AR97,PROGRAM=PROG880A
DFHPCT    TYPE=ENTRY,TRANSID=AR98,PROGRAM=PROG890A
```

Figure 10.6   This chart shows coding for the Program Control Table.

key. You can also change the contents of an existing record or simply delete it. The term "BROWSE" refers to a particular type of inquiry that gives you the ability to scan sequentially an entire file from beginning to end through the use of a generic or partial key.

The purpose of the Processing Program Table (PPT) shown in Figure 10.5 is to define both an application program to the CICS monitor, as well as a mapset. TYPE=ENTRY is required for every definition on this table. PROGRAM=, as previously indicated, can either be an application program or a mapset to which individual maps (that is screen layout definitions) belong.

Last, PGMLANG or programming language is associated with command level COBOL. This is shown in Figure 10.5.

The Program Control Table (PCT) (Figure 10.6) contains information similar to that of the PPT, except for an additional piece of data that is the transaction Identifier, or briefly TRANSID. What you want to remember is that each TRANSID refers to a specific CICS task. The transaction identifier (TRANSID) is used by CICS to start a particular on-line program. As you can see, both the PPT and the PCT tables are closely aligned.

```
//ARARLIB    JOB   (9000,VARSEGI),NOTIFY-VARSEGI,CALSS=A,
//   MSGLEVEL=(1,1),MSGCLASS=X,REGION=4096,TYPRUN=SCAN
//
//* ALLOCATE ALL LIBRARIES
//
//ALOC        EXEC  PGM=IEFBR14
//SOURCE      DD DSNAME=ARAR.SOURCE.LIBRARY,
//            DISP=(,CATLG,DELETE),
//            UNIT=3380,
//            VOL=SER=PRIV007,
//            DCB=(RECFM=FB,LRECL=80,BLKZISE=3120),
//            SPACE=(3120,(700,70,15))
//DATA        DD DSNAME=ARAR.DATA.LIBRARY,
//            DISP=(,CATLG,DELETE),
//            UNIT=3380,
//            VOL=SER=PRIV007,
//            DCB=(RECFM=FB,LRECL=80,BLKZISE=3120),
//            SPACE=(3120,(800,80,10))
//PROCLIB     DD DSNAME=ARAR.PROC.LIBRARY,
//            DISP=(,CATLG,DELETE),
//            UNIT=3380,
//            VOL=SER=PRIV007,
//            DCB=(RECFM=FB,LRECL=80,BLKZISE=3120),
//            SPACE=(3120,(60,6,5))
//OBJECT      DD DSNAME=ARAR.OBJECT.LIBRARY,
//            DISP=(,CATLG,DELETE),
//            UNIT=3380,
//            VOL=SER=PRIV007,
//            DCB=(RECFM=FB,LRECL=80,BLKZISE=3120),
//            SPACE=(3120,(2800,280,25))
//LINKSETS    DD DSNAME=ARAR.LINKSETS.LIBRARY,
//            DISP=(,CATLG,DELETE),
//            UNIT=3380,
//            VOL=SER=PRIV007,
//            DCB=(RECFM=FB,LRECL=80,BLKZISE=3120),
//            SPACE=(3120,(100,10,10))
//LOADLIB     DD DSNAME=ARAR.LOAD.LIBRARY,
//            DISP=(,CATLG,DELETE),
//            UNIT=3380,
//            VOL=SER=PRIV007,
//            DCB=(RECFM=U,BLKSIZE=23200),
//            SPACE=(3120,(20,4,20))
```

Figure 10.7 This chart lists generated JCL to load and set up various systems libraries.

10.6   Allocating Space for the Systems Libraries and the Data Dictionary

When setting up your libraries for a vendor package, the primary objective is to study and allocate sufficient space for the data library. Data library (see Figure 10.7 under "//DATA"), refers to some library space in which data associated with the application are kept. This requires a relatively good understanding of the overall volume, the number of transactions entering the system, and the daily processing activities. All other libraries (for example, SOURCE, OBJECT, LOAD, etc.) are systems generated. The software keeps track of the number of programs utilized in the system and their relative size, the fixed number of procedures referenced and selected during the systems generation process, and so on. As you can see, looking at Figure 10.7, all these libraries are loaded in a single step with a standard IBM utility (IEFBR14).

Once the JCL's are generated, you need to verify that everything has been entered to your satisfaction, that is, perform a double check—which is why TYPRUN=SCAN was coded in specifying this job. TYPRUN=SCAN will browse your runstream sequentially while generating proper diagnostic messages (and subsequent printouts)—all without physically executing the job.

Note that most of the selection requirements were set up during the systems generation process described in Section 10.2. Among these parameters were the DSNAME, UNIT, or DEVICE specifications for disk storage, a VOL=SER definition to point to the exact location of a file, and in the case of the "DATA" Library some critical space allocations were referenced. The source library, of course, is where each source program or member is kept. Since any change to an existing program needs to be channeled through the source library, you have to make sure that the latest copy, or level of that program is always available. (The "Librarian" or the "Panvalet" Library systems are great for this kind of monitoring activity.) What you need to remember is that, as a rule, you do not want to place changes directly into the vendor's proprietary source code, since such changes would be deleted when a new release is to be installed. (More on this in Chapter 12 under the Exit Point concept.)

For those jobs that run frequently, you probably also need to prepare job control statements called procedures. Procedures can be invoked, executed through a few basic JCL statements, or maintained separately. The idea of segregating "invoking" JCL's from a set of procedures (PROCS) is based on security considerations and is done in an effort to simplify computer operation's role in daily production type activities. PROCS are normally developed and maintained by the analyst, and they can be referenced with a few controlling JCL statements. The library that contains this information is the PROCLIB or Procedure Library ("//PROCLIB"). Space allocation for such a library over and above what is required for the standard application is simply determined by some of the additional subroutines or subprograms you may need to develop from scratch, either to enhance the system or simply to provide for a set of highly customized procedures.

An object module is a sequential dataset that contains relocatable machine instructions, as well as data produced by the computer and passed on to the linkage editor. The object module is simply a set of machine state-

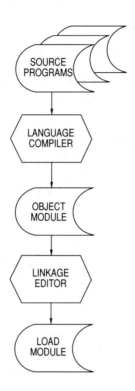

Figure 10.8   This is the system flow from source to load module.

ments translated directly from the source code through the language compiler. The object module cannot be utilized to invoke a task or to run a job because it is still missing vital pieces of data, such as an addressing scheme, symbolics, and other enhancements supplied in the process by the linkage editor. Thus, the object module is simply an input step to the linkage editor that will ultimately translate into a load module. The load module is the final machine format responsible for triggering both batch programs and on-line transactions. An overview of this is presented in Figure 10.8. Libraries associated with these modules are incorporated into //OBJECT and //LOADLIB, accordingly.

Having set up your libraries, you also need to allocate space, as indicated earlier, to your system's data dictionary. You can use several models to accomplish this. In the first model, a data dictionary needs to be installed from scratch. This is characteristic in a situation where a data center has no prior experience with the application package, nor with the particular vendor in general. Since the data dictionary is assumed to be limited in scope (unlike the third model), you can actually accomplish the task through a relatively simple set of procedures without having to redefine every data element used in the system. The physical installation of a data dictionary is normally accomplished through the vendor's own utilities, which are hardly more than some standard IBM utilities, such as IDCAMS, IEFBR14, IEBGENER, and so on.

In the second model, it is assumed that the data dictionary has already been implemented along with a prior application package (assuming an identical vendor), and you only need to follow through the motion of allocating a certain amount of space on a random access device.

Given a somewhat limited fourth generation environment in which to perform borderless inquiries, the two systems now can share valuable data for file maintenance, reporting, and queries, as well.

A more comprehensive approach is highlighted in the third model, where the software can also handle "foreign" files and data elements from other applications. Other applications simply refers to software products by a number of different vendors including your own in-house systems developments. In this kind of an environment, you have to define every field, and procedures that are not part of the original vendor package, including edit rules which would conventionally be defined in the logic of an application program. For example, the field "Department" is defined as a four-position-long numeric field having a range of 1272 to 9999. Criterion, like that needs to be incorporated into a data dictionary, either through vendor provided utilities or in a more practical situation through the vendor's own fourth generation processing language. The definition of these fields is important since they are not defined in the original package, and you are probably the only one qualified to do it.

The data dictionary, and this is a known fact, will keep all vital information centralized. In addition, you also need to define the physical file and all logical views associated with it. Space allocation in reference to the third model is also a great deal more critical, since you have substantially expanded the number of original entries, and only you know space requirements (and edit criteria) for those requirements. This situation where foreign files are also integrated into the dictionary is the key to the completely borderless operating environment.

10.7   Pre-Demo Procedures

10.7.1   Loading and Tailoring Application Procedures

The term "Predemo Procedures" is used to describe generically a set of activities that need to be performed prior to demonstrating the vendor's accounts receivable system using his or her limited database. This aspect will be further reviewed in Chapters 11 and 12. Among these activities are

```
STEP10
FUNCTION NAME      :  VSAM.SER
DEFAULT            :  SER
TASK               :  VALUE FOR THIS OBJECT POINTS TO THE VOLUME WHERE
                      THE VSAM CATALOG IS LOCATED THAT DESCRIBES AND
                      MAINTAINS ALL MASTER AND PERMANENT FILES.
EXHIBIT            :  IF YOUR STANDARD VOLUME SERIAL IS VSAM04, THE
                      FOLLOWING ENTRY IS AN EXAMPLE:
                      VSAM.SER(SER001)
```

```
    VSAM.SER(PRV003)
```

```
STEP11
FUNCTION NAME      :  VSAM.DISK.UNIT
DEFAULT            :  SYSDA
TASK               :  VALUE FOR THIS OBJECT SPECIFIES THE OS JCL UNIT
                      DELIMITER FOR THE DISK DEVICE WHICH CONTAINS
                      ALL VSAM FILES.
EXHIBIT            :  AN EXAMPLE OF THE ABOVE WOULD BE:
                      VSAM.DISK.UNIT(3350)
```

```
    VSAM.DISK.UNIT(3380)
```

```
STEP12
FUNCTION NAME      :  COBOL.LIBRARY
DEFAULT            :  SYS1.COBLIB
TASK               :  THE VALUE FOR THIS TASK SPECIFIES THE LIBRARY
                      IN WHICH ALL COBOL SUBROUTINES ARE KEPT FOR
                      LINKAGE EDITING.
EXHIBIT            :  FILL IN THE NAME OF THE LIBRARY BELOW ON WHICH
                      YOUR COBOL SUBROUTINES ARE TO RESIDE.
                      AN EXAMPLE WOULD BE: COBOL/LIBRARY(SYS2.COBOL)
```

```
    COBOL.LIBRARY(SYS1.COBLIB)
```

```
STEP13
FUNCTION NAME      :  PERM.DISK.UNIT
DEFAULT            :  DISK
TASK               :  THIS UNIT DESIGNATES THE PARAMETER FOR THE DISK
                      WHICH WILL BE USED TO CONTAIN ALL VENDOR PRIVATE
                      LIBRARIES OTHER THAN THE VSAM CLUSTERS
EXHIBIT            :  AN EXAMPLE OF THE ABOVE WOULD BE:
                      PERM.DISK.UNIT(3350)
```

```
    PERM.DISK.UNIT(DISK)
```

Figure 10.9   This shows an expanded version of the genning selection process shown in Figure 10.1.

the loading and customizing of all application procedures, the copying of the installation tape, compiling and loading of all vendor programs and subprograms including his fourth generation technology, and physically generating the screens.

Loading is essentially done with a vendor program reminiscent of a standard IBM utility. This step, of course is hierarchically dependent on the systems generation process that enables you to define specific systems parameters for your telecommunications needs and for every runstream in the system.

If you were to define the term: WORK.DISK.UNIT(TEMP), during the initial generation process, then every time you needed temporary work space on a direct access device, the above macro value would be automatically invoked or substituted into your JCL. The term "TEMP", for example, is nothing else but a macro statement referencing an already established volume serial. Likewise, the name of your sort library would be translated into SYS1.SORTLIB (based on your selection), which means that this symbolic will be substituted every time you are to issue a sort. (In many cases, you may have your own software, which is probably a lot more efficient than some of the standard IBM sort utilities, such as SyncSort, requiring some additional tasks.) SyncSort is one of the products discussed in "Mainframe Productivity Tools for the 90's" by this author.

In Figure 10.9, the chart shown in Figure 10.1 is expanded to include the definition of four (rather than two) macro statements to show you how such a selection during the systems generation process affects a number of subsequently dependent tasks. In step 12, for example, a value of COBOL.LIBRARY(SYS1.COBLIB) was selected in reference to all necessary subroutines and options. This option, in fact, has overridden the vendors own default value of COBOL.LIBRARY(SYS1.COBLIB). As you can see, just by glancing at the chart, VSAM.SER(PRV003) was selected over VSAM.SER.(SER001), and VSAM.DISK.UNIT(3380) over VSAM.DISK.UNIT(3350), and so on.

All the preceding definitions were done in section 10.2, during the systems generation process. Figures 10.10 and 10.11 introduce another set of topics one should be familiar with in implementing a package commonly referred to as Symbolics or Symbolic Parameters. A symbolic parameter "symbolizes" a given value in a procedure (procs) statement.

Conceptually, any parameter that can vary each time the procedure is called is a likely candidate to be coded as a symbolic parameter. For example, if you were to charge computer time to each customer every time you invoked a procedure, you could code this routine one of two ways:

1. ACCT=&ALCNT
2. ACCT= &ACT1&ACT2&ACT3 and so on.

If the first part of a dataset name varies while the last does not, JANDATA, FEBRDATA, MARCHDATA, for example may be coded as: DSN=&MONTH.DATA.

Remember to code two consecutive periods (..), if a period should follow a symbolic parameter. For example, code:&DEPT..POK when the described value is: D58.POK and DEPT=D58 is the value assignment.

```
//VARSEGI JOB (9000,AVRS),NOTIFY=SYSVAR,CLASS=A,MSGLEVEL=(1,1),
//    MSGCLASS=X,REGION=4096,TYPRUN=SCAN
//* THE PURPOSE OF THIS RUNSTREAM TO RESTORE A NUMBER OF MASTER
//* FILES USED IN THE APPLICATION, EXECUTES A SET OF PROCEDURES REQUIRED
//* ELECTRONIC (AUTO) CASH.
//
//
//LOADDB  PROC  MG=,
//        X='UNIV.AR8605',
//        CVOL='VOL=SER=PRV003',  =========>  SEE NOTES ON 1
//        DISK='3380',  ==================>  SEE NOTES ON 1
//        DSX2=,
//        ARAUTOC='DUMMY',
//        ARATTOD='DUMMY',
//        SYSOUTJ='*',
//        SYSOUTR='*',
//        DSCB=UNIV.AR.MODEL,  =============>  SEE NOTES ON 3
//        Y='UNIVT.AR8605',
//        COBOL='SYS1.VSCLLIB' =============>  SEE NOTES ON 2
//
//* THE ABOVE SYMBOLIC PARAMETERS REPRESENTS WHAT WAS ORIGINALLY
//* GENNED INTO THE SYSTEM (SECTION 10.2).
//
//* THE PURPOSE OF THIS PROC IS TO INITIALLY CREATE THE REQUIRED FILES
//* AND BACK THEM UP PERIODICALLY. YOU MAY ALSO RELOAD ANY SPECIFIC FILE
//* IN THIS RUN-STREAM THROUGH A PARAMETER REQUEST.
//*
//LOADMOD  DD  PGM=LOADALL
//STEPLIB  DD  DSN=ARAR.LOAD.LIBRARY,DISP=SHR
//         DD  DSN=&COBLIB,DISP=SHR==========>  SEE NOTES ON 2
//SYSOUT   DD  SYSOUT=&SYSOUTJ
//SYSDOUT  DD  SYSOUT=&SYSOUTJ
//SYSUDUMP DD  SYSOUT=&SYSOUTJ
//SYS005   DD  DSN=SYSIN
//FILE01   DD  DUMMY,DCB=BLKSIZE=80
//FILE02   DD  DUMMY,DCB=BLKSIZE=80
//FILE03   DD  DUMMY,DCB=BLKSIZE=80
//FILE04   DD  DUMMY,DCB=BLKSIZE=80
//
//AR100H   DD  DSN=&MG&Y&DSX2..AR100H,DISP=SHR
//AR200H   DD  DSN=&MG&Y&DSX2..AR200H,DISP=SHR
//AR300H   DD  DSN=&MG&Y&DSX2..AR300H,DISP=SHR
//AR400H   DD  DSN=&MG&Y&DSX2..AR400H,DISP=SHR
//AR897H   DD  &DH897,DSN=&MG&X&DSX2..AR897H(+1),
//             SPACE=(TRK,(30,5),RLSE),&CVOL, ==============> SEE NOTES ON 1
//             DISP=(NEW,CATLG,DELETE),UNIT=&DISK,==========> SEE NOTES ON 1
//             DCB=(&DSCB,RECFM=FB,LRECL=100,BLKSIZE=1000)==> SEE NOTES ON 3
```

Figure 10.10 This shows JCL's generated via a vendor utilities with expanded symbolics.

The ampersand (&) represents part of a symbolic parameter which is followed by a name which may be one through seven characters long. The names for symbolic parameters should be consistent in all the cataloged and instream procedures at an installation. For example, every time a department number is to be assigned to a symbolic parameter in any procedure at the installation, the symbolic parameter could be named &DEPT. Different

```
  1    IEF653I  SUBSTITUTION  JCL - DSN=SYS1.VSCLLIB,DISP=SHR
  2    IEF653I  SUBSTITUTION  JCL - SYSOUT=
  3    IEF653I  SUBSTITUTION  JCL - SYSOUT=
  4    IEF653I  SUBSTITUTION  JCL - DSN=UNIV.AR8605.AR100H,DISP=SHR
  5    IEF653I  SUBSTITUTION  JCL - DSN=UNIV.AR8605.AR200H,DISP=SHR
  6    IEF653I  SUBSTITUTION  JCL - DSN=UNIV.AR8605.AR300H,DISP=SHR
  7    IEF653I  SUBSTITUTION  JCL - DSN=UNIV.AR8605.AR400H,DISP=SHR
  8    IEF653I  SUBSTITUTION  JCL - DSN=UNIV.AR8605.AR897H,DISP=SHR
  9    IEF653I  SUBSTITUTION  JCL - VOL=SER=PRV003,UNIT=3380
 10    IEF653I  SUBSTITUTION  JCL - DCB=(UNIV.AR.MODEL..............)
```

Figure 10.11   This is an explanation to symbolic substitution.

procedures could contain ACCT = (43877, &DEPT) and DSN = Library.&DEPT.Tally. The installation can tell all the programmers the meaning of all the "standard" symbolic names.

Just what is the significance of these symbolics during the systems generation process and why use them in defining certain parameters or procedures? The use of symbolics by the vendor is quite helpful and creative in order to lend an application package a great deal of flexibility in reference to certain terms and certain devices, such as tape drives, disk packs, and libraries. Remember, the First National Bank of Chicago uses different terminology in defining the overall environment than does Montgomery Ward, Marshall Fields, or Standard Oil. Thus, your understanding of this whole process is especially important, because whatever you have "genned" into the system at installation time is what you have to live with unless you decide to reinstall the package from scratch, which is not my definition of a fun-filled event. Figure 10.12 gives you a brief summary of these steps involved in the process of "symbolic-definition."

Once your runstreams are set up with the proper generation criteria, you can go ahead and start customizing them one by one. That means you need to decide on what jobs or steps, if any, will be omitted, and what additional procedures will be added. Looking at this process from a practical point of view, you normally need to include a number of utility steps, some of which may not be defined by the vendor, such as deleting some of the work files before the next production run.

On a secondary level, but equally important, you need to decide on certain run frequencies. What actually constitutes a daily run may very well be completely different from the way it's "demo-ed" or modeled in the initial runstream. Thus, with the preceding background information, it is recommended that you set up your daily runstreams first. Test them thoroughly before you move on to the next application cycle. This is an important aspect. You need to get your most frequent runstreams operational

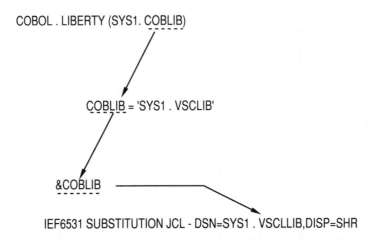

COBOL . LIBERTY (SYS1. COBLIB)

COBLIB = 'SYS1 . VSCLIB'

&COBLIB

IEF6531 SUBSTITUTION JCL - DSN=SYS1 . VSCLLIB,DISP=SHR

Figure 10.12   This is the logical flow of symbolic substitution.

first, in order to get a "breather" in setting up some of the subsequent cycles, such as those of weekly or semimonthly runs, on-demand-type of procedures and so on.

10.7.2   Copy and Use of the Demo Tape

The installation of the demo tape is not an isolated event. It is part of an overall effort to define the complete environment. The tape that contains the vendor's demo system also comes with a number of additional modules or members, such as the source programs, initial job control file and table definitions, and an entire subsystem that defines the fourth generation technology starting with that of a data dictionary and the language compiler.

Avoid embarrassing situations. The first activity on your list should be to copy the demo tape for the purpose of a backup. It is somewhat embarrassing to lose a $29.95 tape that contains a $250,000 system, so that you have to contact the vendor's technical representative for an additional copy. Technically speaking, when you acquire a vendor package, a demo module gives you visibility as to the general features of the package. Once such a system is in place, you can start the process of replacing the demo system with your own data. This is important, since a thorough bench marking of the system, and thus a thorough understanding of it, can only be done accurately through utilizing your own database.

In testing such a system, you can rely on the vendor's own script to attain expected results and correct any possible deficiencies with regards to

```
> GU    001,AT-00189                                    ON R8401

              — AR:M - POSTING CONTROL ENTRY AND STATUS —

    ___   CONTROL GROUP CORP. NUMBER -> 001  AT00189
              DATE ENTERED, OPERATOR -> 031286     20

        YOUR CONTROL TOTAL AND COUNT -> 22,614.00              8
      AR:M'S CONTROL TOTAL AND COUNT  -> 23,614.00              8

                          VARIANCE ->        1,000.00-
                CONTROL GROUP STATUS -> 0
                  — POSTING CONTROL GROUP INFORMATION  —
          POST DURING BATCH PROCESSING  ->
                    TOTAL POSTED SO FAR  ->
        MOST RECENT POSTING TOTALS, DATE ->              000000
        IF WORKSHEET, CHECK REDUCTION ->

          — BILLING TRANSMISSION ONLY —
                          BTP DATE -> 000000
        BILLING BATCH NUMBER -> BPT TIME ->

                          09/12/88  10:11:02    M2LL ACTION ___
```

Figure 10.13 This shows verification of certain control totals using the demo system.

a particular file or job control statements. Figure 10.13 is an overview of this verification process. Actually, the verification of the above should be a joint project between you and the user. You need the user, because of his expertise and accounting experience, to point out the way he or she will be required to do things, which may be different from the way you would normally set up the system.

Figure 10.13 shows a variance of $1,000 between your own control number and another one which is system generated. Keep in mind that there are instances when the vendor deliberately provides you with such variances for highlighting potential problem areas, and with measures you need to take to resolve those problems.

Should you really be concerned with differences and discrepancies between your own test results and those made available to you by the vendor? Discrepancies normally reflect some basic flaws that can be traced back to several sources during the installation process. Actually, you could have misplaced or simply "dummied out" the wrong file while in the process of setting up your batch cycle. When you "dummy out" a file, the system will ignore a particular dataset, but all that without causing an abnormal termination of a runstream.

10.7.3 Screen Generation

Screens, like application programs, need to be generated, which is part of the systems generation process. Screens, regardless of the particular "paint" technology provided, are normally assembler type programs to be reassembled at installation time before you can use them. For such an assembly process, most vendors provide you with a set of customized utilities. Among a variety of screen painters available today (whether they are the product of a fourth generation or conventional technology), they need to arrive at a standard format when interfacing into a particular hardware and telecommunications monitor. For example, if you rely on CICS for your on-line processing requirements (which is fairly standard in the industry), you will need to convert your high level definitions to a machine-readable structure, which is normally an automatic process. Thus, in an IBM environment, you can design and prototype your panels in a real time-like environment. Ultimately, all that format will have to be redefined to the machine using basic mapping support (BMS). BMS, as the name suggests, is an assembler-based technology that is accessible to any transaction-driven program that requires a screen. More recent and advanced packages, like Screen Development Facility (SDF), for example, also generate BMS code, even though they let you design (and conceptualize) any number of maps and mapsets in an interactive environment.

The situation is no different with a fourth generation screen painter software. Your "drawing" or "painting" of a screen needs to be translated into some high-level codes, which, in turn, will translate into more basic, more machine proximity type instructions. As you recall the step-by-step selection process utilized in generating a set of Expert code, which was highlighted in Chapter 7, by merely selecting from among some alternatives, the I.E. environment was able to translate all that process into a formal language. Figure 10.14 shows a menu screen that can be designed and coded in the matter of a few minutes using advanced fourth generation technology. Figure 10.15 is the BMS structure that most packages automatically generate for a standard CICS interface, the end-product of any package to be interfaced into a CICS driven real time environment.

Figure 10.14 is a simple screen definition using one of any number of fourth generation screen painting packages. From the perspective of coding your menu screen, all you need to do is to lay it out the way it would look on the screen. Thus the first, second, and third header lines are formatted, and each field is indicated through a beginning and an ending character. The percent (%) and the plus (+) signs mean a number of things to the fourth generation compiler. It defines not only the length of the constant fields, but their attribute characteristics, as well. The percent and the plus

```
        %   METRA - METROPOLITAN RAILWAY +
                                                                    *


    %  1  EQUIPMENT SUBSYSTEM INQUIRY  +


    %  2  CREW AND EMPLOYEE ROSTER       +


    %  OPTION+          $_$

    %  MAINT CODE      /_$   %MAINTENANCE MODE A=ADD, B=BROWSE+
                             %C=CHANGE, D=DELETE, I=INQUIRY+


    /___$  /__ __ __$


%PF1 RETURN TO MAIN MENU+
```

Figure 10.14   This is a screen painting using a fourth generation software.

```
  1              PRINT NOGEN
  2  TLC1MAP  DFHMSD  TYPE=&SYSPARM,MODE=INOUT,CTRL=FREEKB,LANG=COBOL,   C
                 TIOAPFX=YES
 12  TLC1     DFHMDI  SIZE=(24,80)
 42           DFHMDF  POS=(01,21),LENGTH=28,ATTRB=(ASKIP,BRT,PROT)       C
                 INITIAL='METRA - METROPOLITAN RAILWAY
 53           DFHMDF  POS=(04,15),ATTRB=(ASKIP,BRT,PROT),LENGTH=31       C
                 INITIAL='1  EQUIPMENT SUBSYSTEN INQUIRY'
 64           DFHMDF  POS=(06,21),ATTRB=(ASKIP,BRT,PROT),LENGTH=31,      C
                 INITIAL='2  CREW AND EMPLOYEE ROSTER     '
107           DFHMDF  POS=(08,15),ATTRB=(ASKIP,BRT,PROT),LENGTH=6,       C
                 INITIAL='OPTION'
117  OPTION   DFHMDF  POS=(08,28),ATTRB=(UNPROT,FSET,IC),LENGTH=1
127           DFHMDF  POS=(10,15),ATTRB=(ASKIP,BRT,PROT),LENGTH=10,      C
                 INITIAL='MAINT CODE'
138  MAINTN   DFHMDF  POS=(10,28),ATTRB=(UNPROT,FSET),LENGTH=1
149           DFHMDF  POS=(10,31),ATTRB=(ASKIP,BRT,PROT),LENGTH=33,      C
                 INITIAL='MAINTENANCE MODE A=ADD, B=BROWSE'
160           DFHMDF  POS=(11,31),ATTRB=(ASKIP,BRT,PROT),LENGTH=33,      C
                 INITIAL='C=CHANGE, D=DELETE, I=INQUIRY    '
170  KEY1     DFHMDF  POS=(13,15),ATTRB=(UNPROT,FSET),LENGTH=3
180  KEY2     DFHMDF  POS=(13,17),ATTRB=(UNPROT,FSET),LENGTH=8
190  ERRMSG   DFHMDF  POS=(24,02),ATTRB=(PROT,BRT,ASKIP),LENGTH=60
180           DFHMSD TYPE=FINAL
190           END
```

Figure 10.15 This is the generated code of a screen map converted from fourth generation technology.

sign simply tell the compiler that the field should be displayed in a protected, intensified bright mode. The position of each field is fairly self-explanatory: it will display between the predefined attribute characters. The fourth display line is made up of two types of data. The first one is the header option. Associated with that field and enclosed within two dollar signs ($$) is a one-position-long option field in reference to choice 1 or 2 of the above criteria (e.g. "1 EQUIPMENT SUBSYSTEM INQUIRY,", and "2 CREW AND EMPLOYEE ROSTER").

The two dollar signs that enclose the variable option field tell the compiler that the field is to be displayed as an unprotected, low-intensity, data-entry-type field. It is different, from the other variable fields in that it will initialize the cursor next to the variable option field.

The variable field corresponding to the maintenance code is essentially identical to the option field with the exception that the leading and the ending attributes, a slash (/) and a dollar sign ($), do not require the reinitialization of the cursor in that position.

Associated with the maintenance code is a set of acceptable values, such as an 'A' for an add, a 'B' for a browse, a 'C' for a change, a 'D' for a delete, and an 'I' for an inquiry. Since these values are also part of the data dictionary, any other value entered into the maintenance code field would result in an error condition.

Finally, two more fields are shown toward the bottom of the screen, each designating a key field, which can be entered on the menu screen for directly invoking a particular record. Also, line 24 contains a string of attributes that enables you to produce certain text or messages if one of the conditions defined on the screen fails or if a wrong function key is pressed, etc.

Note that the above narrative of a screen painter refers to a generic model, even though it is similar in many respects to one of the real models (MSA or M&D screen painting techniques presented earlier in this book).

As you can see, a screen such as the preceding one, can easily be coded up in a matter of minutes. The analysis and the evaluation of the symbols are done through a fourth generation compiler, which encompasses a real time interface into a fourth generation data dictionary to provide predefined programming functions there.

To link or activate such a "simplistic" design into a CICS telecommunications monitor, for example, certain required codes must be generated. Figure 10.15 is an overview of some assembler conventions required by the TP monitor.

Actually, a decade and a half ago, you had no vehicle to present a map to the system other than the one shown in Figure 10.15, which is structured in assembler language. To highlight a set of assempler-type instructions on this map, you are referred to lines 117 and 127. The term "OPTION" is a variable field, corresponding to the fourth line of entry in Figure 10.14. DFHMDF simply tells the system that it is one of the component definitions on the map. The field is physically located in line 8 on the screen starting in position 28. Among the field attributes or characteristics are an "unprotected" field necessary for data entry with the modified data tag (FSET) on and the cursor initialized and now situated in position 28. Here the length of the field is a total of one character.

The entry corresponding to line 127 is a constant field that starts in line 10, position 15 for a length of 10. Among the attribute characteristics are field protection and field intensification. The term ASKIP will cause the cursor to skip or omit the entire constant field, since no data entry will be allowed at that point.

Last, the term INITIAL defines a set of constant values or header definitions to the system. Figure 10.15, which shows basic mapping support techniques, has a relatively inflexible format, which makes coding a relatively error-prone process. A misplaced comma or continuation character (C) in column 72 would result in failure to assemble your map.

10.7.4 Comments on Fourth Generation Technology

Vendor packages discussed in this book are normally made up of two basic components such as:

1. an application module that is,

2. enhanced through an associated fourth generation support environment.

Conceptually, some of the vendors require total integration between the application software and that of the new technology: others allow you some leeway in which to segregate the two functions in a number of steps. The basic Millennium product, for example, is such a highly integrated package, that it would be next to impossible to install the basic M&D package in a fragmented manner. To install a fourth generation system is a relatively easy task, the vendor provides you with an extensive set of utilities to get the job done. The vendor even provides you with charts and samples suggesting space and device requirements. An overview of such a chart is shown in Figure 10.16.

Device Requirements

COMPONENT	3330	3340	3350	3375	3380
SOURCE copybook	420	454	287	154	115
OBJECT	911	1418	623	333	250
LINKSET	36	58	25	14	10
LOAD ON-LINE	420	454	287	154	115
LOAD BATCH	977	1521	668	357	268
PROCLIB	55	86	38	20	15
DATA (DEMO SYSTEM)	11	17	8	4	3
GDG"S	729	1135	498	267	200
VSAM WITH INDEXED SPL	5120	17972	3499	1873	1405
VSAM WITHOUT INDEXED SPL	219	341	150	80	60
TOTAL WITH INDEXED SPL	8679	13115	5933	3176	2381
TOTAL WITHOUT INDEXED SPL	3778	5484	2584	1383	1036

Figure 10.16   This depicts the space/file/device requirements during package installation.

The preceding figure shows space requirements in terms of tracks for the system although you may convert them to cylinder, if it makes it easier for you to visualize the overall volume. Because of the variety of devices available, the vendor also provides you with disk units ranging from a 3330 disk drive and including 3340, 3350, 3375, up to a 3380 spindle.

One of the more significant aspects of using a fourth generation technology has to do with the language compiler. Some fourth generation languages have their own compilers, while others utilize conventional languages to accomplish the same. In order to develop a routine that will "automatically" insert a title header on your report (such as a company name, a page number including the word "page," a current system date, and a report identifier), you need to code a set of macro-like procedures. In the above case, you need to develop instructions that would include the following:

- printing a report title retrieved from the data dictionary,
- getting the current date from the system,
- computing page numbers, that is, setting up the initial counters for that,
- accessing the report identifier; this too is done with a data dictionary entry,
- setting up a line counter for calculating page overflows, and
- evaluating conditions for resetting the above counter such as subtotals, last record conditions, and data field control breaks.

This body of code, as I mentioned before, may be developed with a conventional language or simply through a fourth generation compiler. The end-product, however, needs to be compatible with the operating system. In an IBM environment, for example, this is a bi-level conversion process starting with basic assembler that is to be converted into a machine-language (binary) equivalent.

Summary

This chapter focused on technician's responsibilities during the implementation process. So far, two conceptually similar, but implementation-wise different fourth generation business systems have been discussed. Both of these vendor products were highlighted in detail to convey the technical aspects (and philosophies) of McCormack & Dodge and the MSA Corporations.

Vendor packages do not follow the peculiarities of a system cycle. They essentially entail the requirements study phase and some modest programming activities either to customize or to enhance certain features inherent in the package. Systems testing takes on a totally different aspect, and it is normally marked by the following activities:

1. The testing of a demo module provided by the vendor mainly for tutorial reasons.
2. The testing of a limited portion of the system identical to the vendor's demo module, but utilizing the user's own database. This, in fact, requires the reinitialization of all demo files to create a "near" production environment.

3. Last, the saving of all interim files other than those that are transaction related. In an accounts receivable system, for example, the user normally enters permanent customer-related information on the customer master. Assuming that these are valid customers, you need to develop a routine to save that information when switching to a live, production environment. Transactions, on the other hand, need not be saved, since they are normally copies of past activities modified in some fashion. Fourth generation business systems deliver more than conventional utilities. They deliver an entire support environment in which to operate, modules such as those containing an entire I.E. subsystem, the Millennium software, DCI, SDT, PDL, or the Financial Controller Package and so forth.

The Application System Generation Process in essence is nothing more than a set of choices presented to the analyst for his or her review and decision. Among these choices, you need to pick criteria applicable in your specific environment. Each criterion is presented in the form of a questionnaire-like statement, which, nonetheless are macro-oriented symbolic parameters. The purpose of these symbolics is to generate a number of machine-readable commands or Job Control Statements (JCL's) and thereby allowing the system to substitute each parameter automatically.

A third step in the implementation process is to build the required direct-access files, a process referred to as creating VSAM clusters. The term "clusters" simply means datasets, a nomenclature, designed to differentiate what IBM calls a virtual storage access technology from a sequential access type files. Just like creating generation data groups, you need to rely on the same type of general utility (IDCAMS) to develop clusters for them. Actually, VSAM files can be used for both on-line and batch systems, although most vendors utilize VSAM KSDS technology in conjunction with interactive, real-time applications. When you define a VSAM cluster, you need to do it through the DEFINE CLUSTER command. All VSAM datasets must be catalogued in both user and master catalogs.

The majority of main frame environments today utilize the CICS telecommunications monitor in providing on-line, real time processing technology for their installation. CICS is a table-driven system. This means that all your on-line processing requirements need to be defined to the system through a set of tables. Among these tables are a File Control Table (FCT), a Processing Program Table (PPT), and a Program Control Table (PCT).

Note that these tables are already coded for you by the vendor, and by selecting certain options during the genning, or systems generation process, you can easily supply the system the missing information required by the

FCT, such as the DSNAME. When setting up your libraries for a vendor package, the primary objective is to study and allocate sufficient space for the data library.

The source library, of course, is where each source program or member is kept. Since any change to an existing program needs to be channeled through the source library, you have to make sure that the latest copy or level of that program is always available. (The "Librarian" or the "Panvalet" Library systems are great for this kind of monitoring activity.)

The object module is simply a set of machine statements translated directly from the source code through the language compiler.

Screens, like application programs, need to be generated, which is part of the Systems Generation process. Screens, regardless of the particular "paint" technology provided are normally assembler-type programs to be reassembled at installation time before you can use them. For such an assembly process, most vendors provide you with a set of customized utilities. Among a variety of screen painters available today (whether they are the product of a fourth generation or conventional technology) they need to arrive at a standard format when interfacing into a particular hardware and telecommunications monitor.

Vendor packages discussed in this book are normally made up of two basic components such as an application module enhanced through an associated fourth generation support environment. Conceptually, some of the vendors require total integration between the application software and that of the new technology: others allow you some leeway in which to segregate the two functions in a number of steps. Installing a fourth generation system is a relatively easy task. The vendor provides you with an extensive set of utilities to get the job done, and even provides you with charts and samples suggesting space and device requirements.

Chapter 11

Installing a Fourth Generation Vendor Package—Part I

11.1   Overview

In Chapter 10, an inventory of the technician's responsibilities in installing a vendor package was taken. Among the primary responsibilities are the definition of both on-line and batch files along with a comprehensive backup mechanism. In addition, loading and linking the various libraries and defining a Data Dictionary for the upcoming software were discussed. All of these activities are performed to initialize a demo system used to lay the foundation for a more customized test module and subsequently for the final production environment. These definitions were introduced during the application systems "genning" process to make sure that the proper teleprocessing tables were set up, and that the JCL's used in the various run-streams were defined via the proper symbolics and were consistent with in-house shop standards.

Figure 11.1 gives a brief overview of the initial tasks that normally begin at the time the installation tape and documentation are received. However intimidating all that may seem at first, this is generally an activity not to exceed a week's worth of effort on your part.

Read the System Installation Document
Define all Generation Data Group files for batch processing
Define all VSAM Clusters
Define all Libraries: LOAD, SOURCE, etc.
Copy the installation tape and build test files from it
Link all batch and on-line program
Link all fourth generation related technologies (Information
    Expert or Millennium related programs,for example, etc)
Update (or initially load) the Data Dictionary
Prepare all those reports to be generated using fourth generation
    reporting tools (other than the standard reports).
Load the demo files
Run on-line start-up procedures
Run the on-line demo test according to the script
Start post on-line tests
Back up all files that need to be backed up daily/weekly, etc
Set up post on-line reporting
Interface requirements
Run report writer: review and evaluate reports
Back up all vendor libraries
Generate updated documentation from the Data Dictionary
Verify all GDG and VSAM files
Load Company Policy definitions to customize screens and reports

---

Figure 11.1   These are the sequences used in implementing an initial system from the vendor supplied tape(s).

Demo modules are the vendor's "show and tell" of how a system operates, or should operate using a set of script and test files. These files are
built to cover an extensive test environment with predetermined results. By
installing and running such a demo module, you can gain valuable insight
and exposure to the specifics, that is, to the idiosyncrasies of a full-blown
application environment.

A second aspect of a demo module is that you can utilize it as a basis
for a production environment in terms of setting up the various runstreams,
all the backup and restore procedures, systems utilities, and critical restart
sequences. Keep in mind that demo systems are set up to accommodate
probably more steps than will ever be needed to get the job done. If, for
example, you have no need for automatic cash facilities, which is normally
part of a standard accounts receivable package, you might as well weed out
those steps, and everything connected with them (for example, cash edit
and update routines and subsequent reporting).

Eliminating steps requires a good understanding of the application, so
you need to study the system in sufficient detail. You may have to "dummy
out" certain files that are no longer required in the runstreams to avoid a set
of bad condition codes and ultimately the abnormal termination of the job.
Normally, it is a good idea to wait to modify a demo system, until you have
a chance to run and verify it using the vendor's own script. Only when you
are fully satisfied with the results should you transform it into a more
customized, more meaningful test environment. To summarize the preceding material, a demo module is your first benchmark, your first tangible
milestone activity that all the required programs were successfully linked,
and that all of the necessary table entries were created along with other
requirements. A demo system is also a tutorial tool by the vendor to acclimate the user long before such a production system becomes operational.

11.2   Case Study—Part I

11.2.1   Overall Project Description

The purpose of this chapter is to present a case study in which an accounts
receivable (A/R) system, a vendor product, is installed in a fourth generation support environment. To complicate things, a front-end module to such
an A/R system also needs to be developed to provide the user with an
extensive interface mechanism built between the above applications and the
general ledger which is the product of yet a third software company.

The primary purpose of the billing system is twofold—to print invoices and to make sure that data edited in this module is properly validated against a half-a-dozen external and internal files. Among these are a project master and customer files, an invoice file mainly for the purpose of printing invoices, a transaction file, and an internally monitored invoice table that keeps track of the invoice numbers within certain ranges. This is used by the system primarily to generate valid invoice numbers without the user having to enter them manually. The above ranges are referenced by a set of prefixes.

The main purpose of the A/R system, on the other hand is to keep track of the customer's pay habits, apply each payment against one or a set of authorized accounts, and to report on the status of the customer in terms of open and closed transaction items. The A/R system checks, balances, and edits all invoice payments, credits, distribution receipts and/or deductions to the general ledger. As mentioned earlier, the A/R system is a vendor product being supported by fourth generation technology. It is, like the billing system, a mixture of real time and batch processing utilizing mostly VSAM for the A/R database files.The interdependency that exists between the billing and the A/R systems is unusually critical, requiring the parallel development of certain modules. For example, the A/R system cannot function without a billing front-end, so that needs to be developed first. However, the billing system cannot be operational without a customer master database which resides and is maintained in the A/R System.

To introduce an additional complexity into the design, the customer master database also has its own internal hierarchical arrangement; it has a functional dependency on a corporate guidelines file that controls the standard corporate data. Among these elements are the manner in which certain company rules are defined for the customers and the way some of the key reports are generated, including report titles, control entities, financial breakdowns, and so forth. Figure 11.2 is an overview of this critical dependency structure. Note that the sign ------------> represents a batch interface between two systems with the arrow head showing the direction of such an interface. The sign ⬅︎〰️➡︎, on the other hand, represents a bidirectional access where information developed in one part of the system is being utilized in another. Thus, data flow between the two systems (for example A/R and billing) is depicted as a unidirectional, batch flow with the general ledger system being the major target. Interaction between the A/R and billing systems is made up of two parts: a daily batch interface from the billing process into the A/R system, as well as an on-line real time interface to access and utilize certain data elements in the A/R systems.

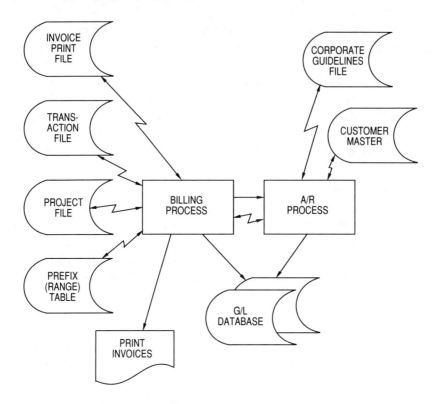

Figure 11.2 This shows the interaction between an in-house billing vendor-designed A/R modules, both feeding the G/L system. (The A/R process is only partially defined at this point.)

11.2.2 Billing System: On-Line Design

The billing system is one of the "building blocks" described in this multi-project environment, which is an in-house application software. It needs to be developed from scratch, and "hooked-up" with a vendor-developed Accounts Receivable system using fourth generation technology. Several aspects of the systems development process deserve consideration this early in the game. First of all, any file structure developed in the billing module is considered "foreign" and inaccessible by the A/R application, since the latter only has limited (fourth generation) capabilities, meaning that it is not totally borderless outside its own area.

The company in process of implementing the preceding two systems utilizes a project file for automatically generating its invoice numbers, all that in an on-line, real time environment. Actually, invoices are created interactively but are printed during the post on-line processing cycle via the invoice master file after CICS is brought down to initiate the batch processing cycle.

A systems flowchart of the Billing module is presented in Figure 11.3. Note that Figure 11.3 is made up of three parts. The first and second parts highlight the on-line (real-time) components of the system. The third part is an overview of the batch procedures.

Path 1 of Figure 11.3 tracks the various steps necessary to create an invoice record that will eventually be printed during the batch cycle. Path 2 and 3 essentially describe some of the maintenance steps necessary to update the project file and the invoice range table.

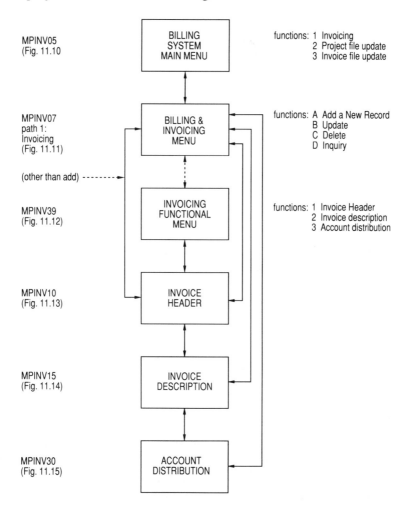

Figure 11.3—Part 1   This is path 1 of the billing on-line module.

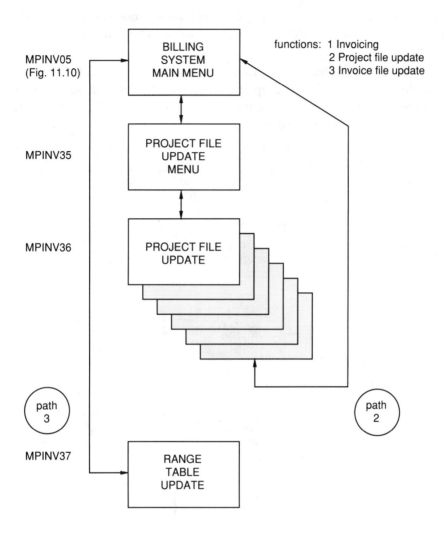

Figure 11.3—Part 2 This shows path 2 and path 3 of the billing on-line cycle.

A complete breakdown of files utilized in this front-end module follows.

A Project File (Figure 11.4); the purpose of this file, as mentioned previously is to control and monitor all the interactive (on-line, real time) generation of invoices. Key to this file is the project number, which is built via an interactive maintenance program. The customer number, which is part of this file, is initially entered by the terminal operator and is checked against the customer master in the vendor system. If no such customer

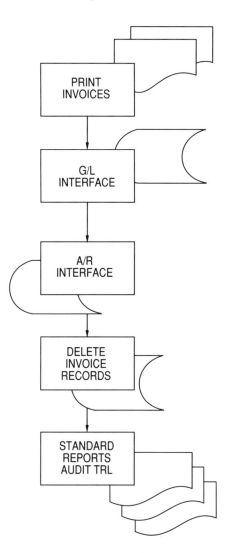

Figure 11.3—Part 3   This shows path 4 of the batch billing subsystem.

exists, the problem needs to be handled in the A/R (rather than in the billing system). The general ledger (G/L) account number will than be validated using parts of the G/L database, which is currently a production system. The transaction file (Figure 11.5) is automatically built during the add operation from the account distribution screen shown in Figure 11.6, displaying a maximum of some twenty debit and credit entries that make up the total invoice amount. Every entry on the transaction file will generate a

```
PROJECT MASTER FILE
-----------------------------------------------------------------
:  FIELD NAME        : KEY COMPONENT :  FROM  :   TO  : DISPOSITION :
-----------------------------------------------------------------

   PROJECT-NUMBER           YES          0001    0006     NUMERIC
   PROJECT-DESCRIPTION                   0007    1107     ALPHANUMERIC
   CUSTOMER-NUMBER                       1108    1121     ALPHANUMERIC
   GL-ACCOUNT-NUMBER                     1122    1129     ALPHANUMERIC
   RESPONSIBILITY-CODE                   1130    1147     ALPHANUMERIC
   BILLING-PREFIX                        1148    1148     ALPHA
   SPECIAL-INSTRUCTIONS                  1149    1289     ALPHANUMERIC

   FILLER                                1190    1300     ALPHANUMERIC
-----------------------------------------------------------------
```

Figure 11.4   These are the components of the Project Master File.

```
TRANSACTION FILE
-----------------------------------------------------------------
:  FIELD NAME        : KEY COMPONENT :  FROM  :   TO  : DISPOSITION :
-----------------------------------------------------------------

   INVOICE-PREFIX           YES          0001    0001     ALPHA
   INVOICE-NUMBER           YES          0002    0005     NUMERIC
   ORGANIZATION-CODE
   DIVISION-NUMBER                       0006    0007     NUMERIC
   DEPARTMENT-NUMBER                     0008    0011     NUMERIC
   GL-ACCOUNT-NUMBER                     0012    0019     ALPHANUMERIC
   PROJECT-NUMBER                        0020    0025     NUMERIC
   ACCOUNTING-PERIOD                     0026    0029     NUMERIC
   DR-CR-AMOUNT                          0030    0040     NUMERIC

   FILLER                                0040    0050     ALPHANUMERIC
-----------------------------------------------------------------
```

Figure 11.5   These are the components of the Transaction File.

corresponding record to be printed on the invoice stub, the key being the invoice number, the organization code, and the account number associated with the G/L. Transaction records are built and disseminated only after the organization code and the account numbers have been validated against the latest version of the G/L showing invoice amounts to be printed on the actual invoice document.

The invoice file (Figure 11.7) is a transient file. After invoices are successfully printed, the records are tagged and subsequently deleted from the system. This procedure also requires the latest version of a customer master file, a copy of which is to be brought forward from the A/R side. The customer master is needed for the customer's description, and possibly for other demographic information.

```
 MPINV30                 ACCOUNTS DISTRIBUTION SCREEN              XX/XX/XX
 INVOICE NUMBER: D DDDD


    DISTRIBUTION          AMOUNT          DISTRIBUTION          AMOUNT
 DIV DEPT  ACCOUNT#  D/C             DIV DEPT  ACCOUNT#  D/C

 XX  XXXX  XXXXXXXX  X  999999999     XX  XXXX  XXXXXXXX  X  999999999
 XX  XXXX  XXXXXXXX  X  999999999     XX  XXXX  XXXXXXXX  X  999999999
 XX  XXXX  XXXXXXXX  X  999999999     XX  XXXX  XXXXXXXX  X  999999999
 XX  XXXX  XXXXXXXX  X  999999999     XX  XXXX  XXXXXXXX  X  999999999
 XX  XXXX  XXXXXXXX  X  999999999     XX  XXXX  XXXXXXXX  X  999999999
 XX  XXXX  XXXXXXXX  X  999999999     XX  XXXX  XXXXXXXX  X  999999999
 XX  XXXX  XXXXXXXX  X  999999999     XX  XXXX  XXXXXXXX  X  999999999
 XX  XXXX  XXXXXXXX  X  999999999     XX  XXXX  XXXXXXXX  X  999999999
 XX  XXXX  XXXXXXXX  X  999999999     XX  XXXX  XXXXXXXX  X  999999999
 XX  XXXX  XXXXXXXX  X  999999999     XX  XXXX  XXXXXXXX  X  999999999


 PF1: BILLING AND INVOICING MENU    PF2: DELETE AN INVOICE
    >>>>>>>>>>>>>>>>>> SYSTEMS OR ERROR MESSAGES <<<<<<<<<<<<<<<<<<<<<<<<<
```

Figure 11.6   This is the layout of the Accounts Distribution Screen.

```
 INVOICE MASTER
 --------------------------------------------------------------------------
 :  FIELD NAME         : KEY COMPONENT :  FROM  :   TO  : DISPOSITION :
 --------------------------------------------------------------------------

    INVOICE-PREFIX           YES          0001     0001     ALPHA
    INVOICE-NUMBER           YES          0002     0005     NUMERIC
    CUSTOMER-NAME                         0006     0035     ALPHANUMERIC
    ADDRESS1                              0036     0065     ALPHANUMERIC
    ADDRESS2                              0066     0095     ALPHANUMERIC
    ADDRESS3                              0096     0116     ALPHANUMERIC
    STATE-CODE                            0117     0118     ALPHA
    ZIP-CODE                              0119     0123     NUMERIC
    BILL-DATE                             0124     0129     ALPHANUMERIC
    BILL-PERIOD                           0130     0133     ALPHANUMERIC
    CUSTOMER-NUMBER                       0134     0147     ALPHANUMERIC
    EXPLANATION                           0148     1248     ALPHANUMERIC
    INVOICE-AMOUNT                        1248     1258     NUMERIC
    PERIOD-DESCRIPTION                    1259     1323     ALPHANUMERIC
    ORIGINAL-INVOICE-NUMBER               1324     1327     NUMERIC
    FILLER                                1328     1350     ALPHANUMERIC

 --------------------------------------------------------------------------
```

Figure 11.7   These are the components of the Invoice Master

Two G/L subfiles are also necessary for the purpose of validating the account number and the organization code. Layout to these files is presented in Figure 11.8, followed by that of the customer master (Figure 11.9).

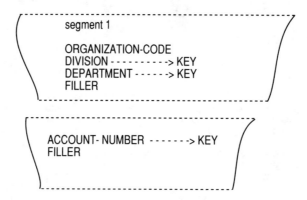

Figure 11.8   These are the key elements to the G/L database for the purpose of validating.

```
COMPANY NUMBER      (KEY)   001    003     NUMERIC       999
SEGMENT NUMBER      (KEY)   004    005     NUMERIC       9
CUSTOMER NUMBER     (KEY)   006    009     NUMERIC       9999
<------------------------------------------------------------>
CUSTOMER NAME               010    039     ALPHABETIC
CUSTOMER ADDRESS:
  STREET                    040    059     ALPHANUMERIC
  CITY                      060    069     ALPHANUMERIC
  STATE                     070    071     ALPHABETIC
  ZIP CODE                  072    081     ALPHANUMERIC
DUN BRADSTREET INFO:
  D B RATED                 082    085     NUMERIC       MMYY
  D B RATING                086    088     ALPHANUMERIC
CREDIT TOLERANCE GUIDES     089    090     ALPHANUMERIC
CREDIT TOLERANCE PERCENT    091    094     NUMERIC       S99.99
TERM CODES:
  REGULAR TERM CODE         095    095     ALPHANUMERIC
  C.O.D.                    096    096     ALPHANUMERIC
  SELL NOTE                 097    097     ALPHANUMERIC
  AGREEMENT                 098    098     ALPHANUMERIC
  DISCOUNT GRACE            099    101     NUMERIC       999
......
  LATE PAYMENT POLICY
......
  FINANCE CHARGE
......
  CREDIT AND DISCOUNT POLICY
......
  CASH TOLERANCE POLICY
......
  DUNNING LETTERS
......
  AGING CATEGORIES
......
  YEAR TO DATE INFO
......
```

Figure 11.9   This is a partial view of the Customer master file and a concatenated key.

Last, you need an invoice range table, which enables you to reassign beginning invoice numbers for printing purposes, and keeping track of the last system generated invoice number (Figure 11.10). With this background, some of the procedures required by the terminal operator will be examined. First, to invoke the billing system, sign-on using your valid operator I.D. and password, then clear the screen, and key in the transaction identifier of the first panel, which happens to be the main menu. This screen is displayed in Figure 11.11. If you have selected code "1" on this menu screen, you will be able to create and process new invoice records necessary for the subsequent printing of this document. In the next step, a secondary menu screen (also referred to as a first level submenu) is invoked by the system that is further illustrated in Figure 11.12 under the billing and invoicing menu screen. A third step in this process is the invocation of the invoicing functional menu shown in Figure 11.13. Note that this panel is only displayed when your selection on the screen was either a "B" (B for updating an invoice record) or a "D" (inquiry). Both the update and the inquiry panels require additional information to establish a specific path. When adding a record to the system, for example, the system is designed to lock you into a specific path, in which you must stay until the transaction is completed. When your processing mode is an "A", the system will walk

```
....5...10...15...20...25...30...35...40...45...50...55...60...65...70
+-----------------------------------------+
   PREFIX      ACCOUNT#    CUR.COUNT    MIN.RANGE    MAX.RANGE
+-----------------------------------------+
     A         12345678      0022         0001         1000
     B         33456772      1009         1001         2000
     C         22345567      3090         3001         4000
     D         33456677      4080         4001         4500
     E         44567782      5001         4501         6000
     F         22390817      6980         6001         7000
     G         22390127      7099         7001         7400
     H         11234556      7509         7401         8000
     I         23000009      8600         8001         8900
     Z                       0007         0001         8000
```

Figure 11.10 This is a prefix or range table. Note that each project has a corresponding prefix and account number on the project master. Thus, all you need to do is to key in the project number (223455) which will point to this table through the prefix and the account number part of the Project Master. When an invoice reaches its max (I=8900) it will automatically roll back to ts minimum which is 8001 in this case. If you need to override this situation, you may do so through the system.

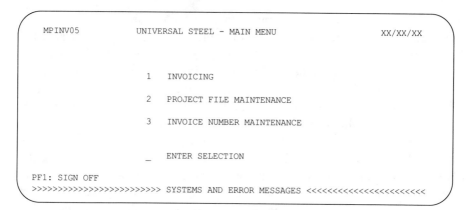

Figure 11.11   This is the layout of the menu screen.

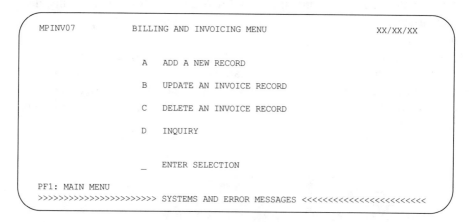

Figure 11.12   This is the layout of the billing and invoicing menu.

```
   MPINV39              INVOICING FUNCTIONAL MENU              XX/XX/XX


                  1:   INVOICE HEADER SCREEN

                  2:   INVOICE DESCRIPTION SCREEN

                  3:   ACCOUNT DISTRIBUTION SCREEN


                  _:   ENTER SELECTION

               _____:  ENTER PREFIX INVOICE NUMBER


   PF1: BILLING AND INVOICING MENU
   >>>>>>>>>>>>>>>>>>>>>>>> SYSTEMS AND ERROR MESSAGES <<<<<<<<<<<<<<<<<<<<<<<<
```

Figure 11.13   This is the layout of the invoicing functional menu.

```
MPINV10                 INVOICE HEADER SCREEN                   XX/XX/XX


        PROJECT NO :_____
        CREDIT MEMO:_         ORIGINAL INV# : ____
        CUSTOMER#  :DDDDDDD   CUSTOMER NAME :DDDDDDDDDDDDDDDDDDDDDDDDDDDDDD
        INVOICE #  :D DDDD    INVOICE AMOUNT:_____
        ACCOUNTING MM/YY: ____   BILLING DATE (MMDDYY) : __/__/__
        PERIOD DESCRIPT : _____

        -------------------- SPECIAL INSTRUCTIONS ---------------------
DDDDDDDDDDDDDDDDDDDDDDDDDDDDDDDDDDDDDDDDDDDDDDDDDDDDDDDDDDDDDDDDDDDDDDDDDDD
DDDDDDDDDDDDDDDDDDDDDDDDDDDDDDDDDDDDDDDDDDDDDDDDDDDDDDDDDDDDDDDDDDDDDDDDDDD

PF1: BILLING AND INVOICING MENU
PF2: INVOICE DESCRIPTION SCREEN
>>>>>>>>>>>>>>>>>>>>>>>>>> SYSTEMS AND ERROR MESSAGES <<<<<<<<<<<<<<<<<<<<<<<<<<
```

Figure 11.14   This is the layout of the invoice header screen.
(Strings of "D" characters represent display/protected mode)

```
MPINV15                 INVOICE DESCRIPTION SCREEN              XX/XX/XX
PROJECT NUMBER: DDDDDD              INVOICE NUMBER D DDDD

>>>>>>>>>>>>>>>>>>>>>>>>>> INVOICE DESCRIPTION <<<<<<<<<<<<<<<<<<<<<<<<<<<<<
XXXXXXXXXXXXXXXXXXXXXXXXXXXXXXXXXXXXXXXXXXXXXXXXXXXXXXXXXXXXXXXXXXXXXXXXXXXXXX
XXXXXXXXXXXXXXXXXXXXXXXXXXXXXXXXXXXXXXXXXXXXXXXXXXXXXXXXXXXXXXXXXXXXXXXXXXXXXX
XXXXXXXXXXXXXXXXXXXXXXXXXXXXXXXXXXXXXXXXXXXXXXXXXXXXXXXXXXXXXXXXXXXXXXXXXXXXXX
XXXXXXXXXXXXXXXXXXXXXXXXXXXXXXXXXXXXXXXXXXXXXXXXXXXXXXXXXXXXXXXXXXXXXXXXXXXXXX
XXXXXXXXXXXXXXXXXXXXXXXXXXXXXXXXXXXXXXXXXXXXXXXXXXXXXXXXXXXXXXXXXXXXXXXXXXXXXX
XXXXXXXXXXXXXXXXXXXXXXXXXXXXXXXXXXXXXXXXXXXXXXXXXXXXXXXXXXXXXXXXXXXXXXXXXXXXXX
XXXXXXXXXXXXXXXXXXXXXXXXXXXXXXXXXXXXXXXXXXXXXXXXXXXXXXXXXXXXXXXXXXXXXXXXXXXXXX
XXXXXXXXXXXXXXXXXXXXXXXXXXXXXXXXXXXXXXXXXXXXXXXXXXXXXXXXXXXXXXXXXXXXXXXXXXXXXX
XXXXXXXXXXXXXXXXXXXXXXXXXXXXXXXXXXXXXXXXXXXXXXXXXXXXXXXXXXXXXXXXXXXXXXXXXXXXXX
XXXXXXXXXXXXXXXXXXXXXXXXXXXXXXXXXXXXXXXXXXXXXXXXXXXXXXXXXXXXXXXXXXXXXXXXXXXXXX
XXXXXXXXXXXXXXXXXXXXXXXXXXXXXXXXXXXXXXXXXXXXXXXXXXXXXXXXXXXXXXXXXXXXXXXXXXXXXX
XXXXXXXXXXXXXXXXXXXXXXXXX^XXXXXXXXXXXXXXXXXXXXXXXXXXXXXXXXXXXXXXXXXXXXXXXXXXXX
XXXXXXXXXXXXXXXXXXXXXXXXXXXXXXXXXXXXXXXXXXXXXXXXXXXXXXXXXXXXXXXXXXXXXXXXXXXXXX
XXXXXXXXXXXXXXXXXXXXXXXXXXXXXXXXXXXXXXXXXXXXXXXXXXXXXXXXXXXXXXXXXXXXXXXXXXXXXX
XXXXXXXXXXXXXXXXXXXXXXXXXXXXXXXXXXXXXXXXXXXXXXXXXXXXXXXXXXXXXXXXXXXXXXXXXXXXXX
XXXXXXXXXXXXXXXXXXXXXXXXXXXXXXXXXXXXXXXXXXXXXXXXXXXXXXXXXXXXXXXXXXXXXXXXXXXXXX
XXXXXXXXXXXXXXXXXXXXXXXXXXXXXXXXXXXXXXXXXXXXXXXXXXXXXXXXXXXXXXXXXXXXXXXXXXXXXX

 PF1: ACCOUNT DISTRIBUTION SCREEN  PF2: BILLING AND INVOICING MENU
   >>>>>>>>>>>>>>>>>>> SYSTEMS OR ERROR MESSAGES <<<<<<<<<<<<<<<<<<<<<<<<
```

Figure 11.15   This is the layout of the invoice distribution header screen.

```
MPINV30                 ACCOUNTS DISTRIBUTION SCREEN              XX/XX/XX
INVOICE NUMBER: D DDDD

   DISTRIBUTION                AMOUNT       DISTRIBUTION                AMOUNT
DIV DEPT  ACCOUNT#  D/C                  DIV DEPT  ACCOUNT#  D/C

XX  XXXX  XXXXXXXX   X   999999999       XX  XXXX  XXXXXXXX   X   999999999
XX  XXXX  XXXXXXXX   X   999999999       XX  XXXX  XXXXXXXX   X   999999999
XX  XXXX  XXXXXXXX   X   999999999       XX  XXXX  XXXXXXXX   X   999999999
XX  XXXX  XXXXXXXX   X   999999999       XX  XXXX  XXXXXXXX   X   999999999
XX  XXXX  XXXXXXXX   X   999999999       XX  XXXX  XXXXXXXX   X   999999999
XX  XXXX  XXXXXXXX   X   999999999       XX  XXXX  XXXXXXXX   X   999999999
XX  XXXX  XXXXXXXX   X   999999999       XX  XXXX  XXXXXXXX   X   999999999
XX  XXXX  XXXXXXXX   X   999999999       XX  XXXX  XXXXXXXX   X   999999999
XX  XXXX  XXXXXXXX   X   999999999       XX  XXXX  XXXXXXXX   X   999999999
XX  XXXX  XXXXXXXX   X   999999999       XX  XXXX  XXXXXXXX   X   999999999


PF1: BILLING AND INVOICING MENU    PF2: DELETE AN INVOICE
  >>>>>>>>>>>>>>>>>> SYSTEMS OR ERROR MESSAGES <<<<<<<<<<<<<<<<<<<<<<<<<
```

Figure 11.16   This is the layout of the accounts distribution screen.

you through a mandatory sequence of three screens, these being an invoice header screen, shown in Figure 11.14, an Invoice Description Screen (Figure 11.15) and an Account Distribution Screen (Figure 11.16). Note that neither an invoice nor a transaction record will be created until all three panels are successfully executed in succession.

11.2.3   Batch Billing

The batch portion, or the off-line cycle, of the billing system is made up of three functions. The first one has to do with the actual printing of a set of invoices, and then, deleting them in subsequent cycles.The second function creates and formats a number of transaction records that are created at the end of the add cycle, provided all verification procedures are acceptable. Once validated, these transaction records will update the G/L master on a detail level. A third function deals with the interface mechanism that is built between this module and the A/R system. All interface requirements are handled in batch mode. Figure 11.17 is an overview of the above situation. Note that the flowchart is a functional review rather than a program-by-program breakdown of the billing cycle, since each box on the diagram can represent either a number of application programs or functional areas.

In the first step, you want to make sure that all files are closed to the on-line processing before initiating the post on-line cycle. Step 2 represents

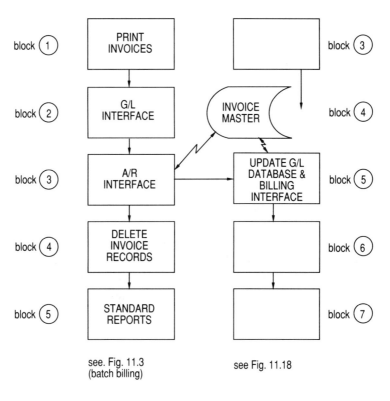

Figure 11.17 This is the interface mechanism between the billing and the A/R systems.

a set of standard procedures possibly to recover a number of on-line trans-actions should there be any problem, for example, a system failure during the processing of those transactions. In step 3, you need to validate all debit and credit transactions that were generated during the add process. Keep in mind that a continuous validation process is required against the G/L files because of the volatile nature of those files, that is, the high number of transactions matched against them. Once the validation process detects no error (step 4), you are ready to reformat those transaction records according to G/L specifications. Note that this process is also responsible for creating a report generator file with pieces of information attained at the various steps of the billing cycle. Step 5 is where the actual interface process is to take place. Subsequently, the printing of invoices are triggered, which is the primary purpose of step 6.

As you can see, this module is fairly involved in terms of logic and file handling. Input to this step is the invoice master, which happens to be simply a transient file, essentially like a suspense dataset, for printing invoices and generating the required audit trails, as the result. Also note that a second interface, this time into the A/R system is completed, where the individual invoice amounts are transferred to the Accounts Receivable database. If the condition code past step 3 is equal to zero (reflecting the successful completion of the prior step), the entire invoice file is deleted before a subsequent run. Last, a set of audit trail reports generated from the report generator file is printed to account for a step-by-step review of the billing cycle.

11.2.4   The A/R System

The A/R system is a recently acquired vendor package made up of both real time and batch procedures. Most of the activities are performed on-line (that is, editing and updating of the data) although standard reporting and a substantial portion of the interface is done in a totally batch environment.

The A/R system overall is made up of three cycles. These are as follows:

1. an on-line preparation cycle,
2. an on-line real-time cycle, and
3. a post on-line cycle.

The on-line preparation cycle prepares or initializes some of the A/R database files for the on-line system. Among these activities, the system purges all credit and customer notes, ages the open item records based on a requested aging date, sets up sequence and alternate search keys.

The on-line, real-time cycle performs practically all the maintenance requirements of the major files that have been referred to as the A/R database files. To be more specific, the system handles cash application, customer inquiry, credit searches and reviews, customer maintenance, the transfer of open items, payment inquiries, and so forth.

The post on-line cycle is responsible for backing up and restoring all major files in the system, for running periodic interfaces between this system and the G/L and providing the user with a set of standard reports.

The post on-line cycle is also responsible for a full, on-line recovery of the system, in other words, it backs up all major files that could have been "blown away" during, the time the Telecommunications monitor was disabled. A fourth module, of course, has to do with the vendor's productivity tools, such as generating ad hoc type of reports through a fourth generation language, which is also utilized to update the system's data dictionary.

11.2.5   A/R File Structure

The A/R database is made up of five individual files, all having the same VSAM structure. The corporate guidelines file, which needs to be created before anything else, is functional in the system. The corporate guidelines file essentially identifies the way a particular business is handled in general terms. It defines, overall, how discounts are determined, deductions, terms, tolerance, credit limits, how G/R distributions are handled and so on. All the previously mentioned features are user-defined including certain constants or header information that needs to appear on the top of each report. Obviously, in our particular situation rather than having the title "CASH TOLERANCE REPORT: (and then the name of the software company) printed on the top of each report page, we want to customize it to read "CASH TOLERANCE REPORT: UNIVERSAL STEEL COMPANY" (the latter refers to our corporate title).

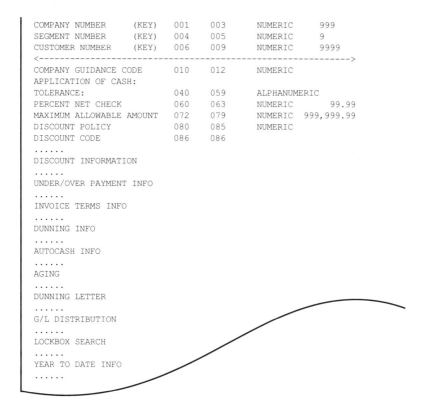

```
COMPANY NUMBER        (KEY)    001    003      NUMERIC       999
SEGMENT NUMBER        (KEY)    004    005      NUMERIC       9
CUSTOMER NUMBER       (KEY)    006    009      NUMERIC       9999
<----------------------------------------------------------->
COMPANY GUIDANCE CODE          010    012      NUMERIC
APPLICATION OF CASH:
TOLERANCE:                     040    059      ALPHANUMERIC
PERCENT NET CHECK              060    063      NUMERIC          99.99
MAXIMUM ALLOWABLE AMOUNT       072    079      NUMERIC   999,999.99
DISCOUNT POLICY                080    085      NUMERIC
DISCOUNT CODE                  086    086
......
DISCOUNT INFORMATION
......
UNDER/OVER PAYMENT INFO
......
INVOICE TERMS INFO
......
DUNNING INFO
......
AUTOCASH INFO
......
AGING
......
DUNNING LETTER
......
G/L DISTRIBUTION
......
LOCKBOX SEARCH
......
YEAR TO DATE INFO
......
```

Figure 11.18   This is a partial view of the corporate guidelines file and a concatenated key.

Conceptually, it is easier to define certain general terms for every customer in the system, than override them as an exception to the rule. A layout of the corporate guidelines master is shown in Figure 11.18. The Corporate Guidelines file is made up of a number of segments, such as discount information, invoice terms, auto-cash, aging, dunning letters, G/L distribution, year-to-date info, and so forth.

A second major file in the system has to do with keeping track of the customer in terms of demographic data and specific policies. The term "overriding" certain terms, or guidelines was mentioned previously. Although general customer policies are set on a company-wide level, it is possible to reapply some of the rules with regards to tolerance or discount procedures to suit a particular (usually high-volume) customer. The customer master includes information with regards to pay habits, rating, tax code, standard industrial classification code and so forth. This information was presented in Figure 11.9. Because of the extent of these files, it normally requires a multiple set of screens to access, define and maintain the above information.

The open items file is the third component on the A/R database. Open items are essentially the charges and credits that are "open" on the customer's

```
COMPANY NUMBER        (KEY)   001   003    NUMERIC       999
SEGMENT NUMBER        (KEY)   004   005    NUMERIC       9
CUSTOMER NUMBER       (KEY)   006   009    NUMERIC       9999
ITEM REF NUMBER       (KEY)   010   020    ALPHANUMERIC
<----------------------------->
DESCRIPTION                   020   040    ALPHANUMERIC
TRANSACTION CODE              041   041    ALPHANUMERIC
ITEM AMOUNT                   052   061    NUMERIC       99,999,999.99
PAYMENT DATE                  062   068    NUMERIC       MMDDYY
PAYMENT AMOUNT                069   077    NUMERIC       99,999,999.99
AGING DATE                    074   079    NUMERIC       MMDDYY
DISCOUNT DATE                 080   085    NUMERIC       MMDDYY
DUE DATE                      086   091    NUMERIC       MMDDYY
ITEM CODE                     092   093    NUMERIC
STATEMENT CODE                094   095    NUMERIC
STATUS CODE                   096   097    NUMERIC
SALESMAN NUMBER               098   104    NUMERIC
STORE NUMBER                  105   110    NUMERIC
PAY FROM LOCATION             111   115    ALPHANUMERIC
PURCHASE ORDER NUMBER         116   122    ALPHANUMERIC
ITEM LOCKBOX                  123   129    ALPHANUMERIC
.....
DISCOUNT INFORMATION
.....
ITEM REMOVAL INFORMATION
```

Figure 11.19   This is a partial view of the closed item master.

```
COMPANY NUMBER       (KEY)   001   003   NUMERIC       999
SEGMENT NUMBER       (KEY)   004   005   NUMERIC       9
CUSTOMER NUMBER      (KEY)   006   009   NUMERIC       9999
ITEM REF NUMBER      (KEY)   010   020   ALPHANUMERIC
<——————————————————————————>
DESCRIPTION                  020   040   ALPHANUMERIC
TRANSACTION CODE             041   041   ALPHANUMERIC
DISCOUNT AMOUNT              042   051   NUMERIC       99,999,999.99
ITEM AMOUNT                  052   061   NUMERIC       99,999,999.99
DISCOUNT DATE                062   067   NUMERIC       MMDDYY
DUE DATE                     068   073   NUMERIC       MMDDYY
AGING DATE                   074   079   NUMERIC       MMDDYY
SALESMAN NUMBER              080   086   NUMERIC
STORE NUMBER                 087   092   NUMERIC
PAY FROM LOCATION            093   097   ALPHANUMERIC
PURCHASE ORDER NUMBER        098   104   ALPHANUMERIC
......
GENERAL LEDGER REF DATA
......
DUNNING INFO
......
```

Figure 11.20   This is a partial view of the closed item history master.

A/R account such as invoices, credit memos, debit memos, unapplied cash, partial payments, etc.

The A/R database comprises two additional files. These are a payment history file and a paid item file shown in Figs. 11.19 and 11.20. Note that the open items file has the same record layout as the paid or "closed" items file.

11.2.6   The A/R Batch Cycle

The batch portion of the A/R system is a great deal more complex to install than its front-end counter part. There are several reasons for that. Batch systems require a more formal approach to customize. Ironically, this is where the "action" is when installing a software package. On-line systems can be accessed by the user in a number of different ways when a procedure is invoked randomly. In atypical batch system however, there is always a set of hierarchical activities that must be done sequentially, such as reporting and initializing files, providing backups and logical interfaces, setting up restart procedures, and so forth. Also, in a typical business environment, the printing of voluminous (standard) reports is still very much a necessity, although this function has been thoroughly enhanced in a fourth generation environment with user-manipulated facilities. Figure 11.21 shows

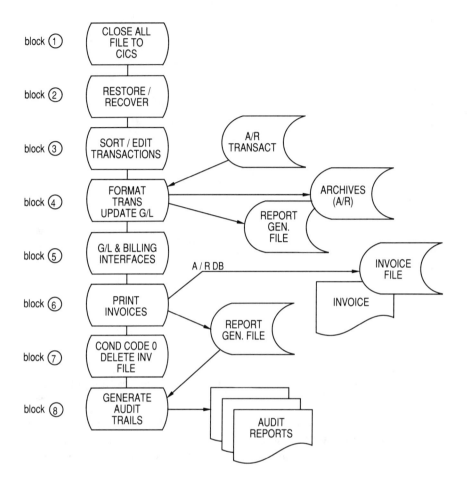

block ① CLOSE ALL FILE TO CICS

block ② RESTORE / RECOVER

block ③ SORT / EDIT TRANSACTIONS

A/R TRANSACT

block ④ FORMAT TRANS UPDATE G/L

ARCHIVES (A/R)

REPORT GEN. FILE

block ⑤ G/L & BILLING INTERFACES

A / R DB

INVOICE FILE

block ⑥ PRINT INVOICES

INVOICE

REPORT GEN. FILE

block ⑦ COND CODE 0 DELETE INV FILE

block ⑧ GENERATE AUDIT TRAILS

AUDIT REPORTS

Figure 11.21   This is a functional overview of the batch portion of the A/R system.

a functional overview of the daily processing job flow for the A/R system. The first block represents a standard set of maintenance procedures including the backing up of key files and recovering certain on-line transactions. This is pretty much the same technique we applied in conjunction with the batch portion of the billing system.

Block 2 is made up of a number of subtasks, such as the formatting of the G/L and report files, which reflects all daily on-line activities. Once these records are formatted, they will be sorted in a number of ways to accommodate G/L and A/R reporting requirements.

Block 3 is further dedicated to reporting. This module extracts certain record types from the Accounts Receivable database and splits them into various reporting segments.

Block 4 represents the interface mechanism between the G/L and the A/R systems. This is the step where each transaction is applied against the distribution master and validates all G/L chart of accounts including the corporate guidelines master.

Block 5 splits the A/R transactions into a number of miscellaneous segments such as bank account maintenance, autocash, G/L, reporting, and so forth.

Block 6 handles the requirements necessary to validate and reconcile cash that is kept on a bank transaction file. The procedures in block 6 also handle cash adjustments and the automatic application of cash when payment is made. The system periodically generates cash activity reports on an on-demand basis.

Block 7 validates, updates (and reports on) all new or changed corporate guidelines data. It sorts and validates A/R transactions into functional areas such as payment history, open item maintenance, cash application, journal write-offs, etc.

Block 8 is a pre-on-line processing phase whose function is to prepare the major files (including the A/R database) for on-line processing.

Normally, these are the last set of procedures built into the batch cycle.

11.2.7   The Interactive A/R System

The on-line portion of the A/R system is a complex mechanism. It is a menu-driven system, thereby allowing the user numerous views or paths to its database and to its data dictionary. This path concept is reflected in Figure 11.22. It would be next to impossible to describe every single aspect involved in the process. For example, a customer inquiry starts with selection 4 (financial systems), which, in turn, invokes a secondary menu. Your selection of 1 (A/R screen) enables you to define one of ten major functions, each of which can be further exploded into subsequent detail. The level of detail, of course, increases with each menu selection until the information is presented on a specialized level, normally geared to a clerk who does nothing else, but processing customer payments, open items, payment history, customer notes, and dunning letters, and so on. Thus, customer inquiry opens into subsequent modules, such as the one presented in 11.23. (An overview of this is also shown in Figure 11.24.) Ironically, because of the overwhelming complexity of most vendor systems, you

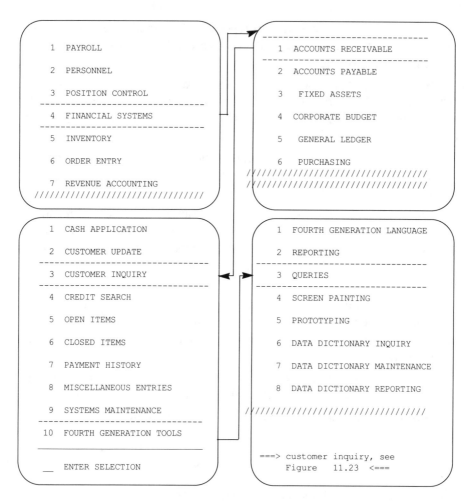

Figure 11.22   This is the path concept in a fourth generation A/R system.

cannot be very concerned about learning all the detail incorporated into such a vendor product—not unless you need to spend an unreasonably long time on such a project the way a technical representative of the vendor company does. Of course, the more you understand the better, even though you need to consider a trade-off point, beyond which your effort may be wasted.

In this particular case study, you need to trace two files without which the billing system would be in jeopardy. These files are the corporate guidelines file and the customer master. You need to be able to answer questions by tracing through the A/R system such as "What happens to the Customer Master and the Corporate Guidelines File after the on-line system is disabled? and "Will there be any further updates affecting these files and from what sources?"

```
 > GU  _____  ON R5001


           ___  AR:M   CUSTOMER INQUIRY   -DESCRIPTION -

     CORP->  _____    CUST->                 SHORT NAME->   _____  LANG->
     TYPE-> _  METHOD-> _  OPENED-> 00000 SHARED DATA->     _____  _____

       NAME/ADDRESS                          ADDRESS

     1 _____        4  _____
     2 _____        5  _____
     3 _____        CITY-> _____
       state-> __  postal->            CTRY-> _____
       CTY-> _____  CITY CD-> __        SOURCE-> _____

       CONTACT NAME                  TITLE           SINCE PHONE
     1 _____     _____      000000_____
     2 _____     _____      000000_____


     SIC--> _____  _____ SUB-> NATIONAL ACCT-> _____  _____
     TAX ID-> _____  AP VENDOR ID-> _____
     DESC-> _____
            _____
                                08/07/88  13:12:01  M2LL ACTION__
```

Figure 11.23   This is the customer inquiry (description) screen.

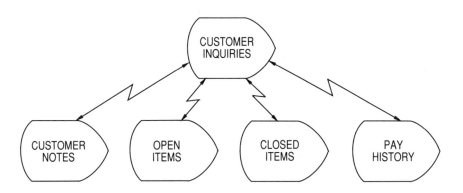

Figure 11.24 These are procedures within the A/R customer inquiry modules.

11.2.8   Implementation Problems

Both the billing and the A/R systems require an extensive interaction, the sharing of common resources, which is the primary purpose of the interface. In order to decide on a proper approach, certain assumptions were made to clarify the environment and some of the potential problems presented therein.

The first assumption deals with the extent of a fourth generation support environment available. That is, how much and how extensive is the fourth generation technology acquired with the purchase of the package? This makes all the difference in the world, whether you can design a borderless system, or one that is only operational among the applications of the same vendor.

A second assumption deals with the fragmented nature of the application software environment. There are three over-riding aspects:

1. The billing system, which is an in-house application software,

2. the A/R system, which is a proprietary product, yet to be installed, and

3. A G/L system, which is another proprietary package fully operational and totally incompatible with the A/R system.

The first problem that comes into play centers around the obvious interdependence that exists between the G/L and the billing systems. The in-house billing system, must validate its own set of distribution codes against the G/L masters. This requires continuous access to a different system. Note that the access is merely for the purpose of validating an account and not for the purpose of transferring data. Invalid distribution codes are also reported in the billing system, the maintenance of which pertains to the G/L.

A second problem relates back to the billing system's dependency on the customer master. In order for you to process an invoice, you need to establish a valid customer account. This too, is outside the scope of the billing system. Once a customer is found and validated, you need to retrieve the customer's name and address from that file along with a half-a-dozen other demographic data fields required for processing an invoice. It is not feasible to create an independent customer master inside the billing module, since such a file needs to be kept in sync with its A/R counterpart, which would otherwise be wasteful and complex.

A third problem is caused by some hierarchical dependencies internal to the A/R system. The problem is that a customer master is contingent on the development of a corporate guidelines file, which essentially defines the entire system in terms of rules and regulations.The corporate guidelines file highlights major policy decisions for a business that can then be overridden on the customer master. Thus, if the discount rate for a certain group of customers is, for example, 6%, and if customer "A" belongs in that category, you need to override his specific discount rate on the customer master file. In order to create a corporate guidelines file, it normally requires a major effort on the part of the user. The corporate guidelines file needs to look at certain policy decisions and procedures in depth while reviewing the organization on several functional levels.

A fourth problem has to do with the dependency of the billing system on the A/R and vice versa. Under problem definition 2, the billing system needs to interact with the customer master file for validating an invoice were highlighted. Once the invoice is validated, you need to "transport" each invoice amount to the A/R system for further review and distribution. This requires an interface program, or two, depending on the extent of the project.

What needs to be interfaced is largely determined by the target system, which happens to be the G/L in this case study. Information expected to be supplied by the various applications may vary in format, that is to say, the G/L may require one specific format when receiving data from the A/P system, another from payroll, and yet a third segment from the A/R or fixed assets procedures.

G/L systems normally deal with distribution codes and debit and credit amounts. Simply, you want to know how much money to apply to what account and whether such an entry is to be debited or credited.Whatever the requirements for data are, you need to provide this exchange of information through your own in-house developed program(s), unless the vendor for both A/R and G/L systems are identical. When that happens, it is normally the vendor who takes responsibility for the overall process.

Timing is another important consideration in defining interface. Most business systems only require the exchange of information between the two systems on a monthly (sometimes on a weekly) basis, normally after the "books" for the current period had been closed. A daily interaction between the G/L and the A/R systems, for example, where you are merely validating some pieces of data against the master file, is a different type of interface, even though you do, in fact, retrieve and utilize information from another system.

11.2.9   Developing an Implementation Plan

To complete an implementation plan, you need to recognize that parts of this project are at different stages of completion. For example, the billing system is in an early programming stage, which is to be reflected in the planning process. The A/R system is a complete product, although some programming requirements are needed in order to accommodate the current procedures. The G/L system is a production system (meaning it is already implemented), but some changes may be directly affecting that system when the new environment becomes effective.

The first stage in planning is to establish a project plan for the billing system, showing all the hierarchical dependencies, which is the purpose of Figure 11.25 and 11.26. Figure 11.25 is an inventory of the new programs that have to be developed from scratch both on-line and batch. Figure 11.26 is part of an implementation plan that describes a task in terms of man-hours, hierarchical dependencies, and personnel assigned to those tasks.

In establishing man-hour requirements, note the following: a day is equivalent to approximately 5.5 or 6.0 man-hours due to the way fringe benefits, such as sick days, vacation hours, holidays, and other nonproductive activities are computed. To simplify the planning process, man-hour requirements are expressed in terms of whole numbers. The term *S next to the hours shown means that a shell of a previous program can be utilized to save time. In an on-line environment, for example (note that the term "shell" is also applicable to batch programs), you can segregate five major functions, which are as follows: add, update, delete, inquire, and browse. Strictly from an efficient programming point of view, you need to keep these functions separate. Once you have completed an add program for example, you can clone it, that is, you can make a copy of it and use it to prepare some other type of program from it, such as an update program, by modifying

```
DESCRIPTION          * PROGRAM * MAP NAME * MAPSET NAME * TRANSID

MAIN MENU            * INV005  * MPINV05  * INVSET      * I005
BILLING & INVOICING* INV007  * MPINV07  * INVSET      * I007
HEADER: ADD          * INV010  * MPINV10  * INVSET      * I010
HEADER: UPDATE       * INV011  * MPINV11  * INVSET      * I011
HEADER: INQUIRY      * INV012  * MPINV12  * INVSET      * I012
DESCRIPT: ADD        * INV015  * MPINV15  * INVSET      * I015
DESCRIPT: UPDATE     * INV016  * MPINV16  * INVSET      * I016
DESCRIPT: INQUIRY    * INV017  * MPINV17  * INVSET      * I017
ACC DIST: ADD        * INV030  * MPINV30  * INVSET      * I030
                     * INV031  * MPINV31  * INVSET      * I031
                                          * INVSET      * I032
                                          * INVSET      * I033
```

Figure 11.25 This is a summary of a program naming convention in the billing subsystem.

TASK #	<——TASK ——>	MAN	TOTAL DEPENDENCY HOURS	STAFF ON TASK	ASSIGNED
001	EDUCATING THE PROGRAMMING STAFF TO FUNCTION IN AN ON-LINE EN- VIRONMENT. projection is based on norm rather than individual skills at the Project Manager's disposal				
002	INVOICING SYSTEM: ON LINE/BATCH PROGRAMMING ACTIVITIES				
002.01	MAIN-MENU : INV005	18		001	
002.02	FUNCTIONAL MENU : INV007	18		001	
002.03	HEADER ADD : INV010	32		001	
002.04	HEADER UPDATE : INV011	18	S* 001-002.03		
002.05	HEADER INQUIRY : INV012	18		001	
002.06	INV. DESCRIPT.ADD: INV015	32		001	
002.07	INV. DESCRIPT.UPD: INV016	18	S*001-002.06		
002.08	INV. DESCRIPT.INQ: INV017	18		001	
002.09	ACCT.DISTRIB. ADD: INV030	46		001	
002.10	ACCT.DISTRIB. UPD: INV031	18	S* 001		
002.11	ACCT.DISTRIB. INQ: INV032	18		001	
002.12	DELETE SEGMENT : INV033	18		001	
002.13	PROJECT FILE MENU: INV035	18		001	
002.14	PROJECT FILE LOAD: INV036	46		001	
002.15	PROJECT FILE UPD : INV037	46	S* 001-002.14		
002.16	PROJECT FILE INQ : INV038	18	S* 001		
002.17	PROJECT FILE BROW: INV039	52		001	
002.18	INVOICE RANGE ADD: INV040	24		001	
002.19	INVOICE RANGE UPD: INV041	24	S* 001-002.18		
002.20	INVOICE RANGE DEL: INV042	18		001	
002.21	INVOICE RANGE INQ: INV043	18		001	
002.22	PRINT INVOICES : INVR001	60		002.01-002.21	
002.23	G/L INTERFACE : INVR002	75		002.01-002.21	
002.24	DELETE INV MAST : INVR003	20		002.01-002.21	
002.25	REPORTING MODULE : INVR004	120		002.01-002.21	
003	PRELIMINARY A/R ACTIVITIES:				
003.01	REVIEW MODIFICATIONS TO THE CUSTOMER MASTER AND CORPORATE GUIDELINES FILE	20			
004	LOAD MASTER FILES				
004.001	LOAD PROJECT MASTER			002.13-002.15	USER
004.002	LOAD CUSTOMER MASTER			003.01	USER
004.003	LOAD CORPORATE GUIDELINES			003.01	USER

TASK #	<---------TASK ---------->	TOTAL MAN HOURS	DEPENDENCY ON TASK	STAFF ASSIGNED
005	COPY ALL FILES: PERFORM A COMPREHENSIVE SYSTEMS TEST USING A CUSTOMIZED VERSION OF BOTH ON-LINE AND BATCH SYSTEMS. EVALUATE RESULTS	72	001 - 005	
006	USER SIGN OFF ON INVOICING SYSTEM			

Figure 11.26   This is a partial implementation plan for both billing and A/R systems.

some of the existing code in the process. Modification of this nature would include the protection of the key field, the redefinition of certain procedures, which, under CICS Command, for example, would correspond to a HANDLE CONDITION.

To develop an update program, you need an add shell (or vice versa), just as you can use an inquiry shell to develop a browse program and so on. This whole concept of "shell preparation" ideally would be performed by the same programmer who is already familiar with the original program to be cloned. To further highlight this process, INV010 (which is an add program) can be modified to an update program with minimum effort. If you were to create a shell out of 002.03 (HEADER - ADD program) to subsequently transform it to an update routine, the following, would be indicated:

002.04 18 HOURS S* DEPENDENCY===>01.002.03

Note that 01 was listed since that program is also dependent on step 1, which represents some educational activities such as reviewing programming conventions and efficiencies with a relatively inexperienced staff.

Time incorporated into the development of each program entails the creation of VSAM clusters (where applicable). To put it simply, the person who develops a certain application program also needs to create its own test data, and preferably a copy library member with which to do the testing.

Staffing assignments have not been mentioned up to this point since most of the specifics involved in picking a team will not be available until some time later. Staffing assignment is simply an expression of priority (and availability) of human resources. Generally, the more people who are allocated to a project, the quicker it will get finished, assuming standard quality and experience on the part of the staff and a hierarchical dependency structure that would nonetheless allow you to work on a number of projects concurrently.

Three of the tasks shown in Figure 11.26 (Part 1 and 2) are completely user dependent. These are the loading (and preparation) of the master files (Task 004) such as the project master file, the customer master, and the corporate guidelines file.

For programming efficiency alone, you can rely on the vendor's demo file in developing your code, but systems testing should be based on a more customized set of data. This would preferably be built by the user out of his or her own test material, which will eventually be used in a production environment. The loading of the above files is a user-dependent task, and you are encouraged to assign a time frame, a target date to such activities, for your own protection. In practice, no task should be left open ended even if it is not expected to be performed by your immediate data processing staff. The second stage of planning involves the new A/R package laid out in Figure 11.27. This schedule is a continuation of what was presented in Figure 11.26, in fact, it continues with Task 007, which is the installation process.

Task 007	INSTALLATION
007.1	Systems Utilities
007.2	Job Stream
007.3	Source Code
007.4	Batch and On-Line Demo Systems
007.4.1	Load A/R Database Files
007.4.2	Initialize All On-Line Files and Those Used with the Batch System
007.4.3	Run On-Line System Using a Vendor Prepared Script
007.4.4	Run Daily Batch System, Generate Reports, Check Results
007.4.5	Set Up All Additional Run-Streams
Task 008	Evaluate Results (MM)*
Task 009	Define Requirements for Customization
009.1	Evaluate Complexity
009.2	Programming Requirements and Specs
009.3	Programming
009.4	Unit Testing of Above (MM)**
Task 010	Develop Interface Mechanism Between A/R and Billing and Between A/R and the General Ledger System
Task 011	Test Interface Programs: Verify Results (MM)**
Task 012	Develop Comprehensive Conversion Mechanism
Task 013	Test Conversion Programs: Verify Results (MM)**
Task 014	Set Up Your Own Test Environment Using the Demo Model With Corporate Data
014.1	Reinitialize Demo Files
014.2	Load Actual Data On-Line or Through the Conversion Programs and Verify the Result of Each Procedure
014.2.1	Corporate Guidelines File
014.2.2	Customer Master file
014.2.3	Open Items File
014.2.4	Payment History
014.2.5	Closed (Paid) Items
Task 015	Comprehensive Test of All Enhancements (MM)**
Task 016	Run Full Blown Test System, Evaluate Results (MM)**
Task 017	Test Billing and A/R Systems in Unison: Evaluate Results (MM)**
Task 018	Start Paralleling - Evaluate results (MM)**
Task 019	Cut Over to Final Production Environment (MM)**

Figure 11.27 This is the A/R implementation schedule.

As pointed out earlier, in Chapter 10, under the systems generation process, the plan calls for the implementation of all relevant systems utilities (Task 007.01), original job streams (Task 007.02), and the loading of all source code (Task 007.03). This will pave the way for the implementation of the vendor-supplied demo module (Task 007.04), which is made up of the following five tasks:

- 007.04.1 Load all A/R database files. Database files are essentially those that represent original or raw data, such as a customer name or address, open items (items that have not been paid yet) as opposed to temporary or interim files whose contents can be arrived at through calculation or consolidation from existing data.

- 007.04.2 Perform file initialization, which simply means that all major files will be set up containing properly tested data using "representative" test material.

- 007.04.3 Start testing your on-line system based on some predefined script that will enable you to verify expected results.

- 007.04.4 Repeat the same, this time verifying the accuracy of the batch system and subsequently all standard reports generated in the process.

- 007.04.5 Define each runstream in the process, runstreams based on functions (such as an update module, reporting module, etc) and those based on time processing (such as daily, weekly, monthly, and on-demand types.)

- Evaluate all the above activities in Task 008, which is a milestone activity. Milestone activities are designated by (MM)** meaning the completion of a major logical unit in the implementation process.

Every user needs to have some additional features developed over and above what is available in the package. That is basically standard in this business. What makes the process more difficult is the extent of the new features that must be incorporated into the software. If it is a simple matter of the system lacking certain customized reports, for example, most fourth generation report modules (for example, Millennium or I.E.) can handle the problem through an available language. If, however, a great number of procedures are substantially different from what is contained in the package, the new requirements must be developed and incorporated into the system to make it viable. That is the primary purpose of Task 009.

Actually, this process is made up of four sets of activities. These are as follows:

1. evaluating the complexity of the new requirements (Can they be done at all and what would be the most economical way of of doing them?)

2. if the answer to the first question is "yes", and steps to an optimal approach are defined, you need to look at those features in terms of feasibility and technical complexity. (The term "feasibility" is not necessarily a financial term, but one representing some of the processing requirements without which the package is not a viable product for any specific user.)

3. the creation of a set of detailed program specs, and

4. the coding and testing of those programs, the completion of which represents some additional milestone activities (Task 009.4). Note that although unit testing needs to be performed within the 009 series, a full-blown systems or integration test of those enhancements will not be practical until Task 15 is implemented.

In a mixed environment (that which utilizes a variety of vendor packages and vendors), the design of an interface mechanism is crucial. Just how elaborate this mechanism should be is largely dependent upon the extent of the fourth generation technology used in the software; whether it is an all-encompassing support system, such as SDT or Extended I.E., or simply a system geared to perform only within a framework of the same vendor. To build an interface bridge between two applications designed by the same vendor is rarely a requirement, since it is in the best interest of that vendor to provide that mechanism for all customers as one of the primary attractions.

Note that both conversion and interface procedures draw heavily from personnel dedicated to the technical support group and to a more loosely defined liaison group.

Summary

Demo modules are the vendor's "show and tell" of how a system operates, or should operate, using a set of script and test files. These files are built to cover an extensive test environment with predetermined results. By installing and running such a demo module, you can gain valuable insight and exposure concerning the specifics, the idiosyncrasies of the full-blown application.

A second aspect of a demo module is that it represents the basic design for a production environment in terms of setting up the various runstreams, steps to backup and restore your files, and your utilities as well as critical restart procedures. A demo system is also a tutorial tool by the vendor to acclimate his user long before such a production system is operational.

The purpose of this chapter is to provide you with background material for a case study. Systems design, unlike mathematical equation, offers dozens, if not hundreds, of solutions for a particular problem.

The interdependency that exists between the billing and the A/R systems is unusually critical requiring the parallel development of certain modules. For example, the A/R system cannot function without a Billing front-end system, thus it needs to be developed first. However, the billing system cannot be operational without a customer master database, which resides and is maintained in the A/R system.

To introduce additional complexities into the design, the customer master database, too, has its own internal hierarchical arrangement. It is functionally dependent on the corporate guidelines file. This file controls the organizational structure of a business entity with rules, standards, titles, financial breakdowns, and so forth.

Several aspects of the systems development process deserve consideration this early in the game. First, that any file structure developed in the billing module is considered "foreign" and inaccessible by the A/R system. The A/R system is a recently acquired vendor package made up of both real time and batch procedures. Most of the activities are performed on-line (that is, editing and updating the data) although standard reporting and a substantial portion of the interface are done in a totally batch environment.

The A/R system overall is made up of three cycles. These are as follows:

1. an on-line preparation cycle,
2. the on-line real-time cycle, and
3. a post on-line cycle.

The A/R database is made up of five individual files, all having the same VSAM structure. The corporate guidelines file essentially identifies the way a particular business is handled in general terms. It defines, overall, standard methodologies to calculate discount rates, the application of payments, tolerance, credit limits, distribution policies, and so on.

A second major file in the system has to do with keeping track of the customer in terms of demographic data and specific policies.

The open items file is the third component on the A/R database. Open items are essentially the charges and credits that are "open" on the customer's A/R account such as invoices, credit memos, debit memos, unapplied cash, partial payments, etc.

The A/R database comprises two additional files. These are a payment history file and a paid item file. Most interface requirements are done through certain batch modules along with file backups and recoveries. Remember that, in a typical business environment, the printing of voluminous (standard) reports is still very much a necessity, although this function has been thoroughly enhanced in a fourth generation environment with user-written reports and queries. Both the billing and the A/R systems require an extensive interaction, the sharing of common resources, which is the primary purpose of the interface.

Chapter 12

Installing a Fourth Generation Vendor Package—Part II

12.1   Overview

The purpose of this chapter is to provide you with a method of approach (and some creativity) in helping you to define and resolve problems. Rather than a text book kind of solution to the case study in Chapter 11, some problem analysis on your part will facilitate the understanding and conceptualization necessary to implement a particular project.

To achieve a detailed application review of the two major systems in Chapter 11, the problem may be approached in one of three ways:

1. Fully utilize a vendor-developed demo module, which was a first alternative for implementing an in-house billing system. The efficiency of this approach is that you do not need to modify the demo system, but simply use it as is. This would immediately enable you to have access to the customer master segment of the A/R system without having to customize the vendor-provided database. With respect to the G/L files, you need to recreate them in a test environment using some of the vendor's own transactions. This is necessary since the recently copied G/L files contain production type transactions incompatible with the vendor's data.

    When creating a database from the various parts of the system, you need to do substantial background study to create a "representative" model. A representative model, means addressing most, if not all, the issues where a systems needs to be tested and verified for accuracy. Volume in itself is insignificant, since out of, for example, 10,000 transactions, you may not run into some of the "weird" conditions until some special quarterly or semiannual processing is to take place, or where some of the criteria have changed due to the modification of a vendor system. To develop such a representative "cross section," you need some strong user participation, and an intimate knowledge of certain idiosyncrasies.

    Creativity is needed, since some of the G/L files would have to be recreated (rather than simply loaded using the vendor's database). This means you have to know what you can salvage out of this production environment intact and what has to be customized to accommodate the new application. Under the circumstances, this first approach would guarantee you instant access to the customers' database, from which you could extract all the required demographic components prerequisite for the billing system, and particularly for generating an invoice.

    There are both advantages and disadvantages to this approach: the advantage is that you will be able to work continually on the billing system, which is quite important, since the billing system, by far, has the longest critical path. Quite clearly,the disadvantage is that too many procedures, not yet developed in a number of application programs, need to be simulated and interim files be built, which will not remain functional once the new system is implemented.

2. A second alternative focuses on implementing an A/R system first. This would be accomplished simply by omitting the vendor's database and by moving directly into a conversion process using your own data. This solution is designed to enable you to "ease" into production mode without having to reinitialize your files once you are satisfied with the vendor's own controlled environment.

    Of course, you still end up having to copy some of the essential datasets from the G/L system, mainly for reasons of security, since production files, or "live data" are not permissible for testing and prototyping a new system. One of the significant advantages of this approach is that it provides an intense learning experience which otherwise would require substantial time and effort. By concentrating on the A/R vendor package alone, you are able to spec out (and even program) some of the procedures necessary for customizing and/or enhancing your package. This may be a long, drawn-out procedure, even though it would probably not be so complex of a process as developing a new billing system practically from scratch.

    Thus, the apparent disadvantages of the above approach would be the temporary "shelving" of the billing system, which has a significant critical path—a serious mistake looking at it from the viewpoint of project management.

3. The third alternative has to do with the simultaneous development of both billing and A/R systems. Logically, this would be an ideal arrangement from an efficiency point of view—disregarding the budget, and, assuming that you have "idle" resources that can be put to the above task. Actually, alternative 3 would resolve all task-dependency problems through careful planning, so that task "C," for example, would not have to be put on the back-burner simply because of unavailable resources that should have been assigned to tasks "A" and/or "B" which could easily be performed in a parallel development. (This latter approach is probably the most practical one, even from a budgetary point of view.) Thus, the advantage of this approach would be speed in implementing the project and a high level of efficiency in handling internal task dependencies. (Because of this, the project would also be under a tighter control, resulting in better follow-up techniques and possibly quality assurance.)

The disadvantage, is the immediate need for substantially more resources and a bigger budget up front. The key phrase is "up front,"
since the first two alternatives are just as expensive, if not more so, than
the last, but requiring a more reasonable spread of personnel resources
(for example programmers, analysts, project leaders, etc.) throughout
the implementation cycle.

12.2 Generic Features in Systems Development

12.2.1 Key Definition

In Figure 12.1, when the terminal operator enters a project number on the
screen (simply to create an invoice record), he or she is initiating a transaction to retrieve a specific record off the project master. The inquiry key is
built from the data entered by the terminal operator on the screen that
initiates the search. If the condition has a false value, meaning that the
record cannot be located on the file, the transaction is to display a warning
message on the screen. If, however, the search results in a direct hit, or a
true condition, you need to build yet another key for a second inquiry to
access the customer master through the Project record. (See some of the
record layouts and screen designs for the preceding files, available in
Chapter 11.)

During the search, a record may or may not be located depending on a
number of conditions.

As you can see, keys are one of the most critical elements in establishing viable relationships among the various applications. You need to have a
very keen understanding of how a particular key is structured and used in a
given system. Most record keys are built in a vendor system to accommodate a maximum size. This is due to the broad user base ranging from
super-sized companies such as Standard Oil on one end of the spectrum to a
150-bed hospital or a junior college.

The MSA A/R system (release 8701), for example, gives you a maximum length of 35 positions on the customer master database, which is a
concatenated key. To be more specific, this key is made up of a two-
position-long company number field, which may have a constant value in
your business, and a segment number, designating one of the many record
types on the A/R database. Other key components are a 14-character-long
customer number, a two-position segment code, and a reserved key area

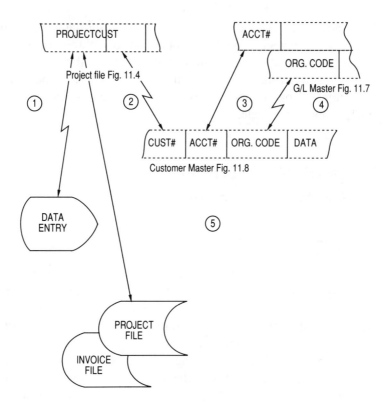

Figure 12.1 This illustrates the complete transaction cycle to perform an interface interactively.

(for a possible expansion of the original key definition) encompassing the next 16 positions.

Given the preceding key structure, how would you arrange your own customer key to fit into the above pattern? Figure 12.2 shows a layout of the concatenated key (each key component being separated by a blank column for clarity) and the building mechanism to produce such a key using a set of CICS Command level instructions.

12.2.2   Writing Exit Point Routines

Chapter 11, mentioned a particular way of producing a record with all the required data elements in place and properly formatted for the receiving system. A more efficient way of handling such an interface is to embed

```
The Customer Account        The same key corresponding to
key, as appears on the      the initial input data (left)
input record                in the vendor record


    0101  ————————>  0 12 0 0000000000101 01
    0102  ————————>  0 12 0 0000000000102 01
    0103  ————————>  0 12 0 0000000000103 01
    0104  ————————>  0 12 0 0000000000104 01
    0105  ————————>  0 12 0 0000000000105 01
    0106  ————————>  0 12 0 0000000000106 01
    0107  ————————>  0 12 0 0000000000107 01
    0108  ————————>  0 12 0 0000000000108 01
    0109  ————————>  0 12 0 0000000000109 01
    0115  ————————>  0 12 0 0000000000115 01
```

```
        COBOL DATA DIVISION shell for defining the key.


01 KEY-DEFINITION.
    05  FIELD1                   PIC X.
    05  COMPANY-NO               PIC X(02).
    05  SEGMENT-NUMBER           PIC X.
    05  CUSTOMER-KEY-COMPONENTS.
        10  ZERO-FILL            PIC X(09).
        10  CUSTOMER-KEY         PIC X(04).
    05  SEGMENT-CODE             PIC X(02).
    05  EXPANSION-AREA           PIC X(16).


01 STORE-CUSTOMER-RECORD         PIC X(500).
01 LEN                           PIC S(4) COMP VALUE +35.

CICS Command Level Statements to convert the initial key:


MOVE '0' TO FIELD1.
MOVE '12' TO COMPANY-NO.
MOVE '0' TO SEGMENT-NUMBER.
MOVE ZEROS TO ZERO-FILL.
MOVE CUSTOMER-INPUT-KEY TO CUSTOMER-KEY.
MOVE '01' TO SEGMENT-CODE.
MOVE SPACES TO EXPANSION-AREA.
EXEC CICS READ DATASET('CUSTREC')
INTO (STORE-CUSTOMER-RECORD)
RIDFLD(KEY-DEFINITION)
LENGTH(LEN)
UPDATE
END-EXEC.
```

Figure 12.2   This is a process to convert to an expanded key.

some of the procedures into one of the vendor-written edit programs to validate the incoming data, as if it were part of the vendor's own application. This would accomplish several things. Since some of those procedures are already developed in the vendor's own system (some, not all), you could greatly simplify the process of customization. Second (and this would reiterate the first suggestion), you could easily curtail redundant coding, which is time consuming and expensive. Since you do not routinely modify any vendor-written code internal to an application system, how would you go about achieving results?

The answer lies in developing your own procedures through various exit points that are vendor-provided linkage areas to accommodate a degree of flexibility currently unavailable in his system.

Most vendor packages are quite dynamic in the sense that they are subject to periodic revisions and enhancements by a particular vendor. These enhancements are necessary for several reasons, one of which is to keep things current in the application system.

Payroll systems, for example, are notorious for existing and operating in a volatile environment and being at the whim of local and federal lawmakers. In one state, for example, a fixed percentage of state income tax may be completely replaced by a graduated income tax, much like the federal tax apparatus. Vendors, as a rule, do not provide for unique situations such as that, which only effect a limited number of people. Rather, this is left to the data center. Any program developed and embedded into the vendor's own procedures would be discarded at the time a new release were to become effective. To avoid that, you need to develop your own procedures and develop them independently rather than consolidating them into the vendor's own body of code. This is facilitated though a technique referred to as exit point programming.

Exit points are vendor provided areas of communication between the vendor's program and your own procedures. They are unlikely to be dismantled by the vendor, as a rule, regardless of the extent of change or enhancements in an upcoming release. Figure 12.3 is an overview of this concept.

The procedure shown on the left, which is a vendor-provided application program to edit the A/R database, has an exit point set up immediately following a number of "housekeeping operations." This exit may or may not be physically hooked up with an external program module. If it is, you will be able to leave the preceding program, perform a set of customized procedures in your respective application, and then, branch back to the original vendor code that triggered the operation, following the next sequential instruction. If, on the other hand, the program is not hooked up with an external source, you simply ignore the first occurrence of the exit point.

Regardless of how often a vendor does produce a new release, he or she will not tamper with his original exit points in the system. The vendor may revise, delete, or enhance some of his own procedures (for example, a new way of restoring the A/R database, or initializing a temporary file), but will under no circumstance move the location of the exit points. In Figure 12.3, exit point 1 is hooked up with three external "bubbles." (Here, a "bubble" is

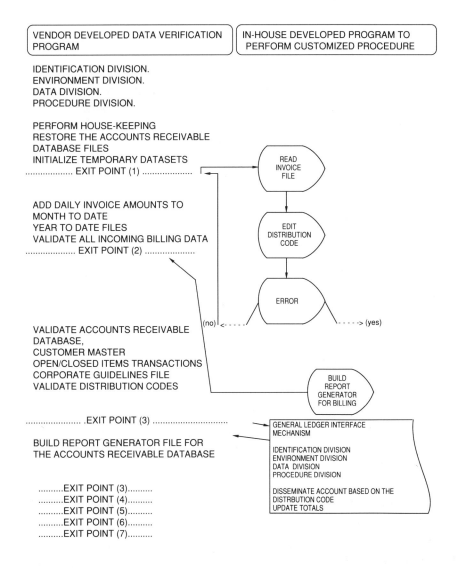

Figure 12.3   This illustrates exit point mechanics and usage.

defined as a set of procedures pertaining to an application program.) The first one of these bubbles reads the invoice file, which, as you will recall from Chapter 11, is created during the billing process. The second bubble checks all the distribution codes that the A/R system needs for a subsequent interface with the G/L. The third bubble determines whether the procedure will return to the invoking program, or remain "put" in the external module. You want to be able to record certain error conditions and, thus, not return to the initial program until a second record is read successfully and edited.

After verification, the main line logic continues (adding invoice amounts to a month-to-date and to a year-to-date file, as well as validating data brought forward from the billing system) until a second exit procedure occurs. In Figure 12.3, a second such exit point is used to create a report generator file for billing.

Following the return from a second exit, the main program is to validate the A/R database, which is made up of a number of segments, such as a customer master, a corporate guidelines file, and an open and a closed items file, etc. Note that all aspects of these were reviewed in Chapter 11. Just at that point, a third vendor exit is used to establish lines of communications with the G/L, and to perform some of the required data validation.

12.2.3   Procedures to be Eliminated

Since most vendor packages encompass a great deal more than what you likely need, it is important to weed out those procedures that do not relate to your business. Sometimes this is easier said than done. The simple example of this is when a program, or an entire runstream, needs to be eliminated. In this case, you simply discard the program (or runstream), while making absolutely sure that some of the interim files that would normally be created at this point and passed onto subsequent procedures will not cause unpredictable results when deactivated.

Whether changes encompass a program or a run-stream, you may "Dummy-out" any number of such files in your JCL's that are simply irrelevant in a given situation. "Dummying out" a file is an override to your Job Control statement to nullify or ignore an otherwise functional dataset. Without such an override, your task would have an abnormal termination.

A more complicated aspect of weeding out unrequired procedures has to do with partially changing an existing set of procedures that are normally part of a single application program.

Suppose, for example, that your company only ages receivables up to 60 days, at which point (and based on past experience), the particular account is turned over to a collection agency. In the current A/R system, the standard aging categories, as initially set up by the vendor are as follows:

1 to 30 days anticipated pay cycle

31 to 45 days unpaid – send reminder

46 to 60 days unpaid – send level 1 notice

61 to 90 days unpaid – send level 2 notice

91 to 120 days unpaid – send level 3 notice

over 120 days unpaid – turn account over to collection

To complicate things even more, assume that starting with the 46-day aging cycle, or delinquency, there are a number of severity levels associated with the dunning process. Assume a company policy of only aging recievables up to 60 days, after which they are to be turned over to a collection agency. Then procedures covering events from the 61st day to the 120th day would be redundant and should be taken out of the system. The way to delete these procedures does make a difference—they ought not to be done through programming changes affecting the existing code for the following reasons:

- when the vendor completes a new release of the preceding system and all those "commented out" statements will magically reappear,

- you will lose, as a result, valuable vendor support should anything go wrong with that particular (or other related) procedures.

So what do you need to do to resolve this kind of a problem? First of all, you may be able to utilize the above exit point concept recently discussed. Should you rely on such programming techniques, you can simply "loop" around the rest of the standard vendor procedures once you have performed the final 60-day aging criterion against your account. Since exit points are only available at certain physical locations in your program, and perhaps, there is none available at that particular procedure, you probably need to exit the program prior to this aging mechanism. This needs to be reviewed closely and evaluated individually under the circumstance. Ironically, this means writing more code even when you need to eliminate unnecessary procedures.

12.2.4   Enhancements—A Dictionary Solution

In the previous sections, enhancing or modifying a system through the exit point mechanism was discussed. Exit point programming techniques are normally used in more complex situations, when the only alternative left is to develop extensive procedures from scratch. However, in more practical situations, you can either add or modify certain rules associated with a data element, such as changing values and ranges, relationships, computational requirements and so forth.

In an A/R system, such as the one described in detail in Chapter 11, you can easily modify a range for the aging criteria of your receivables, if such is required. In Section 12.2.3 (Procedures to be Eliminated) some company policies associated with aging receivables up to, but not exceeding 60 days before the account is turned over to an outside collection agency were pointed out. This simply means that the range, or the categories defined (for example, 1 to 30 days, 31 to 45 days, etc.) must have an upper limit of 60 days (give or take a couple of days), and the rest of the range is no longer viable. The 60-day upper-limit would result in crediting an uncollectible account to the G/L system. This would also set up some new rules for the severity level of the dunning process; all of that without changing a single line of code. Changing a dictionary statement, or adding new procedures to a dictionary is normally done via the vendor's fourth generation language or in some cases through a set of utility statements.

What is desirable about directly manipulating the data dictionary (as opposed to setting up exit point type of procedures) is the fact that you need not develop an extensive maintenance mechanism for adding, updating, or deleting procedures. Instead, you can rely on the vendor's own apparatus, which normally remains transparent to you.

Dictionary qualities vary even in most fourth generation environments, and some extensive editing functions, for example, may not be accommodated even by the more sophisticated data dictionaries today. As mentioned earlier, a data dictionary has one of two major formats in this kind of an environment. The first one is when it is restricted to a single application, or even to a number of applications by the same vendor. Thus, customizing a particular procedure in the A/R module is a relatively simple process since most of the data (and the rules associated with them) are internal to that system. In a mixed environment, however, where massive changes are required, you need to take a more active role in redefining the dictionary. From time to time, the role and the importance of a data dictionary has been emphasized, as a focal point for defining a database. Software vendors today are continually in the process of enhancing their products, placing more and more emphasis on extensive edit rules and relational operands, rather than incorporating them into the logic of an application program.

The advantage of this approach is that you only need to define a set of procedures once, rather than fragmenting them throughout the various applications. Also, by placing procedures in the dictionary, you can generate a much speedier systems response. Figure 12.4 shows a "smart" dictionary.

Let me explain what the coding is all about: EMPLOYEE-CLASSIFICA-TION is the full reference name of the field that you can use in an application program in a conventional sense. Query Name (JOBCL), enables you to reference the above field in an on-line real time environment. The term "real time" environment is the key, since a query normally executes on a real time basis, whereas most fourth generation languages compile and execute strictly in batch mode.

Associated with the EMPLOYEE-CLASSIFICATION (or JOBCL) field is a brief narrative describing what the specific field is all about: an indicator reflecting the status of different employee groups.

EMPLOYEE-CLASSIFICATION is a two-position numeric field. Should the terminal operator attempt to enter a nonnumeric field on the screen, the system will simply disallow it, triggering an error message as part of the same display. If you were to generate a report (or at least a view of it), this field would bear the predefined header for the column 'STATUS'. If this is omitted, the system would automatically grab the query name (JOBCL) and display that as part of the column header for both viewing and printing. Further note that the proper range for the data element is between 01 (lower limit) and 75 (upper limit). Thus, an entry of 00 or 76 would result in an error condition even though both fields happened to be numeric. This again, is a fatal error that must be resolved before you can proceed. The term *=01 through 08 is a self-referenced definition. What it means is that when the EMPLOYEE CLASSIFICATION field has a value

```
DATA ELEMENT NAME            :   EMPLOYEE-CLASSIFICATION
QUERY NAME                   :   JOBCL
DATA ELEMENT DESCRIPTION     :   THIS FIELD DESCRIBES VARIOUS EMPLOYEE
                                 CLASSIFICATION POSSIBILITIES (E.G. 01
                                 ENGINEER, 02 DRAFTSMAN, 13 ACCOUNTANT, ETC.)
LENGTH                       :   2 CHARACTERS
DISPOSITION                  :   NUMERIC
HEADER DEFINITION            :   STATUS
VALUE                        :   01 THRU 05
RELATIONAL                   :   *=01 THRU 08;
                                 EMPLOYEE-DEPARTMENT = 1777
                                 *=12 THRU 27;
                                 EMPLOYEE-DEPARTMENT = 1907
UPDATE                       :   NA
COMPUTATIONAL                :   NA
TRIGGER                      :   NA

//////////////////////////////////
            /////////////////////////////////////////////////////
```

Figure 12.4 This is a "smart" dictionary model; a product of extensive software engineering and research.

of 01 through 08, the associated EMPLOYEE-DEPARTMENT must have a prestated value of 1777. Likewise, the EMPLOYEE-CLASSIFICATION field, with a value range of 12 through 27, must correspond to Department 1907 to avoid any systems-generated error message.

The previous data dictionary prototype is simply a model that has been summarized based on a composite of dictionaries available on the market today.

12.2.5 Customizing through the Corporate Guidelines Delimiters

This mechanism is available to you mostly through the installation process to customize your standard reports (and screens) that will be generated through the system. When you are customizing with a set of corporate guidelines delimiters, you can only implement procedures (or policies) that are initially vendor defined. If you need something other than what is packaged for you, you need to go outside these delimiters. Figure 12.5

```
                        UNIVERSAL SOFTWARE COMPANY
                         — PAYMENT TERMS DEFINITION —


   CORP—> _____    TERMS—> ____  FROM ____  000000   TO ____  000000
   DESCRIPTION__          _____


    — CUTOFF —                      — DAY —    —— MONTH ——

    BASE VAL VAL        AMT   BASE  ADD # BASE   BASE    ADD#  WHICH  ACTUAL
         1   2    —RATE—BASIS  DATE  DAYS MONTH  MONTH  MONTHS DAYS   DATE  DUE

   1 _   __  __   _____  _   _  ___   __    __     __    __   ____  __

   2 _   __  __   _____  _   _  ___   __    __     __    __   ____  __

   3 _   __  __   _____  _   _  ___   __    __     __    __   ____  __

   4 _   __  __   _____  _   _  ___   __    __     __    __   ____  __

   5 _   __  __   _____  _   _  ___   __    __     __    __   ____  __

   6 _   __  __   _____  _   _  ___   __    __     __    __   ____  __

   7 _   __  __   _____  _   _  ___   __    __     __    __   ____  __

   8 _   __  __   _____  _   _  ___   __    __     __    __   ____  __
```

Figure 12.5   This is a standard payment terms definition screen.

shows a standard screen that needs to be customized. (The screen is actually one of M&D's screens used in the standard A/R application). To customize such a panel through the corporate guidelines delimiters, you want to be able to evaluate (and answer) some of the following questions: (This, by the way, is a user-related aspect of working with the corporate guidelines delimiters.

Here are some of the questions to resolve as a user.

- Do you use already established payment terms? If you do, you need to decide if they are set up correctly in the old system or in your general accounting procedures, or simply, if you need to change them. This is a procedural customization that can take place right at this point. (As you can see, this type of customization or enhancement needs to be completed by the user rather than by data processing personnel.)

- Are you going to interface with a Billing System? Since the answer is yes, you may continue with another line of questions, as follows:

  Do you or do you not use financial charges or chargeback invoices? If your answer is "no," that is, if you do not use such a mechanism, you may not need to establish payment terms in the A/R module. If payments come through the Billing System with due dates, such transactions can be posted. However, if you want the A/R system to calculate due dates based on your payment terms, they must be defined in the A/R system. You may establish as many kinds of payment terms per corporation as you can forsee using. You may later select one of these as the default payment terms for all customers and transactions within the corporation. However, you can override this default at either the customer or transaction level as necessary. Payment terms are established on the payment term definition screen in this particular system.

The above mechanics of customizing a single procedure (for example, the payment terms procedures through the corporate guidelines delimiters) only represent a tiny portion in the overall process. Unlike the application systems generation process, this one is extensively user dependent and can be overwhelmingly complex. You can, however, achieve a high degree of customization of your system while gradually transforming the vendor's generic module into a fairly specific set of procedures. Again, the only criteria for you to observe is that you are bound by the constraints of the vendor, that is by procedures the vendor has developed and made available for you in the system. If you are a government or a state agency requiring an extensive encumbrance accounting module, you are on your own, and you need to develop such tasks through exit point programming, or simply through a different subsystem.

12.3   Solving Multiple Interface Tasks

In discussing multi-level interfaces there are two major issues involved. The first issue is highlighted in Figure 12.6, which is the way the user, the accountant perceives such an event. A second issue, which is presented in Figure 12.7 is, on the other hand, the way a data processing technician visualizes interface, that is in terms of paths, data elements, record layouts, and devices on which all permanent files are kept. Looking at this process from the user's point of view, Figure 12.6 gives you a somewhat linear path. The two major events of the interface entail a flow of transactions from the billing and A/R systems into the G/L. All of that can actually be summarized in a set of journal entries. From billing to G/L, you debit A/R (reference number 10097100, which is part of the distribution code) and credit sales (70014310) both for the total of $25,000.

Under normal circumstances, most transactions interfaced into the G/L system require relatively few pieces of data. Among these are an account reference number or distribution code in order to identify a particular element, the amount, which is part of the above transaction, and the type of such transaction: whether it is a debit or a credit amount. Likewise, recording a flow of information from the A/R system into the G/L can be expressed in debiting both the cash (08719211) and the discount expense (30078111) accounts against a single credit to the receivables for $25,700.

Events between the billing and the A/R functions are not carried on the books in terms of journal entries. Interaction between the two systems are done to convey some basic data flow between billing and the receivables, such as invoice and batch amounts, data pertinent to developing an aging mechanism, and so forth.

Figure 12.7, on the other hand, is the data processing technician's view of the interface. Here, as you can see, both billing and receivable layouts need to conform to a "fixed" record format acceptable to the G/L system, which will, in turn, have each account posted and classified according to a valid distribution code.

12.4   Testing Environments

Just like the interface activities, testing is also a multitask project. It is proportionately complicated by the volume of enhancements required by the process of customization. Left in its original format, most software packages would require limited testing; unfortunately, this is seldom the

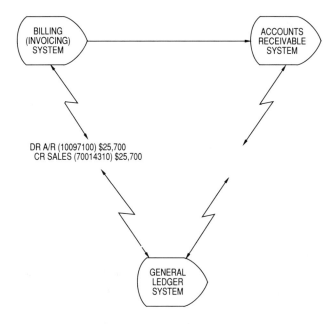

Figure 12.6 This is the accountant's (user's) view of the interface mechanism.

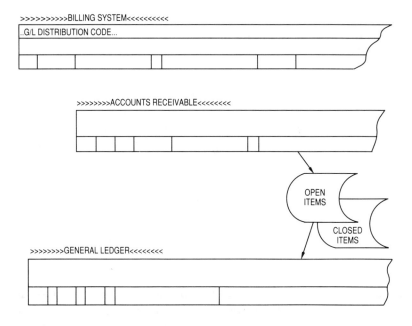

Figure 12.7 This is the DP technician's view of the interface.

case. Customized application programs that are not part of the vendor's original release should be tested in an isolated manner (unit testing) against a set of criteria developed in-house. This is important, especially from a project management point of view, because of the lengthy critical path assigned to these activities.

Once unit testing is verifiable, you need to go ahead with more testing yet. The purpose of these second-stage testing procedures (beginning integration type test) is to make sure that the recently developed application code indeed functions and is compatible with the vendor's software. In an on-line real time situation, for example, the most critical step in the process is the definition of the communications areas where messages are constantly sent and received by the invoking and invoked transactions. Figure 12.8 is an overview of an in-house program that conditionally triggers three types of transactions—all resident in the vendor's software.

Figure 12.8 shows part of an on-line program where the LINKAGE SECTION contains an 85-character-long message. This is transmitted from one of the vendor-developed application programs into the in-house system. Unit testing of this latter program is critical for a number of reasons.

First, you want to make sure that your timing is flawless, and that the message is already built in the communications area by the vendor prior to receiving it.

Second, you want to test and verify the alignment of the particular message, that the two programs, in communicating, share identical layout, very much like using copy-lib for defining a record.

Once the message is picked up in the communications area, it will be used to update the invoice master, which is external to A/R system. The idea is to generate a composite screen partly from the COMMAREA and partly from the additional data that can be attained from the invoice master. This has the same effect as if you were reading (and processing) two separate files through an on-line program (Figure 12.8). The outcome of the previous processing could be a screen like the one presented in Figure 12.9.

Note that our sample program also interacts with another application program that builds an alternate key from the current communications area. Instead of utilizing 85 characters, as in the first instance, the second program only requires a total of 34 characters, which is the combination of the customer number and name.

When testing the interaction between these two programs, you want to make sure that the proper message is generated by your own application, and that you have properly invoked the vendor's load module through a LINK or an exit control (XCTL) statement. You might want to utilize

```
      LINKAGE SECTION
      01  DFHCOMMAREA.
          05  PASS-INFO              PIC X
          05  RECORD-KEY.
              10  COMPANY-NUMBER     PIC X(03).
              10  SEGMENT-NUMBER     PIC X(02).
              10  CUSTOMER-NUMBER    PIC X(04).
          05  CUSTOMER-NAME          PIC X(30).
          05  CUSTOMER-ADDRESS.
              10  STREET             PIC X(20).
              10  CITY               PIC X(10).
              10  STATE              PIC X(10).
              10  ZIP-CODE           PIC X(05).
      ************************************************
      *    05  INVOICING-DATA        PIC X(100). * ------------>
      ************************************************
      PROCEDURE DIVISION.
           ..............
           ..............
           IF PASS-INFO = 'R' GO TO RECEIVE-MAP
           EXEC CICS SEND MAP('DEMOGR1')
           MAPSET('DEM1SET')
           CURSOR
           END-EXEC.
           MOVE 'R' TO PASS-INFO.
           EXEC CICS RETURN TRANSID ('PGM1')
           COMMAREA(DATA-COMM)
           LENGTH(85)
           END-EXEC.
      RECEIVE-MAP.
           MOVE ' ' TO PASS INFO.
           EXEC CICS RECEIVE MAP('DEMOGR1')
           MAPSET('DEM1SET')
           END-EXEC.
      START-BUILDING-MAP.
           MOVE COMPANY-NUMBER TO COMO.
           MOVE SEGMENT-NUMBER TO SEGMO.
           MOVE CUSTOMER NUMBER TO CUSTO.
           MOVE CUSTOMER-NAME TO NAMEO.
           MOVE STREET TO STREETO.
           MOVE CITY TO CITYO.
           MOVE STATE TO STATEO.
           MOVE ZIP-CODE ZIPCO.
           IF INVNOL NOT > 0 GO TO ERROR-DISPLAY.
           EXEC CICS HANDLE CONTITION
           NOTFND(NO-SUCH-RECORD)
           END-EXEC.
           EXEC CICS READ DATASET('INVOIC')
           INTO(STORAGE-AREA)
           LENGTH(LEN)
           UPDATE
           END-EXEC.
```

Figure 12.8 This highlights some testing considerations for on-line programs.

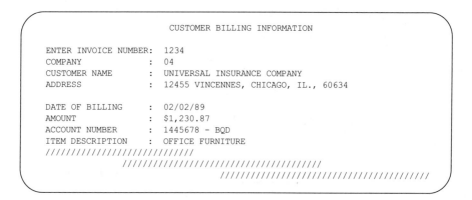

```
                    CUSTOMER BILLING INFORMATION

ENTER INVOICE NUMBER:   1234
COMPANY             :   04
CUSTOMER NAME       :   UNIVERSAL INSURANCE COMPANY
ADDRESS             :   12455 VINCENNES, CHICAGO, IL., 60634

DATE OF BILLING     :   02/02/89
AMOUNT              :   $1,230.87
ACCOUNT NUMBER      :   1445678 - BQD
ITEM DESCRIPTION    :   OFFICE FURNITURE
/////////////////////////////
                /////////////////////////////////////////
                        /////////////////////////////////////////////
```

Figure 12.9 This shows composite data retrieved from the vendor master and from the invoice files.

Execute Diagnostic Facility (EDF) or Intertest in debugging the problem to monitor the path between the two application programs for the first time. When you use such a productivity tool, you can normally prevent "bombing out" in the middle of a transaction because of problems due to some incompatible procedures between the two tasks. In another situation, you may want to send to the vendor's application program, for example, a 100-character-long message containing invoice-related data. Actually, the transmission only pertains to the record key and the invoice data; all other demographic information can be blanked out, so that the message may be reformatted, if necessary.

The PASS-INFO field, was initially set up to control the pseudo-conversational aspect of CICS, , which is the performance of the "send" and the "receive" cycle. An overview of this testing process is further highlighted in Figure 12.10.

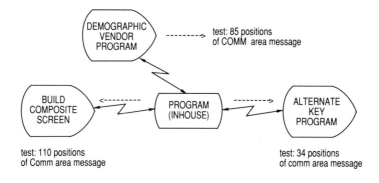

Figure 12.10 This summarizes the three steps in testing critical interactions.

Summary

The purpose of this chapter is to provide a method of approach (and some creativity) in helping to define and resolve problems.

The following viable alternatives are explored in this chapter.

1. Fully utilize a vendor-developed demo module which was the first alternative for implementing an in-house billing system. The efficiency of this approach is that you do not need to modify the demo system, but simply use it, as is. This would immediately enable you to have access to the customer master segment of the A/R system without customizing the vendor provided database. With respect to the General Ledger files, you need to recreate them in a test environment using some of the vendor's own transactions. This is necessary since the recently copied G/L files contain production-type transactions incompatible with the vendor's data.

2. A second alternative focuses on implementing an A/R system first. This would be accomplished simply by omitting the vendor's database and by moving directly into a conversion process using your own data. This solution is designed to enable you to "ease" into production mode without having to reinitialize your files once you are satisfied with the vendor's own controlled environment.

3. The third alternative has to do with the simultaneous development of both billing and A/R systems. This is by far the most efficient approach, provided that there is enough money available in the corporate budget to accommodate such an alternative.

This would also provide a great deal more fexibility in handling dependency situations characteristic of such a project. Because of this the project would also be under tighter control, resulting in better followup techniques and quality assurance.

Glossary

Glossary

Access List A set of security rules defined by the organization authorizing some specific users or user groups to have access to certain dataframe(s).

Allow Defines a list of users or user groups and the access type allowed for each. This statement (reserved word) works in conjunction with IF…and ELSE conditional logic (Chapter 9).

Alternate key Refers to a data set which is now organized using a different key or sort sequence than the primary key (Chapter 4).

Application System Generation A set of choices presented to the analyst for his review and the actual decision or selection process in questionnaire-like statements reminiscent of macro instructions, or symbolics (Chapter 10).

BMS Basic Mapping Support is an assembler-based technology for developing (painting) screens (Chapter 10).

Borderless	Design means that there are no "boundaries" or "borders" among the various applications. It is as though the data processing needs of an entire organization were handled through a single physical database (Chapter 1).
Browsing	Paging multiple Help screens (Chapter 4) meaning to sequentially process each screen. Also refers to a particular type of inquiry that gives you an ability to scan sequentially an entire file from beginning to end through the use of a generic or partial key (Chapter 10).
CDB Database	A control database that defines all other databases on the Millennium system (Chapter 4).
CDD Database	Data dictionary database that defines every data field and query definition that has to do with the application (Chapter 6).
CGI Database	A subroutine library that contains procedures that are referenced by the different PDL programs via an INCLUDE or AN $INCLUDE command (Chapter 6).
CGS Database	Performs like an internal library where all PDL programs are kept and maintained.
CICS Tables	The CICS telecommunications monitor is controlled through a number of tables such as the File Control Table (FCT), where all file-related information is defined. Some of the other tables used by this monitor are a PPT or Program Processing Table, a PCT or Program Control Table, a DCT, or Destination Control Table, and so on (Chapter 10).
CME Database	Works in conjunction with the CMENU (Menu definition screen), CMEXX, and the CMELS screens (Chapter 4).

CNO Database   Optimized search field database enables you to access your source files with search indexes (Chapter 4).

Command Line   Enables you to display, update, or place a query against any specific M&D database in your application system using on-line, real time technology (Chapter 3).

**Command
Qualifier**   Represents the key to an existing record to be accessed (Chapter 3).

Common Section   Pertains to calculations, selections, and exclusion criteria, value assignments and so on. This section is an optional feature in the Expert Language (Chapter 2).

**Concatenated
Key**   A record key containing more than one key component. For example, the key to your personnel file is the employee's social security number, and his department code.

CVS Database   Contains all the variable records required to be referenced (for example, displayed, updated, etc.) in your system (Chapter 5).

Data Dictionary   Is a collection of descriptions of the data, not the actual data. It is a central repository of rules, definitions, and values made up of four basic components in the MSA environment, such as items, groups, records, and dataframes. The data dictionary is the place where you can define all you need to know about a piece of data, such as the name of the data, its length, decimal position, print mask, column heading, code translation, etc. (Chapter 7).

Database   Formal database technologies referred to in this book are: DB2, an IBM relational database; IMS or Information Management System, also a product of the IBM Corporation, which is a hierarchical database; DATACOM, a relational database, a product of ADR or Applied Research Corporation; and IDMS/R another relational model by Cullinet.

Dataframe MSA's term for physical parts or for an entire database (Chapter 7).

Data Library Library space in which data associated with the application is kept (Chapter 10).

Default Defines an access type for all users not specifically mentioned in the access list (Chapter 9).

Demo Module An initial system made available by the vendor of that package for testing, bench marking, and for tutorial purposes (Chapter 10). By installing and running such a demo module, you can gain valuable insight into and exposure to the specifics, that is, to the idiosyncrasies of a full-blown application environment. Also, you can utilize it as basis for a production environment in terms of setting up runstreams, backup and restore procedures, utilities, as well as critical restart sequences (Chapter 11).

Direct Access As in paging multiple Help screens (Chapter 4), meaning to invoke any particular screen randomly in a multipage environment.

Dummy When "dummying" out a particular file, the system will ignore that dataset, without causing the abnormal termination (ABEND) of a runstream (Chapter 10).

Exit Points Customizing a vendor program, or a set of procedures is done outside such an application system through exit points. Exit points are available in the vendor's source code for calling a customized module. This is necessary in order

	to avoid any future complications at the time the vendor is to issue a new release (Chapter 12).
Expert Language	MSA's fourth generation language used for a variety of tasks (Chapter 2).
Expertlink	MSA's fourth generation linkage used to provide for up and down loading between the mainframe systems and their personal computer (PC) counterpart. Up and down loading may be accomplished one of two ways: Selective Screen Transfer (SST) to utilize only selected information, and Database Sharing, where an entire file is involved in the data transfer (Chapter 2).
Extended I.E.	Extended Information Expert environment enables you to perform completely borderless inquiries (and processing) utilizing not only MSA, but "foreign" files, as well (Chapter 7).
Fatal Messages	Indicated that an error occurred from which you can only recover by correcting the problem, thus resubmitting the entire transaction (Chapter 4).
Fourth Generation Business Systems	Reflects a number of evolutionary methods to evaluate and process a set of user requirements. It is made up of a number of building blocks, for example, screen painting facilities, generation language, security, up and down loading to PC microcomputers, Help procedures, etc. (Chapter 1).
Fourth Generation Languages	Represent a mere building block in the overall architecture of the above support environment. Fourth Generation languages are procedural with so many automatic functions unavailable in a conventional environment (Chapter 2).

Generation Data Sets   Also referred to as GDG's, are chronologically and functionally related datasets. GDG's simplify the batch aspect of the system since they enable you to retain different versions of the same file without altering the dataset name (Chapter 10).

Generic Key   A partially defined key. The more complete the generic key, the more specific is the search and the quicker the response (Chapter 4).

Globals   Are values that are maintained by the system using predefined formats for administering security procedures within the Expert Dictionary (Chapter 9).

Group   A collection of items, which is hierarchically the second level that defines the Expert Dictionary (Chapter 7).

Help Subsystem   A mechanism to explain to the user the type of error that needs to be corrected and what you can do to resolve the problem (Chapter 4).

Informational Messages   Indicate to you the status of a system, even though they do not interrupt the processing of your activities (Chapter 4).

Information Expert   A term used for MSA's fourth generation processing environment (Chapter 7).

Input Section   One of the sections used by the Expert Language to define the I.E. environment the incoming data (Chapter 2).

Item   Represents the lowest, most basic form of information kept within the Expert Environment. It normally denotes a field name (Chapter 7).

KSDS
Key Sequenced Data Set (A VSAM type) that enables you to access randomly a particular record either with a "primary," or with secondary or alternate keys.(Chapter 10).

Libraries
Used in the I.E. system as follows: a Public Library: accessible by anyone who has access to the I.E. environment a Semi-Private Library: which is partially restricted and is normally within the jurisdiction of the system Administrator (see System Administrator) and a Private Library which is fully restricted (Chapter 7).

Link Level Indicator
Enables you to develop screen relationships and screen paths. Thus, you can exit a current screen, branch to another, perform various tasks, the return to the initial screen (Chapter 3).

Load Module
The "final" machine format responsible for triggering both batch programs and on-line transactions (Chapter 10).

Menu Screens
They provide you with an ability to find your way through a maze of complex procedures (Chapter 4).

Message Area
Provides you with proper diagnostics within the Millennium based systems, for example, SDT and PDL (Chapter 3).

Migration Technology
A software of procedure to move from one set of computer environment to another. PDL is one of such tools (Chapter 6).

Millennium
Provides an extensive support for all McCormack & Dodge applications. Millennium also provides groundwork for other extended products, such as SDT (Chapter 3).

M&D	McCormack & Dodge Corporation, one of the software companies whose product lines are explored in this book (Chapter 1).
MSA	Management Science of America, one of the software companies whose product lines are explored in this book (chapter 1).
Nonstructured Dataframe	Contains one or more records defined to the Expert Dictionary. When triggering such a data frame, I.E. presents one record at a time for processing and printing. If you have more than a single record type in a dataframe, the system will make no attempt to distinguish one record from another (Chapter 9).
Object Module	A set of machine statements translated directly from the source code through the language compiler (Chapter 10).
PDL	Procedure Development Language, M&D's fourth generation language (Chapter 6).
Primary Commands	Allow you to display records, execute queries, leave processing steps, etc. For efficiency, they are also thoroughly enhanced with a number of associated subcommands, allowing one to refine every command in terms of adding, deleting, replacing, moving, updating, inserting, and displaying information without having to write code to accomplish this (Chapter 3).
PROCS	(Or Procedures) Developed and maintained by the analyst. They can be referenced with a few control statements. The idea of segregating, invoking JCL's from a set of procedures (or PROCS), is based on security considerations and is done in an effort to simplify computer operations file in daily production type activities. The library that contains this information is called the "PROCLIB" (Chapter 10).

Question Mark
A "wild card" When used in any specific position, it will satisfy the search requirements for that particular character.

Queries
Provide you with the ability to retrieve information on-line. You can choose what you need to see and process in order to attain an up-to-the-minute response at your terminal (Chapter 2).

Quick
Commands resemble macro instructions to achieve specialized tasks (Chapter 3).

Records
The third components in the Expert Dictionary makeup. They are the logical collections of groups (and items) pertaining to a logical view of the data (Chapter 7).

Redirection
Accessing a application screen from a Help panel, that has additional information about that particular data: thus the term "redirecting" the Help (Chapter 4).

Report Request
A request that describes a specific report or reports including a set of processing criteria, computations, and so forth (Chapter 7).

Report Request Section
Deals with the physical definition of your output reports using the Expert Language (Chapter 2).

Report Series
Pertains to a number of report requests that utilize the same dataframe and are submitted to the I.E. processing environment concurrently (Chapter 7).

Screen Painting
A tool in the hands of both the data processing technician, as well as the user. Fourth generation screen painters are simplistic, yet powerful, and they expedite the process of designing and prototyping user requirements (Chapter 2).

SDF	(Or Screen Development Facility) Enables you to develop (paint) a screen and verify its layout interactively (Chapter 10).
Secure	Statement points a dataframe to an access list or to a security group (Chapter 9).
Security Groups	Represents a collection of dataframes that have a common security need (Chapter 9).
Source Management	The I.E. source management provides you with a way of entering and processing I.E. commands via a full screen text editor. Syntax checking is done interactively to verify that data were entered in a correct format, and that the proper commands were initiated (Chapter 7).
Support Facility	Module is an on-line real time dialogue manager supported by a number of utility programs (Chapter 7).
Step-by-Step	Programming method used by MSA to produce a fourth generation source code via a number of selection process (Chapter 7).
Sticky Cursor	A concept enabling you to retrieve a piece of information from one screen and insert it into another as the need arises (Chapter 4).
Structured Dataframe	Contains a natural structure of hierarchy defined to the I.E. environment. Structured data frames usually contain at least two or a number of different record types. The set of records is determined by the ORGANIZED BY and the CONTAINS AT LEVEL clauses of the data frame definition (Chapter 9).

Symbolics Lend an application a great deal of flexibility.

System Administrator A function similar to a database administrator in a formal DB environment to manage and assign resources in the system (Chapter 7).

Text Editor Checks the syntax of a particular statement or command. An input statement is available for entering specific instructions. Columns display those members that are shown on the text editor screen. Scroll is invoked when you require forward or backward motion on the screen. Page means that you can move in a specific direction a full screen or a "page" at a time. Half means that you can move in a specific direction a half a screen or page at a time. Line numbers are automatically generated by the MSA text editor (Chapter 8).

THP Database Stores the vendor's help procedures for a given application. This database is associated with the THPBR screen (Chapter 4).

THU Database Sets up your customized Help functions here (Chapter 4).

VSAM Clusters Simply means VSAM datasets, a nomenclature designed to differentiate what IBM calls a Virtual Storage Access Method technology from the sequential access type.

Warming Messages Indicate a number of potential problems for correction. They do not, however, prevent you from processing a transaction.

Index

Index

D

E